AVID

READER

PRESS

# MYSTERY

A SEDUCTION,

A STRATEGY,

A SOLUTION

# JONAH LEHRER

**AVID READER PRESS**

New York   London   Toronto   Sydney   New Delhi

AVID READER PRESS
An Imprint of Simon & Schuster, Inc.
1230 Avenue of the Americas
New York, NY 10020

First Avid Reader Press hardcover edition August 2021

AVID READER PRESS and colophon are trademarks of Simon & Schuster, Inc.

For information about special discounts for bulk purchases, please contact
Simon & Schuster Special Sales at 1-866-506-1949 or
business@simonandschuster.com.

The Simon & Schuster Speakers Bureau can bring authors to your live
event. For more information or to book an event, contact the Simon &
Schuster Speakers Bureau at 1-866-248-3049 or visit our website at
www.simonspeakers.com.

Interior design by Carly Loman

Manufactured in the United States of America

10   9   8   7   6   5   4   3   2   1

Library of Congress Cataloging-in-Publication Data has been applied for.

ISBN 978-1-5011-9587-7
ISBN 978-1-5011-9589-1 (ebook)

*For my family*

O known Unknown! from whom my being sips
Such darling essence . . .

—JOHN KEATS, *Endymion*


Art has something to do with an arrest of attention in
the midst of distraction.

—SAUL BELLOW


The one thing people never forget is the unsolved.
Nothing lasts like a mystery.

—JOHN FOWLES, *The Enigma*

# CONTENTS

# THE MYSTERY OF MYSTERY

The most beautiful thing we can experience is the mysterious.
It is the source of all true art and science. He to whom the
emotion is a stranger, who can no longer pause to wonder and
stand rapt in awe, is as good as dead: his eyes are closed.

**—ALBERT EINSTEIN**

## The Case of the Missing Writer

On the night of December 3, 1926, Agatha Christie put her young
daughter to bed, grabbed her fur coat and suitcase, and left the
house in a gray Morris Cowley. She told the maid she was going
out for a drive.

The next morning, Agatha's car was found near a chalk pit. It
had been driven down a rutted dirt road, before careening off the
track onto a grassy slope. The lights were left on; the brakes had
never been applied.[1] According to the *New York Times*, the Morris
Cowley had been found with its "front wheels actually overhang-
ing the edge. The car evidently had run away, and only a thick
hedge-growth prevented it from plunging into the pit."[2]

Agatha was gone.

At the time, she was a little-known mystery writer. That
spring, she'd published *The Murder of Roger Ackroyd*, her third

novel featuring the detective Hercule Poirot. The book was ingeniously constructed—the narrator turned out to be the killer—but only sold a few thousand copies.* Agatha was disappointed, as she needed money to finance her fancy lifestyle.[3] (She depended on three household servants.) To add insult to economic injury, her husband, Archie Christie, had fallen in love with a younger woman. He kept asking for a divorce.

The police initially suspected suicide. Agatha had visited her chemist a few days before; they had a morbid conversation about the best drafts for a painless death.[4] Near her crashed car, the police found an open bottle of "poison lead and opium." It seemed like a simple tragedy: a spurned wife had taken her own life.

But if Agatha had killed herself, where was the body? The police hired divers and drained a nearby pond. They scoured the Surrey Downs with bloodhounds. After the authorities put out a call for volunteers, thousands of amateur detectives showed up to look for the missing woman. But the crowds found nothing, not even footprints. It was as if Agatha had vanished into thin air.

The police officer in charge of the investigation, Deputy Chief Constable Kenward, began to suspect that Agatha had been murdered. Kenward was the kind of detective that Agatha Christie liked to invent in her novels—a man of deduction, he'd been awarded the King's Police Medal for closing several difficult murder cases. Kenward had a trim mustache, a bulging belly, and a fondness for fedoras.

When it came to Agatha's disappearance, Kenward fixated on the fur coat she'd left behind in the back seat.[5] As Kenward noted,

---

* When Agatha was first reported missing, the papers described her as "a woman novelist" and mistakenly described her most recent book as *Who Killed Ackroyd?*

the temperature at midnight was thirty-six degrees. A damp wind was blowing in from the northeast. Why, then, hadn't Agatha taken her coat? Even suicidal people want to stay warm.

Kenward was also suspicious of the crash. The car had been driven down a hill, but there were no skid marks on the dirt. Why hadn't the driver tried to brake? The canvas roof was still attached, and the paint remained unscratched. It was as if, Kenward thought, someone had carefully driven the car to the edge of the cliff.[6]

And then there was the Archie problem. Kenward knew Archie wanted a divorce. The servants said he'd had a bitter fight with Agatha the day before. When Kenward asked Archie where he'd been the night of her disappearance, he admitted that he was with his mistress at a friend's house. Worst of all, he'd burned the letter Agatha had left for him, telling the police that it was a private matter. Kenward found the husband "vague and defensive."[7]

Yet, Archie had a solid alibi—his friend swore Archie had been with him all evening.[8] (The car was in the garage, and he would have heard the dog bark.) And even if Archie *had* snuck out, Kenward couldn't figure out how he'd have returned before morning. It was too long a walk and there was no sign of a second car. And why would the killer have left the poison behind?

Days passed. A reward of £100 was posted, but that only led to errant sightings. Agatha was dressed as a man on a London bus. She was wandering around Battersea. She was on a train to Portsmouth. The more Kenward learned about the case, the more mysterious it became. Every lead was a dead end.

As the press swarmed, Archie panicked. In an interview given to the *Daily Mail*, six days after Agatha went missing, he speculated that Agatha had staged her own disappearance. It was a literary exercise, not a crime. "Some time ago she told her sister, 'I could disappear if I wished and set about it properly,'" he remembered.[9] "They were discussing what appeared in the papers, I think. That shows that the possibility of engineering a disappearance had been running through her mind, probably for the purpose of her work."[10]

The public didn't buy it, but Archie was right: Agatha hadn't been kidnapped or murdered. *She had vanished herself.* As the biographer Laura Thompson observes, Agatha's disappearance was, in many respects, her finest mystery story. She had turned her own life into an irresistible whodunit, artfully placing clues that captivated the public. It was, the *Times* declared, "one of the most sensational disappearances that ever enlivened the columns of the English newspapers."[11]

Before she vanished, the public didn't know who she was. They only cared because she couldn't be found.

On December 14, eleven days after Agatha Christie was first reported missing, a banjo player at the Swan Hydropathic Hotel in Harrogate noticed that a woman on the dance floor closely resembled the missing writer. The musician told the police, who passed on the tip to Archie.

When Archie arrived at the Swan, he was told by the police to wait in the lobby. The hotel manager said that Agatha would soon descend for dinner; she'd already made a reservation. After a few minutes, Archie spotted her on the staircase, dressed for another night of dancing in a pink georgette evening dress. Agatha calmly returned his gaze, then took a seat by the fireplace in the lounge. After a few minutes of awkward silence, the couple headed into the hotel restaurant for dinner.[12]

Although Archie wished to remain silent, the hordes of reporters demanded answers. Agatha's disappearance remained front-page news. To appease the papers, Archie gave a statement to the

*Yorkshire Post*: "There is no question about her identity. She is my wife. She is suffering from complete loss of memory and identity. She does not know who she is. She does not know me. . . . I hope that rest and quiet will put her right."

Archie assumed his explanation would end the spectacle, that he could soon return to his golf game and mistress. However, as Laura Thompson notes, this only proves that "Archie did not have a clue about what he was doing, what he had become mixed up in."[13] Perhaps if he'd read Agatha's fiction, he would have appreciated the appeal of a good detective story.

Agatha, of course, knew exactly what she was doing. As a crime writer, Agatha understood the allure of the unknown: the best stories give us tantalizing clues but withhold the answer for as long as possible. "The detective story was the story of the chase," Agatha would later declare.[14] Not the catch. *The chase*. And she had just engineered the perfect chase.*

Although Archie blamed amnesia for her disappearance, Agatha was writing again within days. Before she crashed the car, she'd been struggling to finish her next detective novel. There were days she didn't think she'd ever figure it out. (Her mother-in-law told the *Daily Mail* that Agatha walked around the house muttering, "These rotten plots! Oh! These rotten plots.")[16] It was so hard making the details line up, telling the story without giving away the surprise.

But something shifted after her return from Harrogate. "That

---

* The crime writer Dorothy L. Sayers, after reviewing the clues of the case, concluded that it was likely a "voluntary disappearance. . . .[It] may be so cleverly staged as to be exceedingly puzzling—especially, as here, we are concerned with a skillful writer of detective stories."[15] Sayers could recognize a good setup when she saw one. And this was a very good setup. Too good, perhaps.

was the moment when I changed from an amateur to a professional," Agatha wrote in her memoir.[17] She was now committed to her craft, determined to apply the lessons of her disappearance to her fiction. There was a strange power in the mystery story: we were hooked by those tales we couldn't solve, drawn to those crimes and plots that kept us guessing.

But the mystery story did not always exist.

It had to be invented.

## The Rue Morgue

In the spring of 1841, at the age of thirty-two, Edgar Allan Poe decided to write a new kind of short story. At the time, Poe was best known for a magazine column on cryptography in which he dared readers to send him a code he couldn't crack. He received nearly a hundred secret messages from all over the country. Poe solved them all, except for one. And that coded message he proved to be "an imposition," a jumble of "random characters having no meaning whatever."[18]

Unfortunately for Poe, his column only paid a few dollars a page. As his editor observed, "The character of Poe's mind was of such an order, as not to be very widely in demand." Poe's desperate need for money led him to try writing fiction, as he searched for a tale that could pay his rent and bar tab. He gave his first story a salacious title—"The Murders in the Rue Morgue"—and an intriguing protagonist, Monsieur C. Auguste Dupin, a young bachelor living in Paris who is also able to crack the most inscrutable codes.

The story takes places during a recent summer, when the evening papers arrive with news of an extraordinary double murder.

The mother's body was found in the garden, "her throat so entirely cut that, upon an attempt to raise her, the head fell off and rolled to some distance." The daughter, meanwhile, had been rammed up the chimney, killed by brute force. While the police initially assumed the motive to be theft, no valuables were missing. After a lengthy and fruitless investigation, the police concluded that "a murder so mysterious, and so perplexing in all its particulars, was never before committed in Paris."

Dupin is drawn to the mystery. He tells the narrator that they should visit the crime scene for themselves; perhaps they will stumble upon an overlooked clue. If nothing else, Dupin says, "an inquiry will afford us amusement."

After a lengthy examination of the bloodied apartment, and interviews with the neighbors, the narrator is more confused than ever. He concludes the murders are "insoluble." Dupin lets out an exasperated sigh, then systematically lays out his solution to the unusual case.

Dupin begins by summarizing the most perplexing facts of the crime: the needless decapitation, the girl stuffed up the fireplace, the absence of apparent motive. While the cops are searching for a madman, Dupin concludes that the murderer isn't a man at all— he's an orangutan. Furthermore, Dupin has already placed an advertisement in the newspaper for an escaped primate. A few pages later, a sailor shows up, looking for his guilty pet.

Poe's story was an instant success. The ghastly crime and brilliant detective mesmerized readers. Poe even got paid: the owner of the magazine gave him $56 for the tale. But Poe shrugged off the achievement, writing to a friend that "people think them [his detective stories] more ingenious than they are . . . In the 'Murders in the Rue Morgue,' for instance, where is the ingenuity in unraveling a web which you yourself . . . have woven for the express purpose of unraveling?"[19] If Poe was proud of these popular tales, he wrote, it was because he had finally come up with "something in a new key."[20]

What Poe had come up with was the detective story.* His formula went this way: First, there is the impossible crime, followed by the baffled cops. The case appears to be hopeless. But then our brilliant detective appears. He ponders some neglected clues, connects the far-fetched dots, and comes up with an inspired solution. Moral order is restored in the last act, when the guilty soul is found and punished.

This formula has since led to one of the most successful genres of modern culture. From Agatha Christie to Raymond Chandler, Michael Connelly to *Law & Order*, these narratives still obey the tropes and traditions invented by the young Edgar Allan Poe. As Arthur Conan Doyle would later admit, Monsieur Dupin was the first Sherlock. Poe deserved credit for "the monstrous progeny of writers on the detection of crime."

In 1948, nearly a century after Poe's untimely death, the poet W. H. Auden wrote an essay in *Harper's* that tried to explain the enduring popularity of the detective story.[22] For Auden, the subject had personal stakes: "For me, as for many others, the reading of detective stories is an addiction like tobacco or alcohol. The symptoms of this are: Firstly, the intensity of the craving—if I have any work to do, I must be careful not to get hold of a detective story for, once I begin one, I cannot work or sleep till I have finished it." And while Auden dismissed most of these crime

---

* Otto Penzler, the coauthor of *Encyclopedia of Mystery and Detection*, says that Poe was "the first writer to invent the detective story in its pure form. . . . Although there are clearly elements of the detective story in other stories, such as 'The Rifle' by William Leggett, Poe was the first to condense it all and put it all together."[21]

novels as pulpy fictions, he also believed that a close study of the detective story might "throw light . . . on the function of art."

Auden's argument began with a short history of tragedy: "In Greek tragedy, the audience knows the truth." The plot is spoiled at the start. *Oedipus Rex*, for instance, is the story of a man searching for the murderer of the king. It's framed as a cryptic crime story, but everyone already knows how the story ends: Oedipus is the killer he's trying to find.

The genius of Poe was inverting this ancient formula, creating a tale designed to keep the reader in the dark. (The root of *mystery* is the ancient Greek *muo*, which means "to shut the eyes," or "to hide.") While fiction had traditionally relied on predictable beats, Poe's stories were built around the element of surprise. He took the delightful search for clues that had defined narratives since Oedipus but added in an unpredictable ending. (As Auden noted, the entire point of the detective story was that "the audience does not know the truth at all.") And so the reader becomes another sleuth, searching for clues just like the characters on the page.

Poe's insight was that the audience didn't care about the murder. That was just the setup, the inciting incident. What they really cared about was the mystery.

## The Hook

When Edgar Allan Poe invented the detective story, he discovered a new way to hook the human mind. The enduring appeal of Poe's formula raises a larger question: Why is it so compelling? Why do we get obsessed with missing writers and impossible crimes? Why does mystery create a mental itch that must be scratched?

The explanation begins with a strange feature of the dopamine system, an ancient part of the animal brain. While dopamine is often associated with hedonism—it's supposed to be the chemical of sex, drugs, and rock 'n' roll—one of the most important functions of dopamine is the way it controls our attention. In essence, dopamine acts as a neural currency, allowing us to appraise the world and locate the most interesting parts. The feeling of delight is just the brain's way of telling itself to look over there, notice this, focus on that.

So what triggers the biggest spikes in dopamine? It's not predictable pleasures. Rather, it's pleasures that arrive with *a sense of mystery*, or what neuroscientists refer to as "prediction errors."[23] In the lab, scientists trigger these prediction errors by establishing a rewarding pattern—hit a lever, get some sugar—and then introducing a surprise, such as a sweet treat that arrives without warning. (You can also elicit a large dopamine spike with less pleasing shocks, such as loud sounds and flashing lights.) These brain cells are sensitive to surprises because it's an incredibly efficient way to learn, which is why the same quirk of programming exists in fruit flies, mice, and primates.[24]

This mental software has been around for millions and millions of years. The human brain, however, found a way to put this old code to new use. The crucial turn is the ability to find pleasure not just in calories and sex but in ideas and narratives. It doesn't matter if it's a newspaper story about an inexplicable disappearance or an Edgar Allan Poe whodunit: these works still excite the dopaminergic system, which is why we pay attention even when they contain no primal rewards.* As the anthropologist Clifford

---

* Such are the ironies of natural selection: no matter how lofty our ideas get, you don't have to look too far before it all comes back to sugar and orgasms.

Geertz famously observed, "Man is an animal suspended in webs of significance he himself has spun."[25]

But remember, this dopamine system comes with a peculiar feature. Although the human brain is a pattern-making machine, always attempting to solve for $x$ and predict what's next, it's not the accurate predictions that grab our attention—it's those *prediction errors*, the rewards and revelations we can't anticipate. Good art turns this impulse into engagement, establishing a premise and then subtly violating our expectations, postponing the answer for as long as possible. Because it's the questions that keep us interested. Not the expected turn, but the twist we never saw coming. As Stephen Sondheim observed, in a summary of his aesthetic approach, "Art needs surprise, otherwise it doesn't hold an audience's attention."[26]

Prediction errors are just the start of this neural process. If the tale is well told, that initial surprise gives way to a feeling entirely unique to human beings. We stop trying to solve the problem and start surfing the mystery instead, immersing ourselves in what we'll never understand. This feeling goes by many names—wonder, awe, astonishment—but it is rooted in the pleasure of the mysterious. Most animals fear the dark. We find our greatest meaning in it.

In this book, we'll deconstruct the most alluring mysteries. We'll look at how artists, magicians, musicians, teachers, and storytellers use the unknown and uncertain to capture our attention. We have all had the experience of lusting after a mystery, whether it's binge-watching *Law & Order* or being moved by a poem we can't explain. This book aims to provide a theory for why those experiences matter.

We'll begin with the simplest form of mystery, which is the mystery box. In essence, it's the generation of interest by hiding some crucial information from the audience, such as the identity of the murderer or the outcome of the slot machine. The technique helps explain the rules of baseball and the appeal of L.O.L. dolls. It's been used to great effect by Steve Jobs and George Lucas. These boxes arrest us because we want to know what's inside.

But mystery boxes aren't the only way to hook the audience. The second strategy we'll look at is the magic trick. This approach creates questions about the creative process. We see the object vanish, or the woman sawed in half—the mystery is how it happened. It's a technique used by magicians, of course, but also by painters, directors, and architects. They like to make art whose making we can't explain.

We'll turn next to desirable difficulty, the strategy of creating mystery by subverting our expectations. Our culture is overstuffed with content that aims to please. But the stuff that lasts is more difficult, challenging us to make sense of forms we've never before seen. It doesn't matter if it's an Emily Dickinson poem or *Goodnight Moon* or an iconic car advertisement: the work remains interesting because it's a struggle to understand.

And then there's the mystery of a complicated character. From Hamlet to Tony Soprano, the Mona Lisa to Walter White—we are fascinated by those characters full of subtleties and contradictions. They are interesting *because* we can't figure them out. What's more, there's compelling evidence that these imaginary characters teach us how to deal with the mysteries of real people.

The last technique we'll explore is deliberate ambiguity. We'll look at Beatles lyrics and medieval coded manuscripts, romantic sonnets and J. D. Salinger short stories. What these works have in common is the way they suggest multiple interpretations, captivating us with their exquisite uncertainty.

These strategies represent the different hooks of mystery. Although they can take on countless different forms, they share the same goal: hooking the audience with the unknown and unknowable, turning our prediction errors into immersive entertainment.

However, the best cultural mysteries combine these techniques, using multiple hooks to generate a lasting sense of wonder. They might start with a mystery box, but also rely on opaque characters and ambiguity. Or maybe they feature a magic trick *and* deliberate difficulty. Once this happens, the mystery stops being something we solve and becomes an *infinite game*, a work we can return to again and again. The mystery persists.

This ability to grapple with mystery is an essential human skill, a cognitive talent that sets the best thinkers apart. In this book, we'll learn how such passionate curiosity can be taught. We'll visit an inner-city school in Chicago that has dramatically improved its test scores by cultivating a sense of mystery in its students. We'll meet a car mechanic who can solve every mechanical failure because he never stops asking questions. We'll discover why difficult literature makes us more empathetic and playing with infinite games can make us more creative. In the twenty-first century, it's not about what you know. It's about knowing what you don't.

John Keats, the Romantic poet, famously described Shakespeare's greatest gift as "Negative Capability," which he defined as the ability to live with "uncertainties, mysteries, doubts, without any irritable reaching after fact and reason."[27] In Keats's reading, Shakespeare had no interest in simple truths; he wasn't concerned when his plots became confusing or his characters acted in unpredictable ways. Rather, he wanted to hook his audience with the hardest questions, creating whodunits that never reveal who did it. Shakespeare was one of those writers who, as Keats put it, embraced "the burden of the mystery" in his writing, which is why his plays still haunt us.

The success of such art is a kind of mirror: by giving us what we want, it shows us who we are. In this whole universe, we might be the only ones who like to create things we don't understand.

# CHAPTER 1

# THE MYSTERY BOX

Nothing whets the intelligence more than a passionate
suspicion, nothing develops all the faculties of an immature
mind more than a trail running away into the dark.

—STEFAN ZWEIG[1]

Ryan was three years old when he began starring in videos about his toys. The clips are exactly what you'd expect: In his first video, Ryan picks out a LEGO Duplo train at the toy store. He opens the box and clicks the plastic pieces together. He pushes the toy back and forth on the carpet. Then he knocks it over. The video ends, about four minutes later, as Ryan's boredom sets in.

The early archive of Ryan ToysReview is a testament to the fickle preferences of toddlers. There are some Thomas the Tank Engine scenes, messy Play-Doh moments, and assorted Pixar characters in the bath. The videos are shaky, barely edited, and have no narrative beyond the tragic arc of every new toy, which children love most before it's opened.

If Ryan had stopped here, he'd be just another obscure toddler unboxing toys for strangers. (There are tens of thousands of "toy review" channels on YouTube.) But everything changed with Ryan's thirty-third video, created four months after his parents started filming his playtime. For this clip, Ryan's mother decided to do something a little different. The video begins with Ryan sleeping in his bed. His mom wakes him up to reveal a gigantic papier-mâché egg plastered with Disney stickers. Ryan tears open the egg and begins pulling out a random assortment of toys. There's a Fisher-Price garage, dozens of die-cast cars, and a big yellow dump truck. Once the egg is emptied—this takes most of the seven minutes—Ryan briefly plays with the cars on his bedroom floor. It's hyperconsumerism at its most inane.

But this short video is insanely popular. Since it was posted on July 1, 2015, the clip has attracted more than a *billion* views. I've watched it countless times with my young son, who eventually memorized the entire sequence of toys pulled from the egg. ("Next up is Mack the Truck!") Ryan's parents credit the surprise-egg video with launching Ryan ToysReview, one of the most viewed YouTube channels in the United States with nearly 27 million subscribers and more than 42.2 billion views. In 2017, Ryan Toys-Review generated an estimated $26 million in income.[2] Target and Walmart now sell Ryan's World–branded surprise eggs.*

Success breeds imitation. The surprise-toy egg has become a leading category on YouTube Kids. (Because the app allows young children to choose their own videos, it can help us understand what kids want to watch.) There's the "Giant Princess Surprise Egg by Disney Toys Review" (297 million views), the "Truck Car

---

* In recent years, "reveal toys" have become a staple of the toy aisle. From L.O.L. Surprise! dolls, which feature a hidden figurine beneath seven layers of plastic packaging, to Disney "mystery packs," which hide surprise collectibles inside an opaque, shrink-wrapped box, these toys take advantage of our innate curiosity. We buy the packaging just to find out what's inside. From a rational perspective, these reveal toys make no sense, since consumers can't choose their favorites and often get stuck with duplicates. But we're willing to sacrifice the utility in exchange for the delight of surprise.

Toy Surprise Eggs" by ToyPudding (90 million views), and the "GIANT MY LITTLE PONY Surprise Eggs Compilation Play Doh" (121 million views). Each video might feature a different assortment of the latest playthings, but they all rely on the same crude narrative hook: presents are hidden inside an egg. Nobody knows what toy will be pulled out next.

Why are egg videos so compulsively entertaining, at least for young children? The explanation is rooted in the appeal of mystery. The surprise egg, after all, is just a means of producing prediction errors. Will Ryan pull out Lightning McQueen next? Why is there a plane amid the mess of Hot Wheels?

In Hollywood, this is known as the mystery box technique. As defined by the writer and director J. J. Abrams—he's best known for creating *Lost* and rebooting *Star Trek* and *Star Wars*—a mystery box is any contained secret that drives the story forward. It's the meaning of Rosebud and the location of the groom in *The Hangover*; the look of the great white shark in *Jaws*—we don't fully see the beast until eighty minutes into the movie*—and the identity of Keyser Söze in *The Usual Suspects*. And then there's *Star Wars: A New Hope*, Abrams's favorite example. "The droids meet the mysterious woman. Who's that? We don't know. Mystery box! Then you meet Luke Skywalker. He gets the droid, you see the holographic image. You learn, oh! It's a message. She wants to find Obi-Wan Kenobi. He's her only hope. But who the hell's Obi-Wan Kenobi? Mystery box!"[3] Abrams's point is that *Star Wars*, like

---

* Sometimes, the best mystery boxes are accidents. For instance, the shark in *Jaws* is hidden for so long because the robotic fish kept malfunctioning. (The crew nicknamed the movie *Flaws* due to the frequent delays in filming.) But Spielberg realized that we are most scared of what we can't see and turned the broken great white into the most terrifying mystery box.

most suspenseful movies, lurches from one unknown to another, creating narrative moments in which information is intentionally withheld. The story is compelling because of what it hides.

Abrams first discovered the power of mystery boxes as a child, when his grandfather gave him Tannen's Magic Mystery Box. "The premise behind the Mystery Magic Box was the following: fifteen dollars buys you fifty dollars' worth of magic," Abrams remembers in his TED Talk on the subject. "Which is a savings." But Abrams has never opened the Magic Mystery Box. It still sits, in the original packaging, on a shelf in his Santa Monica office.

Why hasn't Abrams opened the container of magic tricks? Because he grasps the hook of the mystery box. It's like a surprise egg for grown-ups. "The thing [about the unopened box] is that it represents infinite possibility," Abrams says. "It represents hope. It represents potential. And what I love about this box, and what I realize I sort of do in whatever it is that I do, is I find myself drawn to infinite possibility."

Steve Jobs would understand. He used that same sense of possibility as a sales tool. In 2007, when he introduced the iPhone, Jobs could have begun his keynote with a glamour shot of the new product. Instead, he opened with a Jobsian riddle, announcing that he was introducing three new devices: a wide-screen iPod, a mobile phone, and a breakthrough internet interface. The catch was that the three features were all bundled in the same gadget. "Today, Apple is going to reinvent the phone, and here it is," Jobs said.[4]

But the new phone wasn't there—Jobs still wasn't ready to open the mystery box. ("Actually here it is," Jobs said, coyly flashing a shiny phone to the crowd before hiding it in his pocket. "But we're gonna leave it there for now.") Jobs then launched into a detailed discussion of the competition. It was a classic stall tactic, building the anticipation by concealing what everyone wanted to see. Several minutes later, when Jobs finally displayed a picture of the iPhone, the crowd erupted, their faces filled with the same joyous anticipation as a toddler tearing open a surprise egg full of toys.

The deep appeal of mystery boxes is written into our basic software. When you show two-month-old babies a selection of items, they are far more interested in the unfamiliar ones; they keep staring at what they've never before seen. This pursuit of novelty quickly blossoms into a general interest in everything that seems mysterious. In one study, the psychologist Frank Lorimer followed around a four-year-old boy for several days.[5] Lorimer kept track of every "why" question asked by the child. Lorimer ended up with pages of queries, almost all of which were delightfully random. Why, the boy asked, does the little chicken grow in the shell? Why does the watering pot have two handles? Why doesn't his mother have a beard?*

The chronic curiosity of children can get wearisome. (In the long transcripts of those why questions, one can almost hear the tired sighs of the parents.) But it's also an important reminder of our intellectual beginnings, those early instincts that define us as human beings. When children look out at the world, they don't focus on what they know. They stare at what they don't. And so they keep asking us *Why? Why? Why?*, their developing minds leaping from one mystery box to the next.

This turns out to be a crucial skill: those children most drawn to mystery also do much better in school. That's the conclusion of a longitudinal study by researchers at the University of Michigan that analyzed data from sixty-two young students.[7] They assessed

---

* More recently, a study by Michelle Chouinard and colleagues found that one group of young children asked their caregivers an average of 76.8 information-seeking questions *per hour*.[6]

the young subjects and interviewed their parents multiple times, beginning at nine months of age. They found that interest in the unknown strongly predicted academic performance, even after the researchers controlled for other psychological variables, such as the ability to focus in class. What's more, the correlation was particularly strong among children from poorer families. While these students generally performed worse in school than their peers from wealthier families, this difference disappeared among low-income students with high levels of curiosity.

What explains this finding? One theory is that the enjoyment of mystery is a crucial advantage provided by higher socioeconomic status. If your parents have money, they can afford to encourage your curiosity, investing in piano lessons and museum memberships. They can get you all the mystery boxes you want. Over time, this cultivation of curiosity pays academic dividends— you learn how to learn—which is one of the reasons family wealth predicts classroom performance. However, if poor children can close the curiosity gap, the stubborn achievement gap also vanishes. Teaching children how to enjoy mystery, then, isn't just a nice luxury—it's an essential part of education.

You can see this process unfold in the brain. In a recent study, scientists at UC Davis looked at how states of curiosity change the way we learn.[8] Researchers placed subjects inside an fMRI machine and asked dozens of trivia questions on topics ranging from history ("Who was president of the US when Uncle Sam got a beard?") to language ("What does the term *dinosaur* actually mean?"). After rating their level of curiosity, subjects were flashed a picture of an unrelated face. Then, they received the answer to the trivia question (Franklin Pierce, terrible lizard). When the scanning session was over, the subjects took a test to measure their memory both for the trivia questions and the faces. Did they re-member the answers? Could they recognize the faces?

The trend was clear: subjects were much better at remem-bering those questions that triggered their curiosity. That's not particularly surprising. What was more unexpected, however, was that people were also much better at remembering the unrelated faces they saw during states of elevated curiosity. The fMRI data helped explain why. When subjects were more curious about the trivia, their brains displayed increased activity in the dopamine-rich circuits of the midbrain. These are the same areas that process rewards and respond to prediction errors; they're turned on by all sorts of mystery boxes. But here's the most interesting part: the dopamine surge of curiosity also led to a spike in activity in the hippocampus, a part of the brain that's crucial for learning and memory.[9] William James argued that curiosity began when a per-son experienced an "inconsistency or a gap in . . . knowledge, just as the musical brain responds to a discord in what it hears."[10] The lesson of this new research is that such a gap turns on our learning machinery. We aren't just paying attention to the new informa-tion; we're saving it in our hard drive. The toys we remember are the ones hidden inside the egg.

In many respects, mystery boxes are the simplest way to create mystery. They take some crucial information and hide it. Some-times, this information is hidden inside a giant egg, or by a plot twist involving a princess and her droid. But these different meth-ods share the same goal: to create some epistemic tension, depriv-ing us of the secrets we seek.

However, not all mystery boxes are created equal. If you understand what the mind really wants, and if you're ruthless about the consequences, it's possible to design a mystery box so mesmerizing it can become addictive. People will give you all of their money to keep them in the dark.

## The Case of the One-Armed Bandit

In 1982, an obscure Norwegian mathematician named Inge Telnaes filed a patent that would transform the gambling industry.[11] That wasn't his aim, though. Telnaes was trying to solve a marketing problem for casinos: their slot machines could only feature relatively small jackpots. The problem was rooted in the mechanical design of the machine, which usually featured three reels and twelve distinct symbols (sevens, cherries, etc.). As Telnaes pointed out in his patent application, the payout of a given machine was directly constrained by the number of symbols, so that a gambling device with twenty different symbols, three reels, and a $1 price to play couldn't offer a jackpot bigger than $8,000 or the house would lose money.[12]* Unfortunately, these smaller jackpots weren't very alluring to gamblers. Why play slots when the roulette table offers much richer prizes?

To skirt this constraint, casinos experimented with larger slot machines offering extra symbols. Instead of the usual fruit and sevens, they might also include horseshoes, diamonds, and dollar signs. However, gamblers rightly sensed that these extra symbols diluted their odds. More pictures meant fewer chances to win.

Telnaes's ingenious solution was to make the process virtual. While traditional slot machines relied on a tripping arm that locked into a groove on the slot gears—the ticking sound was genuine—

---

* The math is straightforward: 20 x 20 x 20 is 8000. Given taxes and operational costs, casinos generally had to set their payouts 2 to 15 percent below the maximum payout.

Telnaes imagined a mystery box running on a random-number generator. There would still be reels and pictures of cherries— they would just be an abstract representation of the results spit out by a microchip. (The clicks were now an ersatz soundtrack.) As gaming expert John Robison notes, this innovation introduced an "intermediate step" between the pull of the slot arm and the outcome of the game, since the payout was no longer dictated by those whirring gears. "You can do all sorts of wonderful things in that intermediate step," he wrote.[13]

The first wonderful thing you can do, at least from the perspective of a greedy casino, is advertise slots with huge jackpots. Rather than be limited by the number of mechanical reels, casinos could program the random generator to pick from a number set of any size. Slots could now feature millions of possible outcomes, with each of these outcomes mapped onto a specific set of symbols. Let's imagine, for instance, a dollar slot offering a $1 million payout. That large payout would be linked to a single reel—say, three sevens across—but that reel would only appear if one winning number was generated. The other millions of outcomes would be mapped onto some combination of losing reels, thus allowing the house to advertise a huge payout while still ensuring a healthy profit margin.*

This new bit of programming made slots far more appealing. Although the chance of winning the jackpot on a slot machine

---

* There is something clearly deceptive about this technique. Bally, one of the largest manufacturers of slot machines, was initially concerned that virtual reel mapping was too misleading. In testimony before the Nevada Gaming Control Board in 1983, Bally's president put it this way: "One of the reasons reel-spinning slot machines have been so successful throughout their history is that players can visually see during the course of several handle pulls all of the symbols on all of the reels as they spin. . . . It would appear to us that if a mechanical reel on a slot machine possesses four sevens and it is electronically playing as if there were one seven, the player is being visually misled."[14]

with hundreds of virtual reels might be as low as 1 in 137,000,000, the gaming device felt far easier to beat. (One early analysis of virtual-reel slots found that, if the machines paid out according to the perceived frequency of their symbols, players would actually come out way ahead.) So players kept inserting coins and credits into the mystery box, chasing a reward they'd never receive.

It didn't take long before gambling companies realized how much money they could make with these virtual reels. According to the anthropologist Natasha Dow Schüll, who chronicles the history of the slot machine in *Addiction by Design*, more than 80 percent of spinning slots used virtual reels by the mid-1990s.[15]

However, casinos soon discovered an even more effective use of virtual reels. The key was to manipulate the way players perceived their losses, not just their potential gains. The machines did this through the frequent use of "near misses," a gambling illusion in which people think they *almost* won because the reel stops next to a winning symbol. Look, for instance, at the evil genius of slot machine manufacturer Universal, which developed a two-stage process after each spin. The first stage determined whether the player won. If he lost—and the vast majority of spins are losers—the second stage initiated the near-miss effect, setting up the player to believe he had come exceedingly close to a real payout. (There might be two sevens on the main pay line, and then a third seven just below.) Although near misses cost the casinos nothing, they keep gamblers motivated, persuading people to stick with a game that's stacked against them.

It's now possible to understand why near misses are so compelling. In a recent *Neuron* paper, scientists at Cambridge University showed that near misses on a slot machine task activated the same reward circuitry as an actual win, triggering blood flow to dopamine-rich areas of the brain.[16]

Why are we wired this way? One hypothesis is that enjoying

near misses helps us persist when learning a difficult new skill. Let's say we're practicing a three-point shot in basketball. At first, our shots are going to be all over the place, a seemingly random distribution of bricks and airballs. Yet, as we slowly get better, those shots will get closer to the rim. A few might even go in, which can be pretty thrilling. Near misses, then, keep us motivated as we slowly improve our form. If we only got excited by makes, we'd give up. The brain needs a mechanism to enjoy incremental progress.

Unfortunately, this practical software is cruelly misled by those gambling machines. There is no skill with these mystery boxes; pulling a lever doesn't take talent. Nevertheless, those dopamine neurons activated by near misses—the peppy cheerleaders of the brain—urge us onward anyway, insisting that we keep playing because we keep *almost* winning. Alas, the only thing we're getting better at is losing money.

The larger lesson of slot machines is that culture never stays still—it is constantly evolving to better fit the grooves of the human mind. Over time, slots have become mystery boxes of astonishing power.

The slot machines do this by carefully manipulating randomness to create a tantalizing state of mystery. While pure randomness quickly gets tedious, virtual reels allow the slots to disguise their inner chaos, tricking the brain into seeing subtle patterns. If we keep gambling, we'll get those triple sevens; all those near misses must mean we're getting closer. It's that illusory sense of progress—the promise of a mystery box we might one day open—that makes slots so tragically compelling.

To explain the power of the slot machine is not to excuse it: the casino delivers squirts of chemical pleasure stripped of all context and meaning. Yet, one can see how the appeal of these gambling gadgets also relies on the same basic psychological mechanisms as the toy egg and *Star Wars*. (As the critic Dave Hickey wrote, in an astute observation about Las Vegas and America, "What is hidden elsewhere exists here [in Vegas] in quotidian visibility.")[17] We want surprise and suspense, but we also crave order and closure. The artistry of the mystery box is in the balance: give away too much and we're bored, give away too little and we're lost.

This is known as the inverted-U curve theory of curiosity. It was first identified by the psychologist Daniel Berlyne, in a series of classic studies done in the late 1960s.[18] Berlyne began the experiments by showing people a collection of simple visual patterns, such as four identical squares, or the outline of a sun. Berlyne then introduced complications, such as asymmetry and irregularity. He added in smudges of randomness and extraneous detail.

As subjects looked at these images, Berlyne asked them to rate each for "pleasingness," "interestingness," and on a scale from ugly to beautiful, which he referred to as "hedonic value." He also measured how long the people looked at the patterns.

The results looked like an upside-down *U*, hence the name of the phenomenon:

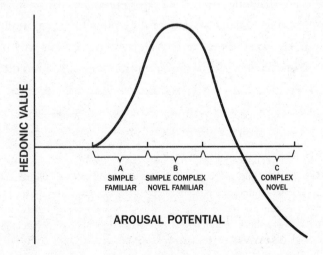

Berlyne found that simple and familiar shapes bored people; nobody wanted to keep staring at a few straight lines. But people also dismissed shapes that were too random and incongruous. Our attention had a hedonic sweet spot, clearly preferring patterns that were unknown but not unknowable. (In Berlyne's formulation, they were either simple and novel *or* complex and familiar.)[19] We wanted a mystery—a new visual form—but one we could still decipher.* And as we'll soon see, the ability to locate the ideal amount of mystery, and to hide it within the right box, helps explain the most popular form of entertainment in the world.

## The Rule Change of 1893

If an anthropologist from Mars studied our culture, our obsession with sports would mystify her. According to one recent measure, ninety-three of the top one hundred American television programs watched live across a single year have been sports related.[21] More people watched the Super Bowl than the Oscars, Emmys, Grammys, Golden Globes, and Tonys *combined*.

Yet, as the Martian would surely notice, these contests have no stakes, at least in the real world; it doesn't matter which team wins. Nevertheless, we lavish vast amounts of attention on these

---

* The industrial designer Raymond Loewy referred to this discovery as the MAYA theory of aesthetics, with MAYA standing for Most Advanced Yet Acceptable design. As the creator of countless midcentury icons—from the Greyhound bus to the Studebaker Avanti to the Lucky Strike logo—Loewy was constantly tasked with navigating the razor's edge of innovation. He needed to invent radically new things, but these new things couldn't be too intimidating. "When resistance to the unfamiliar reaches the threshold of a shock-zone and resistance to buying sets in, the design in question has reached its MAYA stage," Loewy wrote.[20]

freakishly shaped athletes playing with bouncy balls. We spend a fortune on gigantic stadiums and tickets to those stadiums. The games make us cheer and scream and cry.

To explain this peculiar human behavior, the alien anthropologist might begin with a search of the scientific literature. She would come across a wide range of potential explanations. These include the tribal theory—teams are like tribes, hijacking our Neolithic social instincts—and the mirror neuron speculation, which holds that we enjoy watching athletes because our brain imitates their perfect physical movements.[22] We live vicariously through their grace.

These theories are nice. They have a logical sheen. But they fail to explain why some sports are so much more popular than others. After all, not every game makes us care. It's the rare competition that turns us into passionate fans or gets a prime-time spot on national television. So what is it about our most successful sports that makes them successful?

If the Martian tried to answer *these* questions, she might eventually run across a largely forgotten paper by Nicholas Christenfeld, a psychologist who spent his career at the University of California, San Diego.[23] A wiry man, with a chiseled face, twitchy hands, and sardonic sense of humor, Christenfeld is that rare modern scientist who refuses to narrow his interests. He has studied the psychology of *um*s and *uh*s[24]—art historians use more of them than chemists*—and the biases that determine our choice of bathroom stalls.[25] (People are much more likely to choose a middle stall, due

---

* The main reason people in the humanities use more "filled pauses" than scientists is that their technical vocabulary is less precise. Those extra *um*s are a kind of indecisiveness, as their brains search for the best word to use. "Chemists don't have this problem as frequently," Christenfeld says. "*Molecule* has a very specific meaning."

to our deep-seated aversion to edges.) Christenfeld has looked at whether dogs resemble their owners (they do),[26] if it's possible to be tickled by a robot (it is),[27] and the impact of a given name on mortality (men with "negative" initials, such as PIG or DIE, live 2.8 years less on average than matched controls).[28] "If you had to categorize my research, it's about the social psychology of everyday life," he says. "But mostly I'm just interested in the same idiosyncratic questions that everyone is interested in. I mean, who hasn't wondered if dogs look like their owners?"

Christenfeld's interest in sports began in an unlikely place, with a question about the novelist Joseph Heller, the author of *Catch-22*. Simply put, Christenfeld wanted to understand why Heller wrote only one great novel. "Heller wrote other books, sure, but no one thinks they're better than *Catch-22*," Christenfeld says. "Maybe the truth is that Heller only had one great book in him." But how is that possible? If Heller was capable of one masterpiece, shouldn't he be able to write a second?

These questions led Christenfeld to think more generally about the reliability of human achievement. Perhaps Heller never wrote another great novel because creativity is tangled up with luck and contingency. (Even Shakespeare wrote mediocre plays.) "Maybe it wasn't Heller's fault," Christenfeld says. "Perhaps he had the talent, but just didn't get lucky twice."

To explore the role of randomness in the creative process, Christenfeld began looking at one-hit wonders in other fields. Such artists exist in music, of course—Right Said Fred and Vanilla Ice, QED—but Christenfeld also found plenty of scientists whose entire careers depended on a single breakthrough. (They were the empirical version of "Ice Ice Baby.") This doesn't mean these researchers weren't smart. Rather, they just never got lucky enough to hit the achievement jackpot again.

The problem with this research approach is that success in the arts and sciences is full of confounding variables. Picasso created many second-rate sketches, but they're still "Picassos" and thus hang in museums. (His reputation distorts our critical judgment.) As Christenfeld puts it, "If you have one hit, it's often much easier to get that second hit. There's a non-independence problem."

To get around this issue, Christenfeld decided to look at athletic competitions, since the measures of success are far more objective. He began with sprinters. "Take a guy like Usain Bolt," Christenfeld says, citing the world record holder in the 100 and 200 meters. "He's the fastest man alive, but what is the standard deviation of his performances? I mean, if you see Bolt is in a race, are you fairly certain that he's going to win?"

The answer is an emphatic yes; running speed is far more predictable than success in the music industry, science, or literature. During his ten-year peak, Bolt had a winning percentage at major track events of 84 percent. That's a success rate Right Said Fred never dreamed of.

Christenfeld's curiosity is chronic; every answer only leads to more questions. "The predictability of sprinting got me thinking," Christenfeld says, in between bites of panini at the local university café. "The fastest guy almost always finishes first, but is that optimal? If you know who's going to win simply by looking at who's competing, isn't that a little boring?" While people clearly want sports that reward talent, Christenfeld knew that we also crave surprise, the thrill of an unlikely upset. "That struck me as an interesting tension. I began to wonder if there's an ideal level of predictability for these sporting competitions, and if I could find it."

This search for the perfect sport led Christenfeld to assess the statistical reliability of the most popular ones, including baseball, hockey, soccer, basketball, and football. (He assumed that their popularity was not an accident.) Christenfeld randomly divided each of their seasons in two segments and then asked a simple question: To what extent did a team's success in half of its games predict its success in the other half? If a sport is statistically reliable, then it should produce predictable outcomes; the better team should almost always win, just like Usain Bolt. An unreliable sport would be full of one-hit wonders like Joseph Heller and Vanilla Ice, teams whose performances were highly variable and inconsistent.

The first thing Christenfeld discovered is that different sports generate very different reliabilities per game. Major League Baseball, for instance, produces single-game outcomes that are roughly fourteen times less reliable than those of the NFL. (Put another way, the better football team almost always wins, while the better baseball team can easily lose.) But baseball is not all luck and chance. Instead, Christenfeld points out that the randomness of a single baseball game is balanced out by a regular season of 162 games, or ten times longer than the NFL season. What's more, Christenfeld found the same pattern in every sport he looked at, so that season length was always inversely related to single-game reliability. "The sports whose single games reliably assess talent have short seasons, while those whose games are largely chance have long ones," Christenfeld wrote. "Thus these sports, differing enormously in their particulars, converge towards the same reliability in a season." According to Christenfeld, this means that season length is not an "arbitrary product of historical, meteorological or other such constraints." Rather, it is rooted in the desire of fans to witness a "proper mix of skill and chance."

The skill we know about. Christenfeld's research highlights the importance of *chance*. By proving that the most popular sports share a similar level of unpredictability, at least over an entire season, Christenfeld revealed their inherent mysteriousness, which is an essential element of their appeal. "Drama requires uncertainty," he told me. "It requires, at a basic level, that you don't know what's going to happen next." As a result, the most popular sports have evolved to ensure that the mystery remains: the rules of the game intentionally constrain the talent of the players.* "If sports were pure contests of skill, then they'd quickly become genetic tournaments," Christenfeld says. "But that's not much fun, is it? The result is way too predictable."

What fans crave is what Christenfeld calls an "optimal level of discrepancy." Although the better team should *usually* win, the best games are also full of surprises, built around interactions that are inherently unknowable.[29] In Christenfeld's telling, the rules of sports are continually revised to find this ideal balance, the peak of that inverted-U curve. They are mystery boxes, engineered to deliver the right amount of uncertainty just like *Star Wars* or a slot machine. "You can't let any single talent get too dominant, because then you're back to the 'Usain Bolt always wins' problem," Christenfeld says. "The problem is that predictability is boring, even when it's earned."

Just look at baseball. As Christenfeld notes, the mystery of the sport is rooted in its basic mechanics, in which a batter swings a rounded bat at a small ball traveling fast. "The cruel thing about baseball is that the difference between a double down the line and a double play comes down to a few millimeters," Christenfeld

---

* One of the reasons track and field has struggled to compete with other sports, such as soccer and football, is that the outcome is way too predictable. The sheer simplicity of the sport ensures that talent almost always prevails.

says. "This means there's a limit to what even the best players can control."

The history of baseball is largely the story of a game trying to protect this essential mystery. That's what happened during the rule change of 1893, which was a desperate attempt to save the young sport. At the time, the problem with baseball seemed obvious: hitters had stopped hitting. Since 1887, the batting average of National League players had plummeted from .269 to .245, while the number of strikeouts recorded by each team had increased by more than 41 percent. The best team in baseball, the Boston Beaneaters, hit 34 home runs combined over a single season.[30]

The decline of hitters was caused by the rise of pitchers. In the early 1890s, the fastball got faster—Amos Rusie of the New York Giants was reportedly throwing the ball almost a hundred miles per hour*—while the newly invented curve, or "skewball," befuddled batters. The result was a predictable sport: the only players who mattered were the ones throwing the ball. If a good pitcher was on the mound, his team was almost sure to win. These boring games soon led to serious business issues. Attendance at ballparks was in free fall; small-market teams were bleeding money. To stay afloat, player salaries were cut by nearly 40 percent before the start of the 1893 season.[32] It wasn't clear how much longer the sport could survive.

To boost attendance, the owners decided to make a dramatic change to the rules of the game. Pitchers had previously been allowed to pitch from the back of a square box, fifty-six feet away

---

* As John Thorn, the official historian of Major League Baseball, notes, given the distance to the plate, Amos Rusie in 1892 might have been, "from the batter's perspective," the fastest pitcher of all time.[31]

from home plate. The owners decided to push this distance back to sixty feet six inches. Their logic was straightforward: if batters had an additional split second to hit the ball, they might have better luck against the new generation of aces.[33]

Nearly everyone criticized the change. Batters said it wouldn't make a difference: When the speed of a fastball was approaching triple digits, what's the point of four measly feet? (Besides, the trickery of the skewball didn't depend on speed.) Pitchers, meanwhile, claimed the rule change was unfair—it wasn't their fault that batters couldn't hit their pitches. Traditionalists fretted that the young game was being ruined, and small-market teams wanted to return to the hitter's paradise of underhand pitching.

But the new rules worked. Given the biological limits of the human arm and the reaction time of the central nervous system, putting sixty feet between the mound and home plate creates a near-perfect mix of skill and chance. Batters can make contact, but they struggle to control the direction of their hits. While the owners almost certainly weren't thinking about the statistical variance of baseball in 1893—they just wanted more offense—they stumbled upon the optimal level of discrepancy, squeezing as much surprise as possible from a hurled ball and a swinging stick.

You can see this in the statistics—the new pitching distance reduced the strikeout rate by 37 percent and dramatically increased the variability of hitters. One way to measure this variability is by looking at on-base plus slugging percentage (OPS).* More variable at bats produce a higher OPS, as the balls get spread around the field. After the rule change of 1893, OPS increased by nearly 26

---

* Slugging percentage is calculated by dividing the total bases (singles, doubles, triples, and home runs) by the total number of at bats.

percent in less than two years, as batters hit far more extra-base hits and home runs. (Those are the most exciting at bats.) This trend has persisted into the modern game: the OPS of National League hitters is still far higher than it was before the rule change.

Another way to detect the increased variability is by looking at the performance of the best pitchers. In 1892, ten pitchers had an ERA of 2.76 or less; these throwers dominated the league. By 1894, not a single pitcher had an ERA that low. The extra four feet might not have turned baseball into a hitter's league, but it did constrain the most talented throwers. And when a game constrains talent, mystery increases.

In many respects, the pitching shift of 1893 invented modern baseball, turning a fledgling game into America's pastime. Since then, the rules of baseball have been remarkably stable.* After the discovery of the ideal mystery box, there was no need to change the dimensions of the field again.**

We think we watch sports because of the skilled athletes; it's fun to witness physical genius. But this theory leaves out the real reason a few select games have come to dominate our culture.[34] It's not because they attract the most talent, but because they find ways to *limit it*. They pit the best athletes in the world against

---

* The biggest changes to baseball since 1893 have been the abolition of the spitball in 1921, the lowering of the mound in 1969, and the use of the designated hitter in the American League starting in 1973. Like the rule change of 1893, these revisions were also designed to reduce the dominance of pitchers.

** It's worth noting the growing concern that pitchers are once again becoming too dominant, largely due to the rise in the velocity of the fastball. (Many relievers now regularly hit 100 mph.) In 2018, strikeouts exceeded hits for the first time ever. This trend has led some to argue that baseball should, once again, increase the distance between the mound and home plate. In 2019, the Atlantic League announced that it will begin experimenting with a mound that's sixty-two feet six inches from home plate.

each other but ensure that the competition also includes enough mystery so that the better athletes don't always win. As a result, these sports give fans what they subconsciously crave: not certain victory but dramatic uncertainty.*

Professional sports have the luxury of developing their mystery boxes over time, slowly tweaking the game until they are perfectly pitched between talent and chance. But not every form of culture can evolve so slowly. In other arenas of life, people must work on much shorter deadlines.

## Something Happened

While walking in Central Park on East Drive, Michael Chernuchin, the showrunner of *Law & Order: SVU*, had the idea for the best script he's ever written. He'd jogged past the spot hundreds of times before—Michael used to run marathons and would circle the park—but now he was older and fifty pounds heavier. Now he walked.[35]

"When you walk is when you notice things," Michael says. "So I'm walking and I look over to my left and see these boulders. And on top of one of these boulders there's a bronze mountain lion. He's ready to pounce. But all these people are going by, pushing

---

* You can see the impact of this uncertainty on television ratings. A team of economists looked at how surprise and suspense shaped viewer interest during Wimbledon tennis matches. Not surprisingly, they found that matches higher in both variables—they were full of outcomes we didn't expect, at least as measured by the betting odds—generated much higher ratings. People didn't want beautiful tennis, or another Roger Federer win in straight sets. They wanted tiebreakers and upsets, a game with an unpredictable ending.

strollers, talking on the phone, totally unaware that there's this lion right above them. . . . I saw that and I thought, 'We're all prey.' And that one line gave me the whole show."

The episode begins, like every *Law & Order* episode, with a victim. This one is a middle-aged woman named Laurel Linwood, catatonic on the floor of the American Museum of Natural History. The victim is discovered by a class of sixth graders on a field trip. After an initial medical exam finds evidence of rape, Laurel is sent to the Special Victims Unit of the NYPD. The detectives ask her questions; Laurel has no answers. "You'll never catch him," she finally tells the cops. "I can't remember a damn thing." It's an impossible crime—the perfect mystery box.

But the police are patient, and the victim slowly recovers shards of her memory: the smell of Old Spice, his fancy watch, the bar where they got drinks. The SVU detectives fan out across the city, picking up more clues; the box is slowly opened. Then, eighteen minutes into the episode, the cops learn the suspect's name and race to his apartment. It seems like a textbook case.

It's not. "The episode is called 'Something Happened' because that's the essence of our show," Michael says. "Something happened, but what? If we do our job well, you won't know for forty-one minutes." The show is forty-two minutes long.

It's easy to dismiss detective shows such as *Law & Order: SVU*. They can be formulaic and anodyne, especially when compared to the edgy character dramas of cable and Netflix. The good guys win; justice triumphs; resolution arrives before bedtime. But *SVU* has been on the air for twenty-two years. It has run longer than any other drama on television, recently eclipsing the original *Law & Order*. And the show is still going strong—"Something Happened" brought in more than 7 million viewers, a number that doesn't even include its second life in syndication. Dick Wolf is the creator of *Law & Order* and *SVU*. He likes to point out that one of his shows is on somewhere in the world every hour of every day.

Why are the *Law & Order* franchises so successful? How did they become such a staple of modern television? The answer returns us to the mystery box technique, as the television procedural relies on the same psychological tricks as a surprise egg video, baseball, and an Edgar Allan Poe mystery story. The only difference is that, instead of hidden toys and unexpected home runs, *SVU* features sex crimes with surprising twists. We keep watching until the box is opened.

A few weeks after "Something Happened" aired on NBC, I met with Michael at a deli in Studio City, Los Angeles. The show is on winter break, and Michael looks relaxed, obviously enjoying a respite from the hectic production schedule. "Something Happened" got excellent press and high ratings—it was later nominated for an Edgar Award, given out to the best mystery writing—but Michael is already worried about the next episode, and the ones after that. "I've done cable shows, and let me tell you, doing a network show is much harder," Michael says. "You're doing twenty-four, maybe twenty-five stories, and they all have to be self-contained mysteries. You need the setup *and* the ending."

When Michael talks about his creative process, about the long journey from inspiration in Central Park to the finished episode, he returns again and again to the attention span of his audience.*

---

* Michael's fascination with attention is deeply practical, a side effect of his twenty-plus years in the entertainment industry. But it also comes from his father, Paul Chernuchin, an applied psychologist who left his son with a lasting interest in the habits of the human mind. One of Paul's main academic contributions was the Chernuchin Pictograph, a test originally given to prisoners to predict the likelihood they

Tolstoy and Faulkner are his favorite writers—Michael rereads them every year—but he knows that good television has a much quicker pace than *War and Peace*. "The first thing I always tell my writers is you can't be boring," he says. "It doesn't matter if it looks good on the page. If it doesn't keep people from changing channels, then it doesn't work."[*]

*SVU* solves the attention problem by structuring the show around multiple mystery boxes. The first box arrives with the teaser, the segment before the opening credits. Given the structure of the show, the writers have ninety seconds to hook people with a premise. They need a crime that can be explained in a single scene but still generate multiple twists. Their ideas come from everywhere: the *New York Post*, a consulting forensic psychiatrist, local cops, stray conversations, even statues in a park.

Once they settle on the crime, the writers begin plotting out the episode. They usually figure out the end first—the who-did-it part—then begin working backward, looking for ways to withhold information for as long as possible. "Basically, you want a little mystery before every commercial," Michael says. "The question is always the same: How do you break the idea so that people don't see what's coming?"

---

would try to escape. "The test is just a piece of paper with five rectangles and you're supposed to draw pictures," Michael says. "Some people draw inside the boxes, some scribble all over the paper. My father showed that how you treat those rectangles says something interesting about you." According to Michael, the test, which Paul would eventually turn into a test for corporate executives, would go on to inspire the phrase *thinking outside the box*.

[*] What makes Michael's job even harder is the intrusion of commercials. It's not enough to tell a good story—the show has to be so compelling that people are willing to watch eighteen minutes of ads for eczema medicine, home insurance, and family sedans. Netflix and other streaming services, he points out, don't have this problem.

Much of the plotting is written down on colored index cards, each of which contains a short scene description. ("Blood work comes back—not his" or "Carisi talks to Jim, Jim says fuck off.") The cards are mounted on a corkboard, allowing the staff to follow the general flow of the story. Larry Kaplow, a coexecutive producer on the show, takes me through the arc of a forthcoming episode that's still pinned up in his office in the sprawling *SVU* complex in Chelsea Piers in Manhattan. "We've completely restructured this episode twice," Larry says. "You think by now we would have learned how to make the process easy. But it's *never* easy."

Larry has a shock of white hair and the quick wit of someone who writes dialogue for a living. (His wit runs even faster when he's chewing nicotine gum, which seems to be most of the time.) While pointing at the corkboard, he tries to explain how the episode evolved. The changes can be sorted into two main categories: removing scenes that gave away too much and adding threads designed to mislead. "The investigation is what pulls people along," Larry says. "You have to always know what they [the audience] know and make sure they don't know it too soon. If they know what's going to happen"—if they can guess what's inside the box—"then what's the point of watching? But those tricks also can't feel cheap or like they don't make sense in terms of the characters. . . . Nobody wants to feel manipulated, or that you hid something for no good reason." The show might be formulaic, but the best episodes hide the formula.

That's what Michael tried to do with "Something Happened." He imagined the story as a case study in interrogation, with most of the action unfolding in a single room, just two women talking about terrible events. This meant he couldn't rely on any so-called

CSI cheats. "You know, when they come in at the last act and announce that they found a hair and it's a perfect match," he says. "So unsatisfying."

If the first mystery box is a classic whodunit setup—we're searching for the rapist—the second mystery box arrives soon after the cops arrive at his apartment. Instead of arresting the suspect, they find him dead in his bed, scissors plunged into his skull. From this gruesome image, the show cuts to commercial.

The detectives initially assume that Laurel must have stabbed her rapist in self-defense; the killing was justified, an innocent prey striking back at her predator. However, as Detective Benson continues to interrogate Laurel, she keeps talking about her father. He also smelled like Old Spice, she says, just like her rapist. He also wore a fancy watch. As these details emerge, Laurel shows flashes of rage. Why is she so angry? And what does her father have to do with the rape? These questions set up the third mystery box.

After the last commercial break, the truth comes out: Laurel's father raped her sister. After some wily interrogation, Detective Benson coaxes out a confession. Laurel killed the man in the bar with scissors because he resembled her monstrous parent. "The episode works because it's so unexpected," Michael says. "The character begins as the prey, one of those antelope trying to run away from the lion. But then at the end you realize that she's the lion. She's the predator hiding in the park. It's a complete reversal."

After talking to Michael, I go back and rewatch "Something Happened." This time I notice the artistry of his misdirection, the sly way he lays down track for an ending we never see coming. The show is a slew of grisly mysteries, artfully timed to keep us watching the commercials, but Michael's ending still feels emotional and earned.* "I love fooling the audience," Michael says. "And if I do my job, I also show you how much fun it is to be wrong. Because really that's why you watch: you *want* to be wrong. I mean, you also want to know, but you only care because you don't know, at least not yet."

---

* Evidence suggests that an interest in violent dramas, horror films, and "prepper movies" comes with psychological benefits. According to a research team led by Coltan Scrivner at the University of Chicago, fans of dark entertainment exhibited less psychological distress during the COVID-19 pandemic. One likely explanation is that exposure to scary mysteries allows people to "practice effective coping strategies that can be beneficial in real-world situations." Their "morbid curiosity" teaches them how to cope with unknown risks and practice resilience; make-believe traumas can help protect us from real ones.[36]

# CHAPTER 2

# THE MAGIC GASP

Art is magic delivered from the lie of being truth.

—THEODOR ADORNO

I only asked for wonder.

—RABBI ABRAHAM JOSHUA HESCHEL

I first met Mohan Srivastava in 2010, after a friend of a friend told me that Mohan had found a way to defeat a scratch lottery. I was skeptical of the claim. The lottery is a random system, run by professionals. No way could an amateur identify the secret pattern that marked winning tickets. There wasn't even a pattern to find.

During our first conversation, at a Chinese restaurant in the Toronto suburbs, Mohan explained why I was wrong: "The lottery pretends to be random, but the reality is that the lottery company has to very tightly control the number of winning tickets. There's nothing random about it." Mohan has graying hair, a neatly trimmed beard, and the disinterested wardrobe of an academic. He works as a geological statistician, summoned by companies all over the world to assess the value of their underground assets. It's a difficult art, as Mohan has to infer the unknown—say, how much gold is beneath a stretch of the Mongolian desert—from a scattering of drill data and theories about ancient geology. When Mohan starts talking about one of his favorite subjects—statistics, Alice Munro, the history of precious metals—his sentences accelerate until the words run into each other. It's the slight stammer of a fast mind.

Mohan's lottery story begins in June 2003, when his squash partner gave him a few tickets. After scratching off the latex coating, Mohan became fascinated by the algorithm that laid down the lottery numbers. How did it generate millions of unique tickets while also ensuring the correct payout percentage? (Lotteries are highly regulated and generally have to pay out at least 50 percent of ticket sales.) After thinking about the statistical problem for a few minutes, Mohan settled on a likely solution: he was confident he knew how the lottery software worked.

Mohan returned to work. He forgot all about the lottery. But then, as he walked home later that evening, something strange happened. "I swear I'm not the kind of guy who hears voices," Mohan says. "But that night, I heard a little voice coming from the back of my head. I'll never forget what it said: 'If you do it that way, if you use that algorithm, there will be a flaw. The game will be flawed. You will be able to crack the ticket. You will be able to plunder the lottery.'"

The North American lottery system is an $83-billion-a-year industry.[1] The sheer size of the lottery system convinced Mohan that his internal voice must be wrong: "Like everyone else, I assumed that the lottery was unbreakable. There's no way there could be a flaw, and there's no way I just happened to discover the flaw on my walk home."

Yet the voice refused to be silenced. Unable to sleep, Mohan surrendered to wakefulness. After a few hours, he realized that his inner voice was right: the tic-tac-toe lottery was breakable, as the visible numbers revealed essential information about the digits hidden underneath. Nothing needed to be scratched off—if you knew the secret code, you could pick the winners just by looking at them.

The trick is ridiculously simple. Each ticket contained eight tic-tac-toe boards, and each space on those boards—seventy-two in all—contained an exposed number from 1 to 39. As a result, some of these numbers repeat multiple times. Perhaps the number 17 repeats three times, and the number 38 repeats twice. A few numbers, however, appeared only once on the entire card. Srivastava's startling insight was that he could separate the winning tickets from the losing tickets by looking at the number of times each of the digits occurred on the tic-tac-toe boards. "The numbers themselves couldn't have been more meaningless," he says. "But whether or not they were repeated told me nearly everything I needed to know." Mohan was looking for *singletons*, numbers that

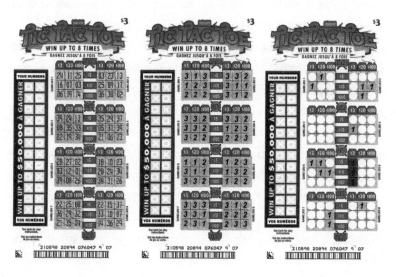

The ticket above shows how the singleton trick works.[2] The ticket on the far left is the actual ticket as displayed before sale. The ticket in the middle reveals how Mohan transformed each number in the original ticket by frequency. The ticket on the far right shows the location of the three singletons (18, 20, and 30) in a row. This ticket is almost certainly a winner.

appeared only a single time on the visible tic-tac-toe boards. He realized that the singletons were almost always repeated under the latex coating. If three singletons appeared in a row on one of the eight boards, that ticket was almost certainly a winner.

The next day, on his way into work, Mohan stopped at the gas station and bought more lottery tickets. These tickets also contained the telltale pattern. The day after that he picked up even more scratchers from different stores. He broke these tickets, too. After analyzing his results, Srivastava realized that the singleton trick worked about 90 percent of the time.

What did Mohan do with this illicit knowledge? Although his first impulse was to plunder the lottery, Mohan realized that he'd have to spend all day staring at tickets in convenience stores. He preferred his day job. Besides, it didn't seem fair to leave only the losers behind. Mohan ended up working with the Ontario lottery system as a consultant to fix the problem.

Mohan would later break several other lotteries, including a Colorado scratcher and a Super Bingo game. There were plenty of other tickets that he couldn't defeat, but still managed to use statistical analysis to increase his odds of winning. (I first wrote about Mohan's exploits in *Wired*.)[3] While Mohan thinks the lotteries have gotten better in recent years, he still worries that organized crime is using these games to launder money. "If you can increase your odds of winning by even a small percentage, then the lottery is a perfect way to clean your dirty profits," he says. "Think about it. You can buy and cash in the tickets just about anywhere. They're an untraceable currency. And they're run by the government."

The scratch-lottery story captures the tilt of Mohan's mind. He's a deductive sleuth in the mold of Sherlock, only he isn't drawn to murder or mayhem—he's fascinated by the enigmas of everyday life. When Mohan encounters an alluring puzzle, he's liable to become obsessed. He buys every book on the subject, scours online chat rooms, and stays up way too late thinking about possible solutions. "There have been moments when I wish I could stop working on one of these puzzles and get some sleep," Mohan says. "But once a problem gets a hold on me, I generally have to figure it out."

That's what happened on July 2, 2014, when Mohan and his young son, Ravi, watched the celebrated German magician Jan Rouven perform at the Riviera in Las Vegas. Most of the act was standard Vegas Strip magic—big props, clouds of smoke, and a loud, thumping soundtrack. (That year, Rouven received the Merlin Award for Illusionist of the Year, the most prestigious award in the magic community.) "It was good stuff," Mohan remembers, "but most of the tricks I could guess how they were done. If you know the principles, you've got a pretty good idea of what's going on."

Rouven's encore, however, was different. For his last trick, the magician came out alone, his only prop a large wooden jigsaw puzzle, enclosed within a frame. Mohan sat up straight in his seat—he wasn't expecting the finale to be an illusion he'd never before seen. Rouven began with a grandiose introduction: "I'd like to tell you a story about life. About what defines life. About ourselves." He then explained the metaphor of the wooden puzzle: "Just as this wooden frame encloses all the pieces of this puzzle of life, we all store our defining elements perfectly inside us, leaving no space for anything else."

Rouven lifted the frame off the puzzle, handing it to a volunteer from the audience, and began describing some of his most cherished memories: a first kiss, his first bicycle ride, the first time he invented his own magic trick. As he recalled these events,

Rouven picked up pieces of the puzzle, holding them in his hands. Each piece, he said, represented one of these memories.

The best illusions build slowly; their languid pace heightens the anticipation. For the first few minutes of Rouven's encore, as he spouted clichés about life, the audience didn't even know what the trick might be.

Once the puzzle was disassembled, Rouven began to put it back together. He turned to the audience and flashed a wry smile, a signal that they should pay close attention to what happened next. He pulled an extra puzzle piece from a small black bag. This wooden block had never been part of the original puzzle. He looked at his fully assembled puzzle, a seamless rectangle, and placed the extra piece beside it; the new block stuck out beyond the perfect rectangle. Rouven started moving the pieces around, a blur of motion. After ten seconds, the rectangle was remade, only now it also included the extra piece. Rouven paused for a beat, making sure the audience had time to appreciate the trick: he had incorporated an additional wooden block into the puzzle.

Rouven looked satisfied, pleased with himself. "But never, ever, take things for granted," he warned, before removing an even bigger wooden block from the black bag. Once again, he placed this large extra piece beside the completed puzzle. Once again, it stuck out awkwardly from the rectangle. Once again, Rouven stacked the pieces in his hands before sliding them around like a two-dimensional Rubik's Cube. Once again, he incorporated the extra piece into the perfect and seamless rectangle.

The audience assumes Rouven has simply expanded the size of the puzzle; it's a cleverly designed trick, but there's no magic. Rouven lets the audience enjoy their assumption for a few seconds as he prattles on about the journey of life. Then, just when they think they've seen the trick, Rouven summons back the volunteer holding the puzzle frame. There's no way the frame could still fit, since they've just watched Rouven add two large additional pieces.

You can probably guess what happens next: Rouven carefully slides the wooden frame right over the puzzle pieces—it fits perfectly.

"What immediately appealed to me about the trick was the simplicity of it," Mohan says. "It was hard to imagine where the magic was hidden, since there was so little to the trick, just some wood pieces and a frame."

The next day, as Mohan and Ravi drove across the Mojave Desert, their road-trip conversation centered on alternative solutions to the trick. The obvious suspect was the frame. Perhaps it was expandable? But they both knew the volunteer from the audience had been holding it the entire time. Unless she was a confederate, or Rouven expanded the frame while placing it over the puzzle, they didn't see how it could explain the trick. The other possibility was that the original puzzle had some slack; some hidden space might have been around the edges, which is why Rouven could add two more pieces and still make it fit. But they were also skeptical of this explanation, since those extra pieces were quite large. "Ravi and I just kept talking about it," Mohan remembers. "Turning it over in our heads, trying to figure out how Rouven pulled it off."

This is how magic works—it draws us in with mystery, creating a performance we can't explain. A puzzle expands but still fits within the frame; a woman is sawed in half but stays whole; the Statue of Liberty vanishes from view. It's the ultimate prediction error, since magic plays with our most basic assumptions about how the world is supposed to work. As the magician Mike Close once said, a good illusion "gives you the gift of a stone in your shoe."

The magic trick is the model for the second kind of mystery hook, which is the subject of this chapter. If the mystery box is all about hiding information, the magician creates mystery by hiding his *technique*. It's not the outcome that's uncertain—it's the *process*, the means of production. He shows us what's inside the box. We just have no idea how it got there.

You can see the source of this fascination in the brain. A recent study by German neuroscientists showed people short videos of magic tricks while lying inside an fMRI machine.[4] In one clip, the magician pours a glass of water into a mug. After waving his hand above the mug, he empties the mug onto the table: the liquid is now an ice cube. In another trick, an orange tossed into the air suddenly becomes an apple. There were vanishing coins, transposed cards, bouncing eggs, and floating balls.

To help distinguish the neural changes induced by the magic, and not just by the physical movements of the performer, the scientists also showed the clips to a trained magician. There were two important findings. The first was the activation of brain areas associated with cognitive conflict and error detection, such as the anterior insula and frontal gyrus. These are core parts of what neuroscientists sometimes refer to as the "Oh, shit!" circuit, those wires that help us process twists we didn't expect and coins that disappear into thin air.[5]

But the best magic isn't just about showing us moves that violate our predictions. According to the fMRI data, magic also triggers persistent activation in the caudate nucleus, a brain region that plays a key role in the dopamine system. This area appears to make magic more than an intellectual exercise, transforming the trickery and deceit into a feeling of wonder. Because the magician didn't show a spike in caudate activity, the scientists speculate that this brain area is reserved for the awe of amateurs, those inexplicable moments when the liquid becomes ice, or the rabbit disappears into the hat.[6] For the professional, there was no marvel: he knew what was happening since he had made it happen before.

The simultaneous activation of the "Oh, shit!" circuit and the caudate helps explain the spellbinding nature of a magic performance. We see an obvious error—the world isn't supposed to work like this—but we don't suppress the dissonance. Instead, we lean into it, focusing intensely on the mystery.[7] "At the center of the magical experience lies a cognitive conflict, and the stronger the conflict, the stronger the experience of magic," writes the neuroscientist Gustav Kuhn. "Magic is the experience of wonder that results from perceiving an apparently impossible event."[8] The mystery is not a whodunit. It's a how-the-hell-did-he-do-it?

But this raises a larger question: Why is magic so hard to decipher? Why can't we detect its techniques, especially since most illusions rely on a short list of secrets? The main reason for our failure is the bias of functional fixedness, which is the tendency to assume that familiar objects can only be used in familiar ways.[9] A hat is for wearing on the head—it can't contain a hidden compartment for a rabbit. Coffins don't have trapdoors and shoes don't have magnets. When it comes to these everyday objects, we struggle to imagine alternate uses and strange variations.

Magicians make a living by exploiting this blind spot.* Charles Morritt, one of the greatest magicians of the late nineteenth century, began his career with a mind-reading act. While Morritt wandered amid the audience, asking people to show him the con-

---

* One of the most common performance tropes of magic is the so-called inspection. A magician will invite an audience member up to the stage to look at the prop. Such inspections reinforce the bias of functional fixedness, since we see the object performing its typical function (the hat is put on the head, for instance) and feel assured it's just a standard object.

tents of their pockets and purses, his blindfolded sister sat on the stage, guessing what he was looking at. Previous magicians had relied on an obvious code—the performer in the crowd would use his banter to give away the answer—but Morritt and his sibling stripped away all the extra conversation.

How, then, did his sister know what Morritt was seeing? After choosing an object from the audience, Morritt would make a discrete noise, such as clicking his boot on the floor. The magician and his sister would then start counting in synchrony, before Morritt stopped the count with another acoustic cue. Perhaps he'd cough or say "Thank you" to the owner of the object. Based on the amount of time that unfolded between these two sounds, his sister would know exactly what he was holding. Four seconds might be a wallet, while twelve seconds could refer to a silver watch. The routine had no margin for error: a single errant beat could turn a necklace into a pack of cigarettes. What made the trick possible was the bias of functional fixedness: the audience couldn't imagine that the silence was actually the cipher.

Morritt's most celebrated trick was a vanishing. The performance began with an assistant in a clown costume, holding the reins of a gray donkey named Solomon. The clown pulled Solomon into a raised wooden crate—the donkey was trained to resist, if only to get some easy laughs—before the clown closed the doors, locking the animal inside. (Morritt used a raised crate and fabric hoop to make sure we knew there was no trapdoor.) After a few seconds, Morritt then pulled the doors open, revealing an empty interior. The donkey had disappeared.

Solomon was still there, just briefly hidden. Once the donkey was locked inside, men beneath the stage pulled on ropes, opening a trapezoidal box at the back of the crate. (Jim Steinmeyer, a famed inventor of illusions, figured out how Morritt vanished the donkey.) But this wasn't an ordinary box—it's exterior walls were covered in precisely angled mirrors that reflected back empty space. The trained donkey would then step inside, happily eating the food scattered on the floor.

It's another trick whose power depends on functional fixedness. We use mirrors to see reflections. They show us things. They show us ourselves. Morritt's genius reversed this function. Once the trick is revealed, it's fairly obvious. But it never occurs to us that mirrors can have multiple uses, and that a shiny surface can also hide a farm animal. Our fixed thinking keeps us from imagining the answer. The result is an impossible deception, and a precursor to the grand stunt magic of performers such as Harry Houdini and David Copperfield.*

Interestingly, young children are largely immune to functional fixedness.[10] When five-year-olds are given an everyday item, they're far more likely to consider alternative uses. This can also make young children a difficult audience for magicians. Because they aren't blinded by their assumptions about hats and mirrors, they are far harder to impress.

The key to escaping functional fixedness is to return to that childish state of mind. We have to remember that even the most ordinary things can contain the unknown. Mirrors reflect, but they can also vanish. A box is not just a box. It can also be a shelf. It

---

* The trick was so mysterious that it soon gained the attention of Houdini. Although Houdini was famous for his death-defying escapes, he'd grown tired of picking locks like a burglar; he wanted to establish himself as a proper magician. Houdini began asking around for tricks he could copy, looking for "an illusion inventor who can keep a secret." He soon learned about Morritt's vanishing donkey and decided to buy his trick for cash. Morritt took the money, but urged Houdini to think bigger: "If you really want to make headlines with your magic, you shouldn't bother with little tricks, rabbits, pigeons. Make an elephant disappear!"[11]

can also contain a secret compartment. Magic depends on a failure of imagination. It creates a mystery out of our inability to see the possibilities that are everywhere.

Mohan knew all this. As an amateur magician, he was well aware of our human frailties, those mental tendencies that magicians turn against us. But he still couldn't make sense of Rouven's encore. "The simplicity of the parts is what makes the trick so interesting," Mohan says. "It's ultimately just a bunch of wooden blocks. Is there anything less mysterious than that?" But Mohan also knew that, in the hands of a talented magician, even a wooden block can have multiple functions. "Ravi and I didn't solve it in the car leaving Las Vegas. But I knew then that I wasn't going to stop until I figured it out." When Mohan returned to Toronto, he began asking his magician friends for hypotheses. He researched other puzzle tricks in search of relevant principles. But nothing helped; Mohan was stumped. "On the one hand, you know that Rouven didn't find a way to break the laws of geometry. But there's always that moment when you can't figure it out, that you think, 'Well, maybe . . .'" The best magic doesn't just show us the impossible—it almost persuades us to believe in it.

But just as Mohan was on the verge of giving up, he had an idea. "I remember thinking, 'That would be really clever if he did it like that. *Really* clever.'"

## The Realism Trick

Every magic trick is a psychological experiment performed in real time. It's a mental contest between the performer and the audience, a high-wire act in which the magician must hide the mechanics of his or her art. We can see the cards but not the sly fingers; the disappearance but not the mirror; the levitation but not the wires. The magician has to sell us a lie even when we know we're being lied to.

In this sense, magic is an extreme version of other art forms, which must also obscure their tricks to keep our attention. (As the philosopher Theodor Adorno put it, "Art is magic delivered from the lie of being truth.")[12] Consider filmmaking. We demand immersive movies, which means that for two or so hours we are willing to suspend our disbelief. (That's not a famous actor in a plastic costume—it's Iron Man!) However, if a special effect appears fake, or an actor isn't convincing, the cinematic magic disappears, and we suddenly realize we are staring at a flat screen in a dark room full of strangers. It's like seeing the Wizard of Oz behind the curtain. The spell is fragile.

Or look at painting. The psychologist Stephen Kaplan has argued that one of the best predictors of whether people find a picture aesthetically pleasing is its ability to conjure a sense of mystery.[13] How do painters do this? One reliable method is to inspire questions about *how* the art was created. Traditionally, this was done through verisimilitude, creating art that imitated the look of real life. Even if the subject of the painting was straightforward—the Virgin Mother, a still life of fruit, a portrait of a nobleman—we didn't understand how the human hand could create such an accurate representation. In this sense, the painter relies on the same motive for attention as the magician pulling a rabbit out of a hat. We keep looking because we can't figure it out. The canvas refuses to give up its secrets.

One of the first examples of such trickery comes from the Italian architect Filippo Brunelleschi, who stood outside the Baptistery of San Giovanni in Florence sometime around 1412.[14]

Brunelleschi was there to perform an astonishing magic act with his paintbrush. He began by marking a central point for the scene on his canvas. Then, he created a grid of receding lines, all of which connected to this central point. These lines became the spatial grid for the painting. For the sky, Brunelleschi cut out a piece of shiny silver, a mirror to the shifting clouds and light.

To perform the illusion, Brunelleschi drilled a small hole into the central point of the painting. He instructed the viewer to reverse the painted panel, so he was looking through the peephole at the real baptistery. Brunelleschi then gave the viewer a small mirror for his other hand and told him to raise it into view—he was now gazing at a reflection of Brunelleschi's painted scene. Here's the mysterious part: the representation of the baptistery was interchangeable with its reality. The world had been faked, and the audience hooked.

How did Brunelleschi pull it off? The accuracy of his scene depended on the invention of perspective, that grid of lines emanating from a central point. Brunelleschi had almost certainly seen imperfect examples of perspective in ancient Roman paintings; Pliny the Elder referred to the technique as "slanting images." But a profound philosophical shift that transformed Renaissance art also influenced Brunelleschi. For the first time since ancient Rome, artists were painting for human audiences, competing for their favor and attention. (The primary function of art was no longer religious.) The central vanishing point is predicated on this mortal perspective; it is a trick designed to deceive those fallible minds staring at the canvas. (As John Berger observes in *Ways of Seeing*, the convention of perspective "centres everything on the eye of the beholder. . . . The visible world is arranged for the spectator as the universe was once thought to be arranged for God.")[15] Brunelleschi's magic trick, in this sense, was just an extension of humanism, a visual illusion that showed what magic was possible when man performed for man.

But here's the catch about verisimilitude: you can always get more real. Over time, viewers came to take linear perspective for granted. The wonder wore off, so the aesthetic trick became the equivalent of the woman being sawed in half—a performance that no longer impressed, even if we didn't know exactly how it was done. Painters had to develop new tricks for their trade, making works of art whose making we couldn't explain.

In January 1999, the artist David Hockney was at an exhibit of paintings and drawings by French neoclassical painter Jean-Auguste-Dominique Ingres at the National Gallery. As the crowds gathered around Ingres's famous painted portraits, Hockney went to a side room full of sketches. At first glance, the drawings seemed insubstantial, wispy, just charcoal pencil on scratch paper. But they astonished Hockney. "Over the years I have drawn many portraits and I know how much time it takes to draw the way Ingres did," Hockney would remember.[16] These weren't impressionistic sketches: they had an "uncannily accurate" quality, full of perfectly rendered lines and subtle shading. And yet, Ingres made them look easy, completing most of them in an afternoon. After Hockney left the exhibition, Ingres's drawing method became an obsession for Hockney. He was determined to learn the secrets of Ingres's technique.

Hockney began his investigation with a close study of Ingres's pencil marks, enlarging the details with a Xerox machine. "One morning, studying the blowups, I found myself thinking, 'Wait, I've seen that line before,'" Hockney told Lawrence Weschler. "'Where have I seen that line?' And suddenly I realized, 'That's Andy Warhol's line.'"[17]

It was an unexpected epiphany. Hockney knew that Warhol

had relied on a slide projector for many of his drawings, tracing the projected image directly onto paper. This "cheat" created some obvious tells, such as a seamless flow between the lines that describe the subject and its shadow. (When one draws freehand, the shadows are usually done separately, *after* the form is defined.) But Hockney realized that many of Ingres's drawings contained the same characteristics as Warhol's tracings. "All drawn lines have a speed that can usually be deduced: they have a beginning and an end," Hockney writes. After studying Ingres's lines, Hockney came to believe that their obvious speed meant Ingres was tracing, like Warhol.

But tracing with what? Warhol had a light bulb in his projector; Ingres was drawing in the early nineteenth century, the last age of candlelight. After researching the available technology, Hockney decided that Ingres was probably using a camera lucida, essentially a prism on the end of a metal stick. When positioned in front of a subject, the prism creates the illusion of a mirror image on the paper below. (The invention of photography relied on these same spare parts.) As Hockney notes, the camera lucida is not easy to use. If the subject moves, or if the paper slides, the traced marks are useless. However, once an artist masters the trick, he or she can sketch quickly and with a seemingly inexplicable accuracy.

And it wasn't just Ingres. Hockney would eventually conclude that most of the Old Masters also relied on optical science to create mysteries within their art. Take Caravaggio. Hockney was drawn to Caravaggio due to his technical breakthroughs. Never before had someone painted real people doing real things—eating, talking, decapitating—with such astonishing accuracy. As the critic Robert Hughes observed, "There was art before [Caravaggio] and art after him, and they were not the same."[18]

Hockney found the tells in Caravaggio's details. *The Supper at Emmaus* (1601), for instance, is a painting with the clarity of a photographic print: the sheen of the grapes, the foreshortened arms of Christ and his apostles, the mottled shadows on the textured tablecloth. "To any draughtsman, eyeballing that is virtually impossible," Hockney writes. "Perhaps you have to be a practitioner to know this. Art historians don't draw anymore."[19]

And yet, the painting is also riddled with basic errors of composition. Cleopas's hands are of different sizes; Christ exists in a different plane from everyone else; the fruit is luscious but oddly flat. For Hockney, these mistakes are like the misdirections used by a magician—their existence hints at the real explanation, at least if you know what to look for.*

According to Hockney, these details suggest that Caravaggio was relying on some kind of optical device to create his paintings. The most likely tool was a crude camera obscura, in which a system of convex lenses and mirrors project an image onto the wall of a dark room. Caravaggio would have his models pose one at a time, assembling the scene from their individual snapshots. ("For the people of those times, such paintings were motion pictures," Hockney said. "Their eyes were invited to move through the unfolding story.")[20] This helps explain why Caravaggio preferred to work in basements with a single source of illumination: the setup provided the ideal conditions for his primitive camera.

Hockney is adamant that the use of these tools doesn't lessen the genius of these painters. "Optics do not make marks, only the

---

* And then there's the circumstantial evidence. At the time, other artists ridiculed Caravaggio for his reliance on models; they said he couldn't paint without one. One of Caravaggio's early patrons was Cardinal Francesco del Monte, a supporter of Galileo and an expert in the latest lens technology. There are also numerous references to Caravaggio's carrying a "glass."

artist's hand can do that," he writes.[21] What Hockney's hypothesis does reveal, however, is the extent to which artists have always sought out new ways of representing the material world, creating paintings so realistic they become mysteries. And so we marvel at Ingres's perfectly sketched mouth and the uncanny perspective of Caravaggio's lute; the clarity of Vermeer's light and the glittering eyes of Hal's subjects. We keep staring at these fixed images because they feel like magic, works of impossible beauty hanging on the wall. Even when we know how they were done, we still can't believe someone pulled it off.

## The Clueless Code

Bill Tutte and his wife, Dorothea, spent most of their lives in a modest house by the Grand River in West Montrose, a small town in the Mennonite country of Ontario. Tutte enjoyed long walks in the woods with Digby, his boxer, and afternoon games of chess accompanied by a cup of hot cocoa.* He was the kind of man who would apologize before winning: "I'm sorry, but I believe that is checkmate." In the summer, he liked to weed the riverbank, clearing space for his favorite wildflowers.

But mostly what Bill Tutte did was work. A math professor at the University of Waterloo, he was an expert in graph theory, devoting much of his professional life to the four-color-map problem. In its simplest version, the problem refers to the minimum

---

* I first learned about the story of Bill Tutte from Mohan Srivastava. In his teens, Mo lived down the street from Bill and Dorothea. Mo was Bill's afternoon chess partner on weekends and suffered the miserable cocoa that Bill made when Dorothea wasn't around to do it right.

number of colors required so that every country has a color different from all of its bordering neighbors. Tutte spent decades trying
to prove that the answer was four. (In the mid-1970s, a supercom-
puter confirmed that he was right.) Dorothea often lamented his
strict work habits, but Tutte feared losing his mathematical talent.
He was sure it would be gone by the time he turned forty.

What Tutte couldn't tell anyone is that his greatest achievement might have come when he was only twenty-four years
old. At the time the world was at war. Tutte was a code breaker,
tasked with cracking the most difficult Nazi ciphers. In many
respects, a code is like an act of magic, only there is no mystify-
ing performance—just inexplicable information. (The strings of
numbers on a lottery ticket are another code.) We know there
must be a trick—the random symbols have to mean *something*—
we just have no idea what it is. The job of the code breaker, in
this sense, is to reverse engineer the ruse, to figure out the secret
method of encryption.

Tutte had a gift for code breaking. His wartime work was so
valuable that the British government classified it as Ultra, a higher
classification than the standard highest, Most Secret, and retained
this classification for decades. To have discussed this achievement,
even in hushed tones to family and friends, could have earned
Tutte a charge of treason. So, for his entire career as an academic,
none of his colleagues knew that this quiet mathematician had
changed the course of history.

Tutte was born in Newmarket, a small town about seventy
miles north of London. His parents lived in a modest flint cottage
at the end of a footpath; both worked at the local racing stable, his
father as a gardener and his mother as a housekeeper. At an early
age, Bill displayed a gift for numbers, which led to a scholarship to
Trinity College of Cambridge University.[22] Although he majored

in chemistry—it seemed like the practical option—Tutte's joy was mathematical puzzles.*

In 1940, Tutte's reputation for solving these puzzles led to an interview with the Government Code and Cypher School (GC&CS), a division of the British intelligence services devoted to cracking the secret codes of other countries. Tutte aced the interview and was sent to Bletchley Park, a rambling estate that had become the center of the British government's code-breaking efforts. At Bletchley, there were trained mathematicians, but also crossword puzzle experts, national chess champions, Egyptologists, classicists, dictionary editors, corporate managers, and even novelists. Winston Churchill, after meeting this ragtag assortment of code breakers, reportedly told the head of MI6, "I know I told you to leave no stone unturned to get staff, but I didn't expect you to take me literally."[23] Tutte fit right in.

The young Tutte was assigned to Bletchley Park's "Fish" team. Their job was to break a set of German codes that encrypted messages using a rotor machine that mapped each input letter, "plain text," to an alternate output letter, "cipher text." Different models of the same type of cipher machine differed in their complexity: the more rotors, the more difficult it was to reverse the trick and untangle the link between cipher text and plain text. Tutte was given the task of breaking the Lorenz cipher, reserved for use by only Hitler and the generals in his high command. Code breakers called it Tunny, or tuna fish.

The Germans believed this cipher to be unbreakable because

---

* Along with three other undergraduates, Tutte solved a long-standing problem called Squaring the Square, which held that it was impossible to divide a square into a series of smaller differently sized squares. Tutte's solution, which borrowed a principle from electrical-circuit design, showed that it could be done.

the Lorenz SZ40 machine used twelve different rotors, thus generating more than 1.6 quadrillion cipher texts for the same plain text. (As a point of comparison, the Enigma cipher—the one cracked by Alan Turing—relied on a machine using three rotors.) In the early 1940s, there was no conceivable way to break the Lorenz cipher because the initial settings of the rotors would change with every message. It was like watching the same magic trick again and again, except the magician used a different method with every performance.*

The Tunny messages arrived at Bletchley Park in their encrypted form, as pages of printouts with row after row of dots and Xs. Each of those "five-bit" rows corresponded to a particular letter. The letter A, for example, was two Xs followed by three dots; the Cyrillic Ж was one dot followed by four Xs. What made Lorenz so difficult to figure out was that in its cipher, two lines were used for each letter, meaning code breakers had to determine the method for combining each already encrypted letter to spit out the actual letter that was being transmitted.

Unfortunately for the Bletchley Park code breakers, they had no way of figuring out the cryptographic key, or how the rotors changed as the message unfolded, or even how many rotors the machine contained. The method of Tunny remained a mystery, Hitler's secrets hidden behind near-infinite layers of orchestrated mechanical confusion.

On August 30, 1941, the Allies received a crucial break. A German army radio operator in Athens sent a Tunny message of ap-

---

* Further complicating Tutte's task was that the Allies had no working example of a Lorenz machine; they didn't even know what it looked like. (The Enigma machine, in contrast, had been recovered from a crippled German U-boat in 1941, along with the operator's codebooks.)

proximately four thousand characters to an operator in Salzburg, Austria. However, something went wrong in that transmission; Salzburg asked for a resend. The Athens operator now made two catastrophic mistakes. First, he used the same twelve-letter key—HQIBPEXEZMUG—to send the second message. By itself, this wouldn't have given the Bletchley code breakers any clues, since they would have just received the same impenetrable message twice. But the Athens messenger made slight edits to his resend, abbreviating certain words and adjusting the punctuation. (He almost certainly did so to save a few keystrokes.) These changes created a "depth," an essential tool for the code breakers since it allowed them to compare the messages and test out various substitution ciphers. After ten days of painstaking decryption, Colonel John Tiltman deciphered the Athens message. It was the first Tunny code ever deciphered.

The triumph was temporary. Although Tiltman had cracked this message, the Bletchley Research Section still had no idea how the Lorenz machine worked. They could only crack the Tunny code when the German operators made a careless error, giving away a depth by accident. Roy Jenkins, a young Bletchley analyst who would go on to become a prominent British politician, describes what it was like to work on these codes:

"I went to a dismal breakfast having played with a dozen or more messages and completely failed with all of them. It was the most frustrating mental experience I have ever had, particularly as that act of trying almost physically hurt one's brain."[24]

In late November 1941, Bill Tutte received a series of Tunny messages to work on. His Bletchley bosses were not optimistic about his chances. Tutte would later say that his bosses gave him the messages as a "gesture of despair."[25] After all, how could one possibly solve a cipher with more than a quadrillion possibilities? Tunny remained a perfect magic trick.

Tutte's ignorance was his advantage. He was a twenty-four-year-old chemistry student; he didn't know enough about code breaking to realize the hopelessness of his situation. So Tutte treated Tunny like any other mathematical puzzle, trying out various strategies and looking for signs of progress. "I can't say that I had much faith in this procedure," Tutte said, in a 1998 speech, "but I thought it best to seem busy."[26]

Tutte shared a small office with several other members of the Fish team. Their room was spare and simple, just a series of wooden desks set against bare walls. There were no luxuries at Bletchley: if the analysts wanted tea, they had to use their own rationed supply.[27] Jerry Roberts was one of the code breakers who shared the room with Tutte. He marveled at the way Tutte worked: "I saw him staring into the middle distance for extended periods, twiddling his pencil and making endless counts on reams of paper for nearly three months. And I used to wonder whether he was getting anything done."

Tutte was getting a lot done. His most important break came early in 1942, as he tested out countless periods, or numerical frequencies, on the Tunny messages. The tests went this way: Tutte would write out a stretch of Tunny code in rows of various lengths, filling reams of paper with charcoal Xs and dots. Tutte would then search for short repetitions in these vast spreadsheets, as frequent repetitions might signal frequently used words. When Tutte tried out a period of 575—itself a wild hunch, based on multiplying the number of possible keys in the Tunny cipher—he came up mostly empty. However, he noticed a few more repeats on the diagonal, which suggested he might have gotten better results by using a period of 574 instead. After rewriting his spreadsheet from scratch, he "found pleasingly many repeats of dot-cross patterns" that indicated words that were five or six letters long. This was his first insight into the methods of the Tunny code.

But now Tutte had another problem. A period of 574 suggested that the Lorenz rotors had 574 different starting positions. That seemed unlikely, even for an intricate German machine. So Tutte decided (again for reasons he couldn't explain) to look at prime factors of 574, which led him to the number 41. When Tutte analyzed the Tunny code based on that, the improvement was clear: these repeats were real.

Tutte concluded that one of the primary rotors used to determine the Tunny cipher had forty-one starting positions. He then used the same technique—searching for repeats that didn't *feel* random—to figure out the number of positions on the second rotor. Along with other members of the Research Section, Tutte went on to decipher the details on the ten remaining rotors. In essence, he found a way to solve the Lorenz machine mechanisms without ever seeing one. It was one of the greatest intellectual feats of World War II.[28]

How did Tutte do it? His colleagues at Bletchley used to say he had the "knack," that uncanny ability to solve codes by intuition. While most Bletchley code breakers used the conventional tactics of their craft—they exploited depths and other transmission mistakes, which are akin to waiting for a magician to screw up—Tutte took advantage of his mind's exquisite sensitivity to patterns. Tutte realized that, due to a quirk in the rotor settings of the Lorenz machine, guessing the first two wheels correctly would raise the odds of a dot to 55 percent. You could try out different key settings and eyeball the Tunny output for feedback. The asymmetry was slight, but Tutte could usually sense a preponderance of dots.

As Tutte would later note, some at Bletchley Park concluded that his triumph was just a "stroke of undeserved good luck." But Tutte rejected those assertions, pointing out that the ability to notice patterns is itself a kind of "analytic reasoning."[29] He might not have been able to explain the patterns—it took him months to solve the entire machine—but he knew they were there. He could feel them, those subtle clues revealing the tricks of the machine.

The Nazis were convinced that the Lorenz SZ40 was the ultimate cipher, generating an impenetrable code. They assumed the Allied cryptographers would gain no traction, that even those with the knack would fail when faced with the twelve-rotor cipher. As a result, they never worried about a chemistry graduate student using the machine's output to reveal its inner workings. But they failed to account for two factors. The first was the two slightly different messages sent from Athens using the same key, which gave Tiltman the toehold for a near-complete decryption of a long message, and Tutte the starting point he needed to search for patterns in the key. The second was the stubborn genius of Tutte himself. Almost all of his code-breaking attempts led nowhere, failure followed by failure. But he occasionally found a strategy that reduced the mystery, revealing a fragile pattern amid the deluge of Xs and dots. Magic works the same way: if the magician gives the audience the slightest foothold—if they get a glimpse of a wire or see a card vanish up a sleeve—the spell is broken. The wonder ends. The investigation begins.

The breaking of Tunny was a turning point in the war, giving the Allies an invaluable window into German strategy. It shaped the planning of D-Day—Tunny messages confirmed that the Nazis expected a landing much farther north—and allowed the Allies to avoid the best-defended beaches. "This was absolute intelligence gold dust," writes Jerry Roberts. "The information had not come from spies"—which had proven problematic and untrustworthy—"but directly from Hitler via Lorenz decrypts, in the German's own words."[30]

Perhaps the most valuable use of Tunny came on the Eastern Front. In the summer of 1943, roughly 775,000 Nazi soldiers, along with three thousand panzer tanks, began gathering near Kursk, about three hundred miles southwest of Moscow. The goal of the German army was to split the Russian flank, cutting off their main salient, or bulge. But disagreements among German generals led to a spike in messages sent using the Lorenz machines, giving Tutte and his team of code breakers a detailed map of German positions.

The British recognized the importance of Kursk: if the Russians lost the battle, Moscow might fall. As a result, they passed their decrypted intelligence on to the Russian generals. (The Russian commander, General Zhukov, was so impressed by the British memos that he assumed they had a secret agent at the highest levels of the German army.)* This intelligence on the movements of the German army allowed the Russians to establish a fierce line of defense at the points of expected attack. The Russians sent more than three hundred thousand civilians to work. They strung rows of mines, dug antitank ditches, and built concrete machine-gun bunkers. Around Kursk, these "defensive belts" were more than twenty miles deep.

On July 4, 1943, the Germans began their offensive, sending every panzer division on the Eastern Front to the Russian lines. They expected scattered resistance. Instead, they ran straight into

---

* The Russians also received raw intelligence from Bletchley Park via John Cairncross, a double agent who worked on the Ultra ciphers.

a death trap. On July 13, nine days after the battle began, Hitler stopped the German attack. It was the first failed Nazi offensive of the war and set up a Russian counterattack that ended, two years later, in Berlin. The Russians referred to the Battle of Kursk as the Turning of the Tide.

As code breaker Jerry Roberts observes, the military intelligence provided by Tutte's achievement was unprecedented. "It was the first and perhaps only war in which one side had such detailed ongoing knowledge of what the other side was planning, thinking and deciding," Roberts writes. "Without Lorenz decrypts, the war in Europe would have lasted many more years. This was a war which was costing tens of millions of lives a year."[31]

A few months after the war ended, Tutte traveled to Germany. He met with a senior German intelligence official, who showed off the Lorenz machine, explaining how the complex interactions of the rotors created an unbreakable code. Tutte listened, pretending to be impressed. When the German was done talking, Tutte shrugged and said, "No one is ever going to break that." What Tutte couldn't say is that he already had.[32]

Nobody knows why Tutte's work on the Lorenz cipher was kept secret for more than fifty years. (The breaking of the Enigma cipher by Alan Turing was declassified in the 1970s.)[33] One theory is that the British didn't want the Russians to know that they'd cracked the code, since the Russians used captured Lorenz machines during the first years of the Cold War.[34] By the early 1950s, however, the Soviets had adopted their own cryptographic systems. Another theory is that being able to read the Lorenz messages required the Allied leaders—Churchill in particular—to make excruciating trade-offs during the war. Time and time again, they had to consider the risk of acting on their secret Ultra intelligence, and thus giving away its invaluable source. These decisions likely meant that innocent people died, and soldiers were sent to their death, all to protect Tutte's breakthrough.

When Tutte retired in the early 1980s, he was known as a distinguished academic who had made significant contributions to graph theory in general and to the four-color-map theorem in particular. Only after he retired, still holding the secret he was obliged to keep, did the British government declassify his Bletchley Park breakthrough. Tutte was named an Officer of the Order of Canada, and a public memorial to his wartime achievements now stands in his birthplace of Newmarket. In his final decade, he received new accolades from his colleagues and attended cryptography conferences to reminisce about breaking the Lorenz cipher with a sharp pencil and reams of paper.

He remained humble and soft-spoken to the end, eager to share credit and minimize his role. At the cemetery in West Montrose where his ashes are interred, a small polished stone is set into the ground with only his name and the dates of his birth and death. A visitor might notice that this William Tutte, whoever he was, lies beside Dorothea Tutte. With no claim to fame engraved on the stones, few would know that here lies the man whose incandescent curiosity cracked the ultimate code, saving the world with the secrets he revealed.

## The Puzzle of Life

All writing about magic is limited by the first rule of magic, which is that one should never talk about how magic happens. Ever since those ancient street artists baffled strangers for spare coins, magicians have policed their secrets, exiling anyone who dares reveal a method, principle, or tool.

There are good reasons for this self-policing. The thrill of a magic trick is that we can't explain it; the mystery is what generates the feeling of wonder, as confirmed by those brain scans. But the secrecy also exists for another reason, which is that the solution to most tricks is heartbreakingly banal. The Statue of Liberty disappeared because the audience was slowly turned; the vanished donkey is hiding behind an angled mirror; the secret of the card trick is some fast fingers. It's not supernatural. It's just thousands of hours of tedious practice.

When I was with Mohan, the geological statistician who broke the lottery, in Toronto, during the last cold days of a long winter, he kept asking me if I really wanted to know how Jan Rouven performed his puzzle trick. He warned me that I'd be disappointed, that it might be better if I just preserved the mystery. But I was in too deep. *I needed to know*.[35]

Mohan set up the trick in his girlfriend's living room. We snacked on cheese and crackers as he assembled the puzzle. He repeated Rouven's performance, filling in the narrative with his own childhood memories. He took the puzzle apart and put it back together, piece by piece. And then, after adding those two extra blocks, he slid the frame back over the puzzle. Jim Steinmeyer, a celebrated inventor of modern magic tricks, and the man who figured out how Charles Morritt vanished the donkey, says that the best illusions have a particular tell: right before the crowd applauds, there is a brief silence, a "split second when the entire audience shares a gasp of genuine amazement." When Mohan fit the frame over the puzzle, I gasped.

Mohan then let me look over the parts of the illusion. My best guesses were quickly falsified. I held the wooden frame and looked over the wooden pieces; they all seemed solid, ordinary, perfectly muggle. A bit rough, perhaps, but only because they had been fashioned by the hands of a geological statistician who is not a professional carpenter.

"Do you give up?" Mohan asked. I nodded, and Mohan began describing his solution. "When I was thinking back on Rouven's performance, I realized that there's just that one moment when we don't see all the puzzle pieces," Mohan says, referring to the brief section when the magician has stacked the wood blocks in his hand. Although Rouven seamlessly weaves that procedure into the narrative—each piece represents one of his essential memories—Mohan knew that all the talking was just a feint, a clever distraction.

What was Rouven really up to? Perhaps holding the blocks gave him the opportunity to "ditch" one of them, thus clearing space for the extra pieces he would later add to the puzzle. But Mohan realized that it couldn't be a typical ditch, such as palming the piece, since the wooden blocks were way too big. "That's one of the neat things about the trick," Mohan says. "If Rouven had used smaller pieces, it would be easy to just think he hid one or two of them up his sleeve. But by choosing such large pieces of wood, he's leading us away from that explanation."

Mohan was stumped, but he couldn't stop thinking about those seconds when Rouven was holding the disassembled puzzle. Something happened there, he could feel it—he just didn't know what it was. "Magic works because magicians understand our attention," Mohan says. "They know exactly where we're looking." Mohan focused his detective work on where the audience *wasn't* looking, as that's likely where the trick was happening. At the top of the list were the puzzle pieces themselves. "That's the elegance of it. The last place we'd think of hiding the blocks are within another block. And then I thought about how, when Rouven's holding all of the pieces"—they're stacked in his arms—"he might be able to quickly slide one into another." It's an ingenious use of functional fixedness. Blocks are for building; they are solid and sturdy. It never occurs to us that a block could also be a hiding spot.

So Mohan went to his garage, a cluttered corner of which doubles as his woodworking shop. It took a few weeks, but he engineered one of the larger blocks with an empty inside, so that it could swallow a smaller piece. To make the ditch easier, he inserted small neodymium supermagnets into both blocks. The magnets ensure that the disappearance happens fast—once the blocks are near their positions, the invisible force takes care of the rest. Mohan smiled as he explained the supermagnets: "The reason for making the carpentry look rough is to get the audience thinking 'clumsy bits of wood,' which takes their thoughts away from high-tech rare-earth supermagnets." Many of us are familiar with the physical misdirection of magic: the flourishes with the wand, the distractions of the cape and hat. But the best magic also uses subliminal misdirection.

After I returned from Toronto, I found a video of Jan Rouven performing the puzzle illusion. It's an old clip from 2014, taken at a charity benefit for an animal shelter, but it's the only recording of the original trick. In March 2016, authorities arrested Rouven for possessing child pornography; he's been in jail ever since. While the incident ended his career, it increased the "prestige" of Rouven's tricks, since several of them have never again been seen.*

---

* A few years ago, the celebrity magician Criss Angel performed a trick for a television special that, by most accounts, was extremely similar to one performed by Jan Rouven years before. This trick, the Bed of Death, is essentially a version of Russian roulette without a loaded pistol, with Rouven instead strapped to a table beneath five razor-sharp swords connected to a series of ropes. One of these swords

In the video, Rouven's ditch occurs just before the two-minute mark. The ditch is visible once you know what to look for—due to the camera angle, you can see the piece disappear—but that's the point: nobody knows to look. Such are the lessons of magic: it's an art that constantly reminds us how little we know, and that we understand even less. Our brains can't see everything; the world is too big, too full, too strange. So we take shortcuts instead.

Consider a visual illusion known as the Shepard Tables. Look at the picture below and pick the table that is more likely to fit through a narrow doorway:

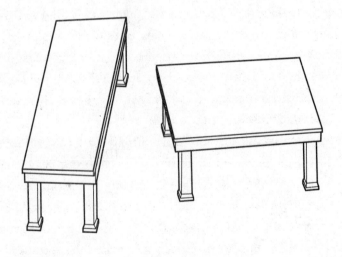

---

is poised directly over the magician's heart. A volunteer from the audience chooses the order of the swords by randomly pulling on various ropes. (The trick is that he or she never chooses the deadly one.) While Rouven's illusion was widely celebrated, Criss Angel's television version didn't go as smoothly. When Angel tried to release the last sword—the one that would have killed him—the sword refused to budge, thus giving away the mechanics of the trick: the rope connected to the dangerous sword is held back by a separate mechanism and thus can't actually be released by the volunteer.[36]

Nearly everyone picks the table on the left. The answer, however, is that both tables have identical dimensions. (The illusion dupes our perception of depth, which estimates size based on foreshortening.) What makes this illusion so compelling is that even after we know the tables are the same, we still see them as different. As the neuroscientist Gustav Kuhn observes, this tension is what makes the picture interesting, turning a simple line drawing into an epistemic mystery. "Even when you know such illusions are present, the mismatch with reality is still there," he writes.[37]

Magic is like that, too. The best tricks can't be spoiled because, even when the trick is given away, we still can't understand how it was done. Penn and Teller used to perform a version of Cups and Balls, a classic sleight-of-hand trick supposedly popularized by ancient Egyptian conjurers. In the trick, in a series of "vanishes" and "transpositions," the balls appear and disappear beneath a series of opaque cups. Teller's ingenious innovation was to use clear water glasses instead. Although it was now possible to follow the balls as Teller palmed them and moved them from glass to glass, audiences still couldn't make sense of the performance. "The eye could see the moves, but the mind could not comprehend them," Teller says.[38]

But then the same could be said of the Old Masters, who turned some lenses and mirrors into visual wonders. To be a great artist is to become a magician. It requires that you devote your life to making the inexplicable look easy. It means spending years practicing tricks that only succeed if nobody notices them. Because if the method works, there doesn't seem to be any method at all. Just a quiet gasp, followed by a lasting sense of mystery.

We crave the gasp. A recent experiment by the magician Joshua Jay and the psychologists Lisa Grimm and Nicholas Spanola showed subjects a series of videos documenting impressive magical feats, such as making a girl levitate. The subjects then had a choice: they could either learn how the trick was done or watch another magic trick. Most people just wanted to see more magic. The experience of mystery was more fun than its solution.

# CHAPTER 3

# THE POWER OF COMIC SANS

It's not where you take things from. It's where you take them to.

—KANYE WEST, ON TWITTER

Trust what is difficult.

—RAINER MARIA RILKE, *Letters to a Young Poet*

## "The Woods Movie"

In the early 1990s, Dan Myrick, a student at the University of Central Florida film school, began complaining to his friends about the sad state of the American horror movie. For Dan, the problem was simple: the movies had stopped being scary. They were bloodier than ever—*Freddy's Dead* featured buckets of red corn syrup—but the violence felt frivolous and campy. "The movies had become so predictable," Dan says. "You could see every move way in advance because you'd seen it a million times before."[1] Krueger had become a cliché.

But Dan wasn't content to be a critic. Along with fellow film student Eduardo Sánchez, Dan began plotting out a new kind of horror film. "We'd have a few beers, smoke a little, and just talk about the movies we wanted to make," Dan told me. The students discovered that they both loved the television series *In Search of . . .* , a syndicated show from the late 1970s that investigated paranormal mysteries, from Bigfoot to ancient aliens. "What we responded to was that authentic search for answers," Dan says. "The show treated the mystery seriously, and that made it scarier than most of the horror crap being made." Dan and Eduardo's big idea was to make a horror movie modeled on an episode of *In Search of . . .* , with their characters attempting to unravel some long-standing enigma. They decided to set their investigation in the woods. ("What's scarier than getting lost in a big dark forest?" Dan asks.) They started calling their project "The Woods Movie."

Now the film students needed a plot, a mystery for their characters to investigate in that forbidding forest. The film students began by inventing a sprawling mythology about the curse of Burkittsville, a small town in north-central Maryland. The curse started with the death of a witch—she was exiled during a harsh winter storm—and the disappearance of her accusers. Decades pass; the vanishings continue. Cut to 1994, when three local college students decide to make a documentary about all these missing people. The students walk into the woods and are never seen again. A year later, an anthropologist discovers their duffel bag, containing video tapes, in an abandoned cabin.

Dan and Eduardo's brilliant conceit was to make a film out of that found footage. "We realized that if you make it feel like a documentary, then all of a sudden there's no safety net for the audience," Dan says. "It doesn't have to have a neat ending. The good guys don't have to survive. Anything can happen because you're free from the old ways of telling the story."

New technology made their new style of storytelling possible. At the time, handheld cameras were becoming commonplace. And it wasn't just random home videos—the same shaky style was also appearing on television, thanks to cable news and reality shows such as *The Real World* and *Cops*. "There was something about the shakiness that just made it feel real," Dan says. "It was so artless, you're like, 'This has to be true.'"

But using a jittery camera wasn't enough. If Dan and Eduardo were going to avoid the predictable tropes of the horror genre—the cheesy soundtrack, the obvious shots, the foreseeable deaths—they would have to pioneer a different kind of movie-making process. Instead of a conventional script (which would feel too contrived), Dan and Eduardo spent weeks coming up with a thirty-five-page narrative outline, a beat sheet that described every scene in the movie. The actors would improvise the dialogue. "We knew that if for even a second, if you felt like these people were acting, if it felt like a movie at all, we were going to lose the audience," Eduardo told *Vice* in 2016. "So it was very important that these actors know how to improv and know how to improv creatively and not overdo it."[2]

Casting took nearly a year. Another month was spent scouting locations. Then they had to get the camera equipment—a Hi8 from Circuit City, which they returned after the shoot—and gear for camping, since they would be spending eight days in the woods. Instead of working directly with the actors, Dan and Eduardo gave them a GPS unit programmed with directions to various hideouts containing their daily instructions. They made the actors hike in the rain and camp in a soggy tent and slowly decreased their food intake during the shoot. The actors had a safe word—if things got too gnarly, they were supposed to say "bulldozer"—but mostly they stayed in character. They were scared kids in the woods pretending to be scared kids in the woods.

When Dan and Eduardo began filming, they assumed the found footage would only be a small part of a larger fake documentary. "We thought we'd also have expert interviews, stuff on the curse, backstory on how the footage was found, things like that," Dan says. "Maybe twenty minutes or so of material with the actors, but we didn't think there was any way you could get away with more than that."

The first review of the raw footage from the woods wasn't promising. "It was rough, rougher than anything I'd ever seen in a movie theater, and it most definitely broke every rule you learn in film school," Dan says. The camerawork wasn't just shaky—it bordered on incoherence, especially when the actors were filming themselves at night. The dialogue was often mumbled and inaudible; most of the scenes lacked structure. At times, the footage was hard to watch. "I mean, there's a reason people write scripts," Dan says. "There's a reason the actors don't normally hold the cameras."

And yet, the subversive insight of Dan and Eduardo was that these same lo-fi "flaws" could make for a terrifying horror film. Before long, they decided to make the entire movie out of that found footage from the woods. "What we discovered is that it's so much scarier to do it this way than to have some slick well-lit forest scene with a bogeyman," Dan says. "You've never seen a horror movie like this before. You have no idea who's going to live or die or what's coming next."

The desire to make a new kind of horror movie even extended to the final scene. In the original cut, two of the students race into an abandoned cabin, desperate to save their missing friend, whose screams they can still hear. They run down the stairs, cameras on. But when they get there, we don't get a glimpse of the witch, or even their tortured friend. Instead, we see one of the students standing in the corner. The last shot of the movie is sideways, as the camera drops to the floor. It's not murder, but the terrifying moment before.

The studio, however, insisted on a less ambiguous ending. So Dan and Eduardo returned to the woods to shoot several alternative takes. They were all more obvious and more gruesome: there was one with a noose, and one with a bloody wound, and one with a student nailed to a wooden stick man. "We hated them," Dan says. "They all felt so conventional." Although the studio executives warned Dan and Eduardo that ending the movie with so much uncertainty would cost them millions at the box office, the young filmmakers insisted on preserving the mysterious ending.

On July 14, 1999, they released "The Woods Movie" in theaters as *The Blair Witch Project*. The movie was an instant hit and went on to gross nearly $250 million around the world. (Dan and Eduardo originally made the film for around $25,000, making it one of the most profitable movies ever made.) It helped that the marketing leaned into the mystery. The distributor didn't want to invest in conventional television spots, so Dan and Eduardo built out their website instead, telling the story of the myth along with additional information about the missing filmmakers. They included archival photos, missing persons signs, and elaborate historical time lines. The result was a fiction that felt real. After the movie came out, the families of the actors received condolence cards.

*Blair Witch* has since inspired two sequels and countless imitators; found footage is now a common trope of the horror genre, from the *Paranormal Activity* franchise to *Cloverfield*. "There's something ironic about our style becoming so popular," Dan says. "We did it because we had to, because we had no money and we didn't think scary movies were scary anymore. But what we unlearned is now its own tradition." Such is the destiny of successful art: it gets copied until it becomes a cliché.

Our culture is full of content that aims to please. It tries to amuse and entertain and pass the time. But the art that changes the world is *subversive*, designed to unsettle and confuse. We've been trained to expect X, so it serves up Y and Z instead. This strategy can produce material that's strange and disorienting, just like *The Blair Witch Project*.

This chapter is about the subversive hook. It's about the unexpected benefits of difficult art, which improves our attention and enhances our thinking. We might not enjoy this kind of hook, at least not at first. We probably wish we were watching a more conventional horror movie, with Freddy Krueger and a predictable ending. But our discomfort isn't a sign of failure. It's proof that the mystery hook is working.

## Desirable Difficulties

You will remember this sentence.

To understand why, it helps to know about the work of psychologist Daniel Oppenheimer. A decade ago, he led a study at a public high school in Chesterland, Ohio.[3] The scientists asked teachers to submit their written classroom materials, such as PowerPoint decks and worksheets. Then, the researchers changed the fonts on the material, transforming the text with a variety of so-called disfluent fonts, such as *Monotype Corsiva* and **Comic Sans** italicized. What makes these fonts disfluent is that they're used less frequently: When was the last time you read a book in Comic Sans? Because all of the teachers included in the study taught at least two sections of the same class, the psychologists could conduct a controlled experiment. One group of students received the classroom materials with the disfluent fonts, while the other group was taught with more typical fonts, like Helvetica and Arial.

After several weeks of instruction, the students were tested on their retention of the material. In nearly every class, the students in the disfluent condition performed significantly better. Comic Sans led to higher grades. Ugly fonts improved their recall.

And it's not just the classroom: the benefits of disfluent fonts apply in many domains. Consider a series of recent experiments led by Adam Alter, a psychologist at NYU, and done in collaboration with Oppenheimer. In his research, Alter relied on a well-known assessment called the Cognitive Reflection Test, or CRT.[4] The short test is designed to measure the extent to which an individual relies on mental shortcuts and quick instincts, giving subjects tricky questions in which their initial hunch is almost always incorrect. Here's a classic question from the CRT: "If it takes 5 machines 5 minutes to make 5 widgets, how long would it take 100 machines to make 100 widgets?" The intuitive response is that it will take the machines 100 minutes. That, however, is incorrect: it will still only take the machines 5 minutes. When Alter gave people the CRT in a disfluent font—he used a tiny print in a light gray—they were much less likely to get the wrong answer. While 90 percent of subjects in an easy-to-read font got at least one of the CRT questions wrong, only 35 percent did so in the disfluent group. The perceptual struggle made them more reflective and thoughtful.

Think, for a moment, about the strange implications of this research. The primary goal of typography is to create legible text. This is especially true in the digital age. Amazon, for instance, brags that Bookerly, its custom font for the Kindle, makes reading easier on the eyes, allowing us "to read faster with less eyestrain." Company logos, meanwhile, are designed to maximize fluency, which is why American Airlines, Jeep, Target, Nestlé, and Toyota all rely on versions of Helvetica. The irony is that the research suggests that the effortless processing might lead to less attention and retention. Easy in, easy out.

Why does disfluency help us learn more and think better? The explanation begins with the natural laziness of the human mind, which is always trying to save energy by *not* thinking. (Your brain requires only about three hundred calories per day for consciousness, or the amount of energy in a candy bar.)[5] This need for efficiency means that we often rely on mental shortcuts, whether it's our shoddy assessments of probabilities or instant judgments of other people. These shortcuts aren't a faster form of thinking. They're a way of skipping thought altogether.

And that brings us back to these ugly fonts. Because their shapes are unfamiliar, because they are *less* legible, they make the mind work a little harder; the slight frisson of Comic Sans wakes us up or at least prevents us from leaning on the usual efficiencies. "The complex fonts . . . function like an alarm," Alter writes. They signal "that we need to recruit additional mental resources to overcome that sense of difficulty."[6]

You can see this extra activity in the brain. Stanislas Dehaene, a neuroscientist at the Collège de France in Paris, has helped illuminate the neural anatomy of reading.[7] It turns out that the literate brain contains two distinct pathways for making sense of words. One pathway is known as the ventral route, and it's fast and efficient. The process goes like this: We see a group of letters, convert those letters into a word, then grasp the word's semantic meaning. According to Dehaene, this ventral pathway is activated by writing in a "familiar format" and relies on a bit of cortex known as visual word form area (VWFA). When you are reading a straightforward sentence, you're almost certainly relying on this speedy neural highway.[8] As a result, reading seems effortless and easy. We don't have to think about those symbols on the page.

But the ventral route is not the only way to read. The second reading pathway—the dorsal stream—comes on whenever we're forced to pay conscious attention to a sentence, perhaps because of an obscure word or unfamiliar font.[9] (In his experiments, Dehaene activates this pathway in a variety of ways, such as rotating the letters or filling the prose with errant commas and semicolons.) Although scientists had previously assumed that the dorsal route ceased to be active once we became literate, Dehaene's research demonstrates that disfluent and unfamiliar writing can change the way we read. We're suddenly hyperaware of the words on the page, forced to work harder to make sense of the text. The difficulty demands our focus.

In 1917, the Russian formalist Viktor Shklovsky wrote an influential essay about the aesthetic benefits of disfluency. He began by observing the natural negligence of the human mind, which is good at *not* noticing things. The function of art, Shklovsky said, is to push back against this tendency, restoring our attention by defamiliarizing reality.* Here's Shklovsky:

"Art exists that one may recover the sensation of life; it exists to make one feel things; to make the stone stony. . . . The technique of art is to make objects 'unfamiliar,' to make forms difficult, to increase the difficulty and length of perception."[10]

Look at poetry, an art form dependent on disfluency and defamiliarization. A poem is writing that often breaks the ordinary rules of writing; the only requirement is that the language feel different. (As the poet and critic Jane Hirshfield writes, poetry reminds us "of the usefulness of the useless.")[11] It's always been

---

* Shklovsky used the Russian word *ostranenie*, which has also been translated as "estrangement" or "making strange."

this way. *The Odyssey*, one of the oldest works of literature, is an epic poem composed in a six-beat line, and its sentences, in a strict rhythm, are distinct from everyday speech. *The Odyssey* also featured a bizarre vocabulary. "The language contains a strange mixture of words from different periods of time, and from Greek dialects associated with different regions," writes the translator Emily Wilson. "The syntax is relatively simple, but the words and phrases, in these combinations, are unlike the way that anybody ever actually spoke."[12]

All this strangeness can make poetry feel abstract and obscure—who has time for such a disfluent art? But it also means that the best poetry can rescue language from our indifference, allowing us to look at old words in new ways. Here's Marianne Moore, in "Poetry":

> I too, dislike it: there are things that are
> important beyond
> all this fiddle.
> Reading it, however, with a perfect contempt
> for it, one
> discovers that there is in
> it after all, a place for the genuine.

Moore is reminding us that these glimpses of the genuine are bound up with the fiddle of the art; it is the disfluency of the poem that compels our concentration, forcing the brain to read with that demanding dorsal route. The weirdness of the words slows us down, giving us a chance to notice the "genuine" we normally overlook.

Perhaps no poet made better use of disfluency than Emily Dickinson. Writing in a time of highly metered poetry, Dickinson resisted every structure and tradition.* She rebelled against the conventions of grammar—she used em dashes like commas and plus signs like ellipses—and deployed words and metaphors in the most unexpected ways. ("Pain has an element of blank," to take a line almost at random.)

This strangeness didn't make her popular. Dickinson only published ten poems in her lifetime, all with an anonymous by-line. When one of her poems appeared in the *Springfield Daily Republican* in February 1866, Dickinson complained that the editors had ruined her verse by taking away the disfluency, stripping away her dashes and math symbols. The published poem, Dickinson wrote, was "robbed of me—defeated . . . by the punctuation."[13] The edits reminded her why she "did not print." Publication required conformity and she refused to conform.

To understand the eccentricities of Dickinson's poetic style, consider the envelope poems, a trove of literary fragments composed on scraps of scavenged paper. (Dickinson had access to lined paper, she just preferred drafting on these carefully unfolded envelopes.) Here are some lines from piece A316.[14]

---

* Compare a typical Dickinson poem to the opening stanza of "The Day Is Done" by Henry Wadsworth Longfellow, the most celebrated American poet of the nineteenth century:

> The day is done, and the darkness
> Falls from the wings of Night,
> As a feather is wafted downward
> From an eagle in his flight.

Longfellow is leaning heavily on the most familiar poetic structures. He uses a simple iambic cadence and the rhyming scheme of a nursery rhyme (ABCB). As a result, the poem is easy to understand on first reading.

Oh sumptuous
moment
Slower go
That I
May gloat on
Thee—
'Twill never
Be the same
To starve
Now I abundance
see[15]

It's a short poem about the shortness of life. Dickinson wants to slow experience down, to "gloat" on the moment, but time keeps rushing on.

Here's Dickinson's genius: the disfluency of her poem also provides the solution, encouraging us to savor the "sumptuous / moment" of her words. By making the form of her poem so unfamiliar, Dickinson teaches us how to "gloat," how to read carefully, how to be mindful of the marks on the page. (She creates her own "abundance.") All it takes is a style we've never before seen.

Dickinson celebrated strangeness. For Dickinson, disfluency wasn't just an aesthetic choice—it echoed her great theme. She wanted her poetry to be difficult because the world was difficult to understand; if her writing was mysterious, it's because everything was mysterious, at least if you looked at it properly. We learn to ignore these mysteries—we are too busy for awe—but she wanted to return us to them. As Dickinson writes in one of her most canonized poems:

> But nature is a stranger yet;
> The ones that cite her most
> Have never passed her haunted house,
> Nor simplified her ghost.

It's sometimes said that Dickinson was a writer born in the wrong century. She was a female poet writing modernist poems during the Civil War; she broke with poetic traditions that would remain entrenched for another fifty years. In many respects, we're still catching up to her, trying to transcribe and understand those verses she wrote down on envelopes, chocolate wrappers, and scattered notebook pages. Because what Dickinson said about the mysteries of nature is also true of her art:

> Those who know her, know her less
> The nearer her they get.

## Goodnight Nobody

In October 1934, Gertrude Stein embarked on a thirty-seven-city tour of America. She'd recently published *The Autobiography of Alice B. Toklas*, her first bestseller, and eager crowds hoped to glimpse this expat intellectual. An electric ticker in Times Square announced Stein's arrival by steamer;[16] journalists clamored for interviews; the *Times* described the "simplicity of her garb," which was "almost like a Nun's."[17]

One of Stein's first public appearances was sold-out, at the Brooklyn Academy of Music. One of the people in the audience that evening was a struggling young writer named Margaret

Brown. A charming rebel, with a pile of messy curls and a closet full of slacks, Brown was enthralled by Stein's criticisms of grammar and punctuation, which the famous writer said got in the way of true understanding.* (In college, Brown had struggled in her English composition class due to her own grammatical failings.)[18] Stein wanted her writing to reveal the limitations of *all* writing, compelling her readers to notice the confining conventions of language. This made her work baffling and pugnacious, but it also expanded the possibilities of art. "When you make a thing," Stein wrote in *The Autobiography*, "it is so complicated making it that it is bound to be ugly, but those that do it after you they don't have to worry about making it and they can make it pretty, and so everybody can like it when the others make it."

Unfortunately, Margaret Brown soon had to abandon her dream of becoming the next Gertrude Stein. After years of writing short stories, Brown still hadn't sold a single piece. Nevertheless, she'd had enough of the suburban life on Long Island and moved to Manhattan, where she applied to Bank Street, a progressive teaching college founded by Lucy Sprague Mitchell. The mission of Bank Street was to create a new kind of education modeled on the philosophy of John Dewey. While traditional pedagogy emphasized rote memorization, Dewey argued that real learning was a by-product of *doing*, and that the classroom should be a hub of verbs. The best way to learn chemistry was by cooking lunch; geometry could be a carpentry lesson; civics should be a student vote. Rather than present knowledge as a static, settled lesson, teachers should emphasize exploration and experimentation.

---

* As Stein put it, "If a reader doesn't know that a question is a question when he reads it, then a question mark can't tell him."

Brown admired this educational philosophy—it reinforced her skepticism of tradition—but she struggled to manage her students. One assessment blamed her for contributing "a somewhat disorganizing influence to the class." Another noted her messy approach to the art closet: she spilled two containers of glue and forgot to clean them up.[19]

But Brown didn't drop out of Bank Street. Instead, Lucy Sprague Mitchell encouraged Brown to return to writing, only with a focus on children's books. Mitchell was tired of fairy tales. She wanted Brown to write books that exposed the wonders of the ordinary world. "It is only the blind eye of the adult that finds the familiar uninteresting," Mitchell wrote. "The attempt to amuse children by presenting them with the strange, the bizarre, the unreal, is the unhappy result of this adult blindness."

As she began working on her first children's book, Brown returned to her favorite writer for inspiration: Gertrude Stein. Like her literary hero, Brown also wanted to challenge the stale conventions of her form. "Everybody said the same thing over and over again with infinite variations but over and over again," Stein once declared. In Brown's opinion, this was particularly true of children's literature, which seemed limited to predictable fairy tales and didactic rhymes. Even toddlers, Brown thought, deserved a little avant-garde.

The Stein influence is most clear in Brown's masterpiece, written in a single morning in 1946. She got the idea for the book from a dream. A little girl is trying to sleep in a green bedroom. The child is frightened by the noises of the night, but finds comfort in her favorite things. When Brown woke up, she wrote down the idea right away. The story—she called it *Goodnight Moon*—began with an introduction to everything in the "great green room." There's a red balloon, some kittens and mittens, and a mother rabbit whispering hush. These words are written in the voice of the good parent, who teaches the child how to name the world. After this soothing introduction, the book starts to circle back, as we say goodnight to everything in the room. *Goodnight room. Goodnight red balloon. Goodnight cow jumping over the moon.*

If Brown were writing a conventional children's book, we'd now repeat the first half of the book, only with a goodnight preface. (Repetition is a fundamental trope of children's literature. So is going to sleep.) But that's not what happens. Instead, Brown introduces us to a new character: the actual moon. (We never met the real moon before, only the crescent moon in the painting.) Then Brown returns to the established pattern, saying goodnight to things we've already seen, such as the jumping cow. But then she breaks again—goodnight light and chairs we don't know— before once again revisiting the familiar kittens, mittens, and bears.

The key point is that Brown dismantles the expected form, which would involve a straightforward repetition. By blending in a collection of new objects, she forces us to pay attention; we can't take the text or its rhythms for granted. This constant back-and-forth between the known and the unknown, the familiar and the strange, makes her simple book compelling. Every page becomes its own little mystery.

The writing gets stranger as the book draws to a close. After saying goodnight to the brush, Brown features a blank page and a goodnight to "nobody." Then, right after we say goodnight to the old lady, Brown expands beyond the green room, flying out the window into the wide world beyond. *Goodnight stars. Goodnight air. Goodnight noises everywhere.*

And so the book ends. Not with the old lady whispering hush—that's the predictable choice—but with an ode to all the noises of the night. As the writer Aimee Bender observes, in an appreciation of Brown, "On some level, it had to have been a felt ending, a note she hit that must have seemed right and took confidence and daring to pull off. The reader has time to linger with that end and accept it—it's not the obvious closing note of the music, it's not the fully resolved major chord. But she trusted it."[20]

Not everyone liked Brown's subversive little story. The head children's librarian at the New York Public Library refused to buy *Goodnight Moon*; she didn't like the trippy pictures and, according to an internal review, found it "unbearably sentimental."[21] But Brown didn't care. She'd learned from Gertrude Stein that a little difficulty can be good. What grabs our attention is not the pattern we expect—it's the one we never see coming. Not the obvious repetition, but a jarring mixture of the new and the old. So the gentle dissonance becomes a cultural lesson for the child. Brown is teaching them the essential template of good art: it evokes a pattern and then finds a way to undermine it, subverting our expectations and assumptions.*

*Goodnight Moon* barely sold any copies for the first several years. Nobody knew what to make of a children's book inspired by the modernists. But something about those unpredictable words was irresistibly mysterious. As the years passed, *Goodnight Moon* gradually became a bestseller; by 1970, sales were approaching twenty thousand copies a year. It has since become one of the most pop-

---

* But these violations should never be haphazard or reckless; *Goodnight Moon* is filled with thoughtful details invented by Brown and her brilliant illustrator, Clement Hurd. When the book begins, the little bunny is already in bed; sleep seems imminent; the hour hand of the clock is at 7:00. But as every parent knows, bedtime can take a while. By the time the little bunny says goodnight to the noises everywhere—and then presumably passes out—the clock is at 8:10, and the moon has risen into the window frame. Such precision is emblematic of Brown's approach. Even her simplest books are exquisitely layered.

ular children's books of all time, with cumulative sales of roughly 50 million copies. Brown never enjoyed her triumph. She died in 1952 of a blood clot, long before *Goodnight Moon* became a classic. But writing the book gave her confidence to break the rules. After delivering the manuscript, Brown painted the walls of her bedroom green.

## The Mystery of the Blind Headline

In May 1947, Bill Bernbach, the creative director of Grey Advertising, wrote a mission statement that would transform his industry. At the time, though, it was mostly seen as an act of career suicide. In the memo to his bosses, Bernbach launched an attack on the business practices of Madison Avenue, which he said were leading to the death of creativity. "Our agency is getting big," Bernbach began. "That's something to be happy about. But it's something to worry about, too, and I don't mind telling you I'm damn worried."[22]

He was worried because getting big meant following the rules of other people, listening to those confident marketing "technicians" who tried to turn advertising into a slick science. "They can tell you that a sentence should be this short or that long," Bernbach wrote. "They can tell you that body copy should be broken up for easier and more inviting reading. They can give you fact after fact after fact." But Bernbach believed that such "facts" were suffocating, inevitably leading to a "sameness, a mental weariness, a mediocrity of ideas." As Bernbach would later put it, "Rules are what the artist breaks; the memorable never emerged from a formula."[23] Bernbach wanted to be an artist.

Not surprisingly, the management of Grey Advertising didn't

think much of Bernbach's cri de coeur. (Those technicians were making them lots of money.) Before long, Bernbach began talking with Ned Doyle, a colleague at Grey, about setting up their own shop. In 1949, they partnered with Maxwell Dane, a business guy with a lease to an empty rooftop office on Madison Avenue. Doyle Dane Bernbach was born. "Nothing will ever get between us," Bernbach said. "Not even punctuation."

The early days were tough. The big agencies routinely dismissed Doyle Dane Bernbach as "two Jews and an Irishman."[24] Their rule breaking turned clients off; amid the postwar boom, it seemed smarter to play it safe and trust the technicians. The agency was kept afloat by billings for Ohrbach's, a moderately priced department store chain, and Levy's Bakery, which sold crusty rye bread. Although the campaigns were small—Levy's only had a $50,000 budget—they established the daring, subversive style that would become a hallmark of the agency.

For Bernbach, such subversion had a purpose. He understood that he was in the business of delivering a message that people didn't want to hear. (They wanted to get back to the television show, not learn about rye bread.) This meant that every spot needed a creative hook, a little mystery that made people look. "Playing it safe can be the most dangerous thing in the world, because you're presenting people with an idea they've seen before, and you won't have an impact," Bernbach said. "Imitation can be commercial suicide."[25]

One of Bernbach's most effective strategies was to create a tension between the picture and the headline. Although every other print advertisement used the picture to reinforce the message of the text—it usually showed a smiling person enjoying the product—Bernbach wanted a mismatch. We saw the image, and we read the words, but, perplexed for a second or two, we struggled to understand how they fit together. The ad required unpacking, provoking questions whose answer was the sell.

This dissonant style reached its creative peak in Doyle Dane Bernbach's work for Volkswagen. In the late 1950s, the German carmaker had a single model available for sale in the United States: the Beetle. Although sales had steadily been growing, the Beetle was about to face a new fleet of compact car competition from Ford, Chrysler, and General Motors. Everyone expected the dated Beetle to be obliterated by these new models, which featured bigger engines, electronic controls, and fashionable fins. Volkswagen tasked Doyle Dane Bernbach with making sure that didn't happen.

At the time, car advertising followed a strict template: a highly stylized image of the vehicle featured a debonair driver and an admiring female, followed by a few paragraphs of text that spelled out the innovations in the latest model.

Bernbach realized that Volkswagen required a different approach. The usual claims made in car advertisements—More power! Smoother ride!—couldn't be said about the Beetle, since it only had forty horses and an antiquated suspension. (He was also limited by the budget: Volkswagen had $800,000 for the entire campaign.)[26] Given these strict constraints, Bernbach and his brilliant creative team (led by Julian Koenig and Helmut Krone) decided to break all the rules. Instead of using a glossy car picture with saturated colors, they used a black-and-white image of the Beetle, set against an empty background. It was a utilitarian look for a utilitarian car.

The most significant breakthrough, however, was the text. The agency was tasked with highlighting the number of industrial inspectors used by Volkswagen. While a traditional print ad might have sold this with a picture of the factory and a few paragraphs about its reliable cars, Bernbach's team created an ad that pulled people in with a puzzle. He juxtaposed a simple picture of the Beetle with the headline "Lemon."[27]*

### Lemon.

This Volkswagen missed the boat.

The chrome strip on the glove compartment is blemished and must be replaced. Chances are you wouldn't have noticed it; Inspector Kurt Kroner did.

There are 3,389 men at our Wolfsburg factory with only one job: to inspect Volkswagens at each stage of production. (3000 Volkswagens are produced daily; there are more inspectors than cars.)

Every shock absorber is tested (spot checking won't do), every windshield is scanned. VWs have been rejected for surface scratches barely visible to the eye.

Final inspection is really something! VW inspectors run each car off the line onto the Funktionsprüfstand (car test stand), tote up 189 check points, gun ahead to the automatic brake stand, and say "no" to one VW out of fifty.

This preoccupation with detail means the VW lasts longer and requires less maintenance, by and large, than other cars. (It also means a used VW depreciates less than any other car.)

We pluck the lemons; you get the plums.

Bernbach's audacious bet was that this subversive ad—why was Volkswagen criticizing its own car?—would hook the attention of readers as they flipped the pages of a magazine. As

---

\* The seamless interplay of visual and text was only possible because Bernbach insisted that the writer and art director work together on the concept. In every other agency, the headline and copy would typically be written first and only then sent to the art director for layout.

Bernbach once observed, "You cannot sell a man who isn't listening." The "Lemon" headline got people to listen.

It also got them to remember. In "The Mystery Box" chapter, we learned about a study showing that the feeling of curiosity was associated with increased activity in the hippocampus, a part of the brain associated with learning and memory. Bernbach's advertisements anticipated this finding. By hooking his audience with questions and jokes, he made sure we didn't forget the product he was trying to sell.

But Bernbach knew that a punchy headline wasn't enough: he wanted every detail of the ad to feel different. ("It's not just what you say that stirs people," Bernbach said. "It's the way that you say it.")[28] Take the design of the words. Bernbach typeset the copy with plenty of widows and orphans, as he wanted the ad to have a less "professional" and less polished look. Even the VW logo was placed in an unusual position, at the border between the second and third columns. These details were unexpected—every other car company justified their text and featured a big central logo—but they added to the sense of intrigue. Because we've never seen anything like this before, we want to know more.

The effectiveness of this marketing strategy has been demonstrated in recent work on disfluent text. In a series of experiments, psychologists at the University of Illinois at Urbana-Champaign showed that giving people writing in an unfamiliar font could help them stay open-minded, inducing a less automatic form of thought.[29] This is the kind of thinking Bernbach needed. Because his firm specialized in so-called challenger brands—companies attempting to grab market share from their more established competitors—he had to invent a visual form that kept his audience from relying on preconceptions. The Beetle wasn't a cheap car with obsolete technology. It was a solid piece of German engineering.

Once Bernbach used the mystery in the message to get the attention of magazine readers, he could educate them about those industrial inspectors. Julian Koenig, his gifted copywriter, wrote the prose in a jaunty, conversational tone. The copy begins, "This Volkswagen missed the boat. The chrome strip on the glove compartment is blemished, and must be replaced." After another few paragraphs about German manufacturing, Koenig delivered the perfect last line: "We pluck the lemons; you get the plums."

It's easy to be difficult. The genius of the creatives at Doyle Dane Bernbach was to create ads that were subversive in extremely precise ways. They broke lots of rules, but each careful transgression reinforced their message. (As Bernbach would remind his team, "The product. The product. Stay with the product.")[30] The vivid headline, the black-and-white photograph, the sans-serif font, even the widows of the layout—these surprising choices all communicated the practical virtues of the Beetle. As Bernbach had written years before in his mission statement, such details defined the art of advertising. "Let us blaze new trails," he wrote. "Let us prove to the world that good taste, good art, good writing can be good selling."

It *was* good selling. Three years after the Big Three introduced their new compact models, the number of imported cars fell by nearly 50 percent. The only exception was the Beetle, whose sales continued to climb.

## The Information Theory of Kanye West

Kanye West had to run away. His troubles began when he interrupted Taylor Swift at the 2009 MTV Video Music Awards. Swift had just won Best Female Video and was a few sentences into her acceptance speech when Kanye ran onto the stage and grabbed the microphone. "Yo, Taylor, I'm really happy for you, I'm gonna let you finish, but Beyoncé has one of the best videos of all time," he shouted. "One of the best videos of all time!"

The furor was immediate. There were reports of Swift crying backstage; the president of the United States called Kanye a jackass; even Beyoncé criticized the intrusion. It got so bad that Kanye had to cancel his international tour with Lady Gaga.

Kanye escaped to paradise. Avex Honolulu Studios, to be precise, a den of recording rooms set in a suburban strip mall, just off the Kalaniana'ole Highway. (Avex is in the back, behind the chain drugstore.) Kanye had booked every Avex studio for as long as necessary, complete with engineers on standby twenty-four hours a day. After a morning game of basketball at the Honolulu YMCA, Kanye and his rotating crew of rappers, producers, and musicians would head into Avex and start playing with sound. The process was the opposite of linear: a track might be finished, then changed and changed again. Kanye would work on a song, then lose interest for weeks; beats would be tweaked, lyrics rewritten; the only constant was change. "I'd never worked the way Kanye was working in Hawaii," Q-Tip remembered in *Complex*.[31] "Everybody's opinions mattered and counted. . . . If the delivery guy comes in the studio and Kanye likes him and they strike up a conversation, he'll go, 'Check this out, tell me what you think . . .' Every person has a voice and an idea, so he's sincerely looking to hear what you have to say—good, bad, or whatever."

Kanye had been on Oahu for a few months when he started working on a new track called "Runaway." A beat from the producer Emile inspired the track. "It was late one night, and we were hanging out [in Avex Studios], and Kanye asked me if I had any beats," Emile remembered. "Pretty low, no big deal, we were just chilling playing some beats." What happened next has become the stuff of hip-hop legend. Kanye listened to the new beat for a few minutes before telling the engineer, "Okay, put it in Pro Tools." (When he said that, Emile remembers, "the room was like, 'Oh, shit.'") Then Kanye stepped up to the microphone and, without hesitating, sang the melody and lyrics of "Runaway."[32]

It's a song built around a stunning inversion. While the pop charts are filled with attempts at seduction, Kanye isn't trying to seduce in "Runaway." He's trying to *repel*, warning this poor lady to escape before it's too late.

Baby, I got a plan
Run away fast as you can
Run away from me, baby, run away.

In case there was any doubt about his sincerity, Kanye goes on to propose a champagne toast for the douchebags, assholes, and scumbags, because he is one of those guys. The typical stance of hip-hop is braggadocio, as rappers celebrate their triumphs and conquests. "Runaway" is not one of those songs. It is an anthem of self-loathing.

This subversive style isn't limited to the lyrics.* As Kanye refined "Runaway" in the studio, he created a track that intentionally

---

* There is no such thing as a Kanye sound. While every Drake album sounds like a Drake album, Kanye reinvents himself with each new release. The chipmunk soul of *Late Registration* gave way to the bleak electronic minimalism of *808s & Heartbreak*, which, in turn, the lush maximalist sounds of "Runaway" and *My Beautiful Dark Twisted Fantasy* surpassed. If there is a recurring theme to these pop masterpieces, it's a skepticism of musical convention. Kanye's only consistency is his refusal to conform.

violates many of the established patterns of its genre. "Runaway" begins with a repeated piano note, a high E-natural played fifteen times. It's a riff on György Ligeti's "Musica Ricercata II," which also features a single note repeated multiple times. The piano melody then dips an octave, returns with a high E-flat, then a low E-flat, then a high C-sharp, then a low C-sharp, and so on. It's a melancholy tune, the keys accented with spite, and Kanye draws it out for nearly forty seconds. It is the least radio-friendly intro imaginable.

Just when we've adjusted to those spare piano notes, a throbbing bassline appears, followed by a sharp snare drum and a looped sample from a live Rick James show. But Kanye doesn't settle for the obvious blend of piano and rhythm. That would time the piano notes to beats one and three of each measure, which are the so-called strong beats. Virtually every pop song obeys this convention, which makes it easier to listen and dance along to the music. Kanye knows this. He has an exquisite understanding of our expectations. And he delights in turning them against us.

Because "Runaway" begins with just the piano, we assume the notes are being played on the strong beats of one and three. There is no rhythm yet, but Kanye realizes that our expectations fill in the void. But then, when the drums enter, Kanye reveals our error: the piano is hitting on the weak beats of two and four. As the musician and podcaster Cole Cuchna observes, in his close analysis of "Runaway," "That's why the drums are always so impactful when they come in, no matter how many times we hear the track. . . . They're always a bit unexpected and it takes our mind and bodies a moment to adjust to the change of the pulse."[33] Most rhythms are easy to ignore, a ticking clock we take for granted. The bumps and thumps of "Runaway," however, violate our musical expectations—their timing is a prediction error. They seize our attention.

Kanye had his beat, this cadence coming in at the wrong time.* But these Honolulu songs had layers of samples and sounds. "Runaway" might begin with a single piano note—the simplest of musical acts—but it dissolves into a sonic collage of dirty drum samples and a mean Pusha T. But what Kanye said about his celebrity persona also applies to his music: "My existence is selvage denim at this point, it's a vintage Hermès bag. All the stains just make it better."[35]

The last few minutes of "Runaway" capture this dissolution. After nearly six minutes of celebrating his own douchebaggery, Kanye returns to the sound of that solo piano. We're prepared for a typical outro, which would repeat the opening melody along with a gentle fade-out, perhaps featuring that same high E-natural. Pop songs are supposed to follow this cyclic pattern.

Kanye does the opposite. He starts off with an inaudible mumble set against two cellos. Some insist Kanye's saying, "I'mma be honest"; others hear, "No pianos." His voice is indecipherable

---

* The human mind is most intrigued by slight rhythmic imperfections. According to a recent study by scientists at Harvard and the Max Planck Institute for Dynamics and Self-Organization, human drummers tend to systematically deviate from the robotic pulse of a metronome or a drum machine, falling ahead or behind of the rhythm by ten to twenty milliseconds per beat. (That's less time than it takes to blink.) However, these human deviations aren't entirely random. Rather, the best drummers tend to deviate from a "perfect" beat by obeying sweeping and subtle patterns. "You can have these trends [with human drummers]," Holger Hennig, a physicist at Harvard, told the *Harvard Gazette*. "For example, the drummer plays ahead of the beat for thirty consecutive beats, while half a minute earlier, he tended to play slightly behind the metronome clicks. These trends are pleasant to the ear."[34] In short, we want the beat to be subversive but not inscrutable. Another little mystery layered in with all the rest.

because it's been highly processed in Auto-Tune, a musical device that's traditionally been used to fix flawed vocals. (Auto-Tune can alter the pitch of a recording to ensure that a singer hits the right notes, shifting the sound to the nearest correct semitone.) Kanye, however, uses Auto-Tune to distort his voice beyond recognition, setting the pitch corrector to its most extreme setting and pairing it with a distortion filter and a fuzz box. The result is a vocal track that sounds like a wailing electric guitar. There are no lyrics, just pure cathartic emotion, channeled into a noise we've never before heard. "The 'Runaway' piece at the end, when it's like my voice being changed into a guitar, when I did that, I was tearing up," Kanye would later say. "Just humming the abstracted notes, I was crying just humming notes. And the notes were more expressive than the words."

## The Mystery of Goose Bumps

In the late 1950s, a musicologist named Leonard Meyer published a series of technical papers that attempted to solve the ancient mystery of music. It's a mystery that has perplexed everyone from Aristotle to Schopenhauer: How did such an abstract art form generate such intense emotions?

To make sense of this mystery, Meyer analyzed a wide variety of songs and symphonies, from Beethoven's String Quartet in C-sharp Minor, op. 131, to the Delta blues. He looked at Brahms piano sonatas and the rhythms of East African folk music, Chinese lute melodies and Italian arias. According to Meyer, the differences between these musical creations concealed their shared aesthetic strategy. While the melodies might not sound alike, they all worked in the same way.

Meyer laid out his evidence most clearly in a 1959 humbly titled paper, "Some Remarks on Value and Greatness in Music."[36] In the paper, Meyer compared a fugue by Johann Sebastian Bach to one by Francesco Geminiani, an obscure eighteenth-century composer. As Meyer notes, both fugues are similar in their basic melodic structure: they begin on the fifth note of the scale, move to the tonic, and then jump an octave. This jump, writes Meyer, "creates a structural gap, a sense of incompleteness. We expect that the empty space thus outlined will be filled in."

The question is how that empty space is filled in. As Meyer points out, Geminiani completes the melody's structural gap in a highly predictable manner, choosing those notes (B, then E) that sound most probable to the ear. "When the theme falls to this obvious consequent with neither delay nor diversion, it seems like a blatant platitude, a musical cliché," Meyer writes. Geminiani has created a puzzle, but its answer is rather obvious. As soon as the gap is opened, we know how it will be closed. The pattern remains predictable.

Bach, in contrast, comes up with a far more difficult melody. While Geminiani moves swiftly to close the gap, Bach moves slowly, digressing into related harmonic areas. He flirts with possible resolutions but then backs away; the music hints at tonics it refuses to deliver; even the rhythms are varied, as Bach introduces new tempos before finally giving us the closure we want. Although Bach's music is much more complicated, it's also much more emotional: the beauty of the work is rooted in the way it provides "temporary resistance" to the questions it provokes. "The greater the buildup of suspense, of tension, the greater the emotional release upon resolution," Meyer writes.[37] While the release generates the aesthetic pleasure, there can be no release without the uncertainty that came before. The meaning of music depends on the way it violates its own form.

To prove his point, Meyer delves into the realm of information theory. "Musical events take place in a world of stylistic probability," he writes. If a single note is played, it can be followed by many different notes; the world of pitches is wide-open. However, as more notes are added, and as the piece develops its keys and themes, the possibilities begin to shrink. We can increasingly predict what sound is coming next, as we use the patterns of the past to forecast the future. According to information theory, such highly predictable systems—say, a Geminiani fugue, or a pop song by the Eagles—communicate a minimal amount of information. Because we already know what's going to happen, the message is mostly irrelevant. As the mathematician and philosopher Norbert Wiener put it, "The more probable the message, the less its information. Clichés, for example, are less illuminating than great poems."[38]

The musical mystery—what we *don't* know—is the primary source of information in the art. By undermining our ability to predict the resolution, by not closing the gap in the expected way, the unpredictable notes force us to notice all the subtleties in the message. All that extra information makes the work harder to solve; the art exceeds our ability to perceive it.* When listening to Bach, we understand less about the music, at least compared to Geminiani's. Kanye makes hip-hop that's impossible to decipher. But such mystery also makes the work worthy of attention.

In a study published in *Nature Neuroscience*, a team of researchers at McGill University looked at individuals who reliably experienced chills, or frisson, in response to music.[39] The scientists

---

* Edmund Burke, in his treatise *On the Sublime and Beautiful*, argued that one of the defining features of the sublime was "obscurity," which he defined as the absence of clarity. "A great clearness helps but little towards affecting the passions," Burke wrote. "It is our ignorance of things that causes all our admiration."

asked these subjects to bring in their playlists of favorite songs—virtually every genre was represented, from techno to tango—and played them the music while their brain activity was monitored with fMRI and PET scanners.

Not surprisingly, the experience of music lit up the cortex, with a large spike in activity in dopamine-rich areas. The more interesting finding emerged from a close study of the timing of this response, as the scientists looked to see what was happening in the seconds before the subjects got chills. In essence, the scientists found that our favorite moments in the music were preceded by a prolonged increase of activity in the caudate, a brain area associated with breaches of expectation. (The caudate, remember, is also turned on during magic tricks that break the rules of reality.)

What kind of musical passages excite the caudate? According to the scientists, the brain area is sensitive to those sections of music in which composers violate "expectations in certain ways or by delaying the predicted outcome (for example, by inserted unexpected notes or slowing tempo)."[40] What's interesting is that it's not the consonant chorus or rousing climax that triggers those chills. It's the difficulty that comes before.*

---

* In a recent paper, "Thrills, Chills, Frissons and Skin Orgasms: Towards an Integrative Model of Transcendent Psychophysiological Experiences in Music," scientists at Wesleyan University attempted to dissect the particular forms of difficulty that are most closely associated with musical chills. One of the most effective techniques is the melodic appoggiatura, a musical flourish in which a dissonant (or nonchord note) appears before resolving into the melody, thus creating extra emphasis. It's Adele's fluttering voice during the chorus of "Someone Like You," or the off-pitch singing of John Lennon during "In My Life." It's Kanye at the end of "Runaway," Whitney Houston's high notes during the chorus of "I Will Always Love You," and Frank Ocean when he shifts into an unexpected falsetto. These musical moments give us chills because they focus our attention on those notes we never saw coming. They amplify the mystery.

This is the paradox of beautiful art: it is often hard to under-stand, or at least a little disfluent. It's not the easy content that touches us deep—it's the difficult stuff, those poems without punctuation and pop songs without precursors. We pay attention to bedtime books that break the rules and horror movies that re-ject the tropes and tricks of every previous horror movie.*

The feeling of beauty is inherently subjective. The dissonance of Kanye might make Kanye cry, but it might sound like noise to you; Bach is sublime, unless he's boring; each of us is moved by specific forms of disfluency and dissonance. Yet, despite these endless variations in taste, a clear theme emerges: *beauty requires work*. It demands a high quality of attention, the willingness to wrestle with material that resists our understanding. Keats may have been wrong: beauty is not truth. Rather, it is the consolation that comes from engaging with material that *obscures* its truth, leav-ing us with memorable questions instead.

It's easy to settle for complacency. The brain is lazy by design; the path of least resistance is to seek out material that we already know how to perceive. But the best art compels us to choose the more mysterious path, delivering sensations that are strange and unsettling. Such art is a struggle. It's a struggle to enjoy and a struggle to explain. The struggle is why it lasts.

---

* As Kanye observes, there's often a hidden cost to this kind of aesthetic innovation: "If you guys want these crazy ideas and these crazy stages and this crazy music and this crazy way of thinking, there's a chance it might come from a crazy person."

# CHAPTER 4

# STRATEGIC OPACITY

The fact remains that getting people right is not what living is all about anyway. It's getting them wrong that is living, getting them wrong and wrong and wrong and then, on careful reconsideration, getting them wrong again. That's how we know we're alive: we're wrong. Maybe the best thing would be to forget about being right or wrong about people and just go along for the ride.

—**PHILIP ROTH**, *American Pastoral*


Only Muggles talk of "mind reading." The mind is not a book, to be opened at will and examined at leisure. Thoughts are not etched on the inside of skulls, to be perused by any invader. The mind is a complex and many-layered thing, Potter.

—**J. K. ROWLING**, *Harry Potter and the Order of the Phoenix*


## Or Not To Be

In the late 1590s, William Shakespeare's touring company was locked in a fierce competition for ticket sales. Another troupe had just built a theater across the Thames; their light comedies were, as Shakespeare had one of his characters lament, "now the fashion."[1] He must have worried that his own company would soon be forced to close.

Shakespeare's solution was new material. To speed up the writing, he decided to adapt an old Scandinavian fable starring a prince named Amleth.[2] It seemed like a safe choice: this story had been performed on the stage a few years before and been a hit. Shakespeare had almost certainly seen the previous version. Some scholars believe he might even have acted in it.[3]

The story begins with the murder of a king, assassinated by his power-hungry brother. The king's son wants justice, and thus blood. The only problem is that everyone knows about the murder—it is a public fact—so Prince Amleth has to hide his fury. To avoid suspicion, he fakes insanity. Once his uncle believes Amleth to be a harmless lunatic, the young man burns down the palace and reclaims the throne.

The tale of the vengeful prince had been told this way for hundreds of years.[4] But Shakespeare decided to make one crucial alteration. In his adaptation of the story, the murder of the king is a secret. (Everyone thinks he died of a serpent bite.) When the play begins, even the son is in the dark.

This might seem like a minor change, but Shakespeare surely grasped the consequences. For one, it transforms Hamlet from a transparent assassin—revenge is all he wants—into a walking riddle. If the king isn't worried about Hamlet's retribution, then why is he pretending to be crazy? Why is he wasting time with all these soliloquies? Why doesn't he just get on with the killing? Before long, these questions lead us to question the prince's actual sanity; we have lost track of how mad he really is. (It's not clear Hamlet knows, either.) Shakespeare has turned a character defined by the most primal motivation into one that's impossible to understand.

This was a strange way of telling a story, especially for a playwright obsessed with commercial success. It's easy to imagine the notes Shakespeare might get from a Hollywood studio. Hamlet is too confusing. The audience will get lost. Shakespeare should stick to the story that works.

But Shakespeare knew what he was doing. When it came to his characters, one of Shakespeare's finest innovations is what he left out, how he removed information until what remained was a mystery. The literary critic Stephen Greenblatt refers to this method as "strategic opacity," noting how Shakespeare liked to excise "a key explanatory element, thereby occluding the rationale, motivation, or ethical principle that accounted for the action that was to unfold."[5] The playwright took this strategy to a new level in *Hamlet*, constructing a drama designed to frustrate every explanation.

The strategy worked: *Hamlet* was a big success, selling out the Globe Theatre in London. What's more, it marked a decisive turn toward mystery that would define Shakespeare's later plays. While the playwright had always featured protagonists behaving erratically, most of these crazy characters were crazy in love. (Romeo and Juliet weren't complicated, just randy.) But Shakespeare's writing after *Hamlet* embraced opacity to an unprecedented degree. As Greenblatt notes, in these adapted masterpieces Shakespeare repeatedly "took his source and deftly sliced away what would seem indispensable to a coherent, well-made play." He removed Iago's motivation in *Othello*—he's now seeking revenge for no particular reason—and deleted the plot point that explains the early actions of King Lear. In Shakespeare's version, we never know why the old monarch is testing the love of his daughters. The result, writes Greenblatt, is a character whose actions are so arbitrary and haphazard they must be rooted in some "deep psychological needs."

Shakespeare's discovery of opacity led to an even more important discovery about the audience. When he stripped away the explanation, Shakespeare realized that people weren't drawn to obvious characters. They didn't want a predictable hero or facile villain. What they wanted was an enigma, the thrill of watching an unknowable being walk the stage.

## A Difficult God

A few thousand years ago, a small nomadic tribe in the Middle East began writing about a being who would change the course of history. This being would become so influential that He shaped the way we conceived of the universe. Some anthropologists speculate that this new literary figure even made modern society possible, creating a shared system of norms and beliefs that allowed us to live together in large urban populations.

The being I'm talking about, of course, is the monotheistic God. He first became famous in the writings of the Jews, who compiled their scriptures while wandering around the desert. While it's hard to compare the Jewish God to the monotheistic deities that came before—most of these scriptures have been lost—it seems likely that He represented a radical approach to religion. For one, the itinerant nature of the Jews meant that their religious text was an amalgam of many other texts, from the Gathas of Zarathustra to the Sumerian myths of Babylon.

These other religious stories had a profound influence on the Old Testament, and not just because they inspired many of the events it describes. (The story of Noah's ark, for instance, is taken straight from the *Epic of Gilgamesh*.) Perhaps their most important influence has to do with the way they shaped the new Jewish God, giving rise to a singular divinity defined by his multitudes.

This God was not a coherent character with a clear narrative arc. Rather, He was a collage of sticky oral scraps, many of which contradict one another. He was a mystery.

The book of Genesis, for instance, begins with an account of creation in which man is formed in the image of a God who calls himself Elohim. But then, in the very next section, we get a second version of creation, this time performed by a God who calls himself Yahweh Elohim, or Lord God. While the first version gave man the entire earth, the second version restricts us to a small garden in Eden and forbids us from eating from the tree of knowledge. (In the first version, there are no rules to follow.) When we disobey God and eat the fruit, Yahweh Elohim erupts in fury, cursing His own children and giving us a starkly different description of our origins. We are no longer made in His image. Now we are made of dust.

The Old Testament is full of these inconsistencies. As the scholar Jack Miles argues, God is the protagonist of the Bible; the text is the story of His evolving relationship to His creation. One might expect this relationship to be rather straightforward—He is, after all, omniscient and omnipotent—but it is marked by tumult and volatility. God gives us free will except when He takes it away; He is forgiving but also prone to punishing rages; He loves us like a child, but isn't afraid to let us suffer. "Tension among these personalities makes God difficult," writes Miles, "but it also makes him compelling, even addictive."[6]

It's the same strategy that Shakespeare used in *Hamlet*. He created a "strategically opaque" prince, stripping away the reveals that would allow the audience to understand Hamlet's actions. This opacity made the character incoherent, but it also hooked the audience: we kept trying to predict his next move. The God of the Old Testament is similarly opaque, which is why He remains so interesting.

Consider the binding of Isaac, one of the strangest scenes in the Bible. It begins with God telling Abraham, His beloved follower, to sacrifice his son. "Take your son, your favored one, Isaac, whom you love . . . and offer him as a burnt offering on one of the heights." It's a sadistic request. God is all-knowing and all-powerful, so why is He testing the faith of His most loyal follower?

But Abraham obeys God. He lies to his wife and son, telling them they are going to the mountains to sacrifice a sheep. As Kierkegaard pointed out, the lie is the tell: Abraham cannot reveal the truth because he knows that God, a supposedly infallible being, is making a profoundly unethical demand. Not even Sarah, his dutiful wife, will understand.

In *Mimesis*, the literary scholar Erich Auerbach engages in a close reading of this bizarre biblical scene.[7] He observes that the Hebrew God is marked by His "heavy silence" and "obscurity." His actions are described, but "what lies between is nonexistent . . . thoughts and feeling remain unexpressed, are only suggested by the silence and the fragmentary speeches." The result is that even a plain reading of the text requires interpretation. Some rabbinical scholars have insisted that Abraham is testing God, going through the sacrificial motions to ensure that Yahweh Elohim would not insist on a murder. For others, the story is a parable about the need for obedience, even when the motives of God are unclear. But nobody knows. If there's a moral, it's a mystery.

One of the central arcs of the Old Testament is toward God's reckoning with His own opacity. (He might be omniscient, but He doesn't always understand Himself.) It's not until the book of Isaiah, one of the later sections of the Hebrew Bible, that God seems to accept His mysteriousness. When the Jews begin to doubt His power, after they are exiled and defeated, God empathizes with their doubt because "his understanding is unsearchable." Later in Isaiah, He describes Himself as "a God who hidest thyself." This makes Him a hard God to worship—His behavior is unpredictable—but it's also the source of His lasting literary power. As St. Augustine said, "If you think you understand God, it is not God."[8]

## The Most Mysterious Smile

In the 1540s, a middle-aged architect named Giorgio Vasari began writing a book about the lives of artists. At the time, it was a radical conceit—artists were seen as mere decorators, the humble servants of lords, merchants, and priests. You wouldn't write a biography of a plumber, would you?

But Vasari saw the literary potential in the artistic life, the romance in their manual labor. In *The Lives of the Most Excellent Painters, Sculptors, and Architects*, Vasari assembled a series of short biographies of the greatest Renaissance creators, from Botticelli to Titian. By humanizing the artist, Vasari hoped to inspire others to pick up the paintbrush and chisel. "I wish to be of service to the artists of our own day by showing them how a small beginning leads to the highest elevation," he wrote.[9]

It's hard to overstate the influence of Vasari's unusual book. Although error and rumor riddle the text, it has defined the way we think about art history. Vasari invented the cliché of the tortured artist—his biography of Michelangelo emphasizes the sculptor's obsessive solitude—and the myth of the natural genius, blessed with a supernatural talent. He also helped set the canon: we worship the artists of the Tuscan Renaissance in part because Vasari canonized them.

One of the paintings made famous by Vasari comes in his

section on Leonardo da Vinci, which is overwrought even by Vasari's purple standards. ("Sometimes, in supernatural fashion, beauty, grace, and talent are united beyond measure in one single person. . . . This was seen by all mankind in Leonardo da Vinci.")[10] After describing many of da Vinci's most celebrated works, such as *The Last Supper* and *The Adoration of the Magi*, Vasari introduces an obscure portrait da Vinci did for Francesco del Giocondo, a Tuscan silk merchant. Francesco asked the artist to paint a picture of his young wife. (He married her when she was fifteen.) While Vasari usually skims over the details of the art—even *The Last Supper* only gets a few sentences—he lingers on the look of this portrait. He describes the "watery sheen" of the noblewoman's eyes, and the delicacy of her eyelashes, and the intense realism of her eyebrows, "in which the hairs spring from the flesh . . . and curve according to the pores of the skin."[11]* He praises her "beautiful nostrils," the rosy tint of her face, and even the bend of her throat, in which, "if one gazed upon [it] intently, could be seen the beating of the pulse." But Vasari saved his highest praise for the woman's subtle smile, a work of artistry "more divine than human to behold."

By the time Vasari wrote about the portrait, nearly fifty years after it was finished, the painting was already in the private collection of the king of France. Almost no one had seen the canvas; Francesco was a forgotten merchant. Nevertheless, Vasari believed that his young wife would live on, that da Vinci had created a portrait "more alive" than reality. Her name was Mona Lisa.

Vasari was right. Five hundred years later, crowds still line up at the Louvre to get a glimpse of her face, now shielded behind

---

* Oddly, the woman in the painting has no eyebrows.

bulletproof glass. (In a typical year, as many as 10 million people see the *Mona Lisa*.) But something about the painting's popularity is ludicrous—it is just a portrait of a medieval Tuscan woman, painted on a poplar panel. There is no memorable action or lofty theme. Yet, as Vasari noted, the portrait is an astonishing technical achievement. Mona Lisa does feel alive. Something about the way she returns our gaze, even in a room packed full of tourists, is uncanny.

What's the *Mona Lisa*'s secret? Why does this remain the most famous painting in the world? Vasari credited the woman's ambivalence, the way her face blended expressions of melancholy and merriness. (According to Vasari, da Vinci hired "persons to play or sing, and jesters," to entertain Mona Lisa during her tedious sitting sessions.) The result is a mood that matches the sfumato brushstrokes, a Renaissance technique in which the portrait is marked by a deliberate blurriness, what da Vinci described as being "without lines or borders, in the manner of smoke or beyond the focus plane." The mystery of Mona Lisa's magic is that her feelings are similarly out of focus.

While art critics have advanced countless theories to explain her enigmatic smile, it turns out to have a clear biological cause. Margaret Livingstone, a neuroscientist at Harvard, argues that the mysteriousness of Mona Lisa's expression is rooted in the way da Vinci confuses our visual system. He offers different interpretations to the two distinct regions of the retina that can process light. The fovea, located in the center of the retina, allows us to focus on details: it picks up bright colors and sharp edges. But we also have a peripheral area, surrounding the fovea, that can detect grays and motion.

When we first look at Mona Lisa, we tend to focus on her eyes. Our peripheral vision notices her mouth. But here's the thing about those peripheral photoreceptors: because they aren't tuned for details, they mostly detect the shadows below her formidable cheekbones. These darker areas suggest a face bent in smile—she must be a happy woman.

Our gaze then turns to Mona Lisa's mouth. That's when we realize she isn't actually smiling; her lips are straight and tight. At this point, Livingstone writes, "her smile fades, like a dim star that disappears when you look directly at it."[12] When our eyes look away from her lips, the shadowy smile reappears. The result is a painting of contradictions, the riddle of a smile that flashes and vanishes depending on the viewer.

There's an interesting parallel here to the "gutter" of comic books, which refers to the empty space between drawn panels. "Despite the unceremonious title, the gutter plays host to much of the magic and mystery that are at the very heart of comics," writes the cartoonist and comic theorist Scott McCloud.[13] As McCloud notes, most of the action in a comic unfolds in the gap between drawings, as our brain creates a character out of a set of still sketches. As a result, the best graphic novelists find ways to use gutters more suggestively, encouraging us to fill in the emptiness with our imagination.

It's an act of imagination that keeps us engaged. We can't figure out Mona Lisa's feelings, which is why we can't stop looking at her face. Likewise, it's the mystery of the gutter that gives comics their kinetic momentum. Just as Kanye and Bach made art out of the gaps in our knowledge—the musical pattern we can't predict—so do characters come alive when we're unable to figure them out.

It doesn't matter if it's Hamlet, God, or a sixteenth-century portrait—it's their mysteries that make them interesting. It's what we don't know that brings them to life.

## A Sentimental Education

Why are we drawn to opaque characters? What makes an unknow-able God so interesting? Why do we prefer paintings and plays about people we can't understand? There's a practical explana-tion, which was eloquently explored by the philosopher Richard Rorty. Toward the end of his career, Rorty became increasingly interested in the ability of literature to educate people about the inner states of others, changing the way "we treat people whom we think not worth understanding."[14] Rorty referred to this as the "sentimental education" of art.[15] A good story, he said, isn't just a pleasing entertainment—it also makes us better human beings.

It's an admittedly pretentious hypothesis; plenty of assholes have read the canon. But Rorty was prescient: an emerging body of evidence links the reading of literature and increased empathy. A recent study showed that people who were more familiar with literature scored much higher on a test of theory of mind, which measures how likely we are to model the thoughts and feelings of other people. (This correlation existed even after controlling for a number of possible confounding variables, such as personality traits, demographics, and choice of undergraduate major.)[16] Other experiments from the same research team have shown a direct causal connection. After people read literary fiction, they scored significantly higher upon retaking the same empathic measure-ment as before.[17]

But not every fiction is equally effective at teaching us how to read minds. E. M. Forster once distinguished between flat and round characters. Flat characters, Forster wrote, "are constructed round a single idea or quality."[18] He cites Mrs. Micawber in *David Copperfield*, who is utterly defined by the sentence "I never will desert Mr. Micawber." As Forster notes, "She says she won't desert Mr. Micawber, she doesn't, and there she is." She has no inner existence outside of that trait. There is no mystery to her. She's flat.

Round characters, in contrast, have an irreducible aspect: they are alive with contradictions. It's Hamlet pretending to be crazy, and God asking Abraham to kill Isaac, and Mona Lisa smiling with her eyes but not her lips. It's Tony Soprano, a sociopathic mobster and devoted family man, and Walter White, a meek chemistry teacher and meth kingpin. These people are round because we can't predict their feelings and behavior. "The test of a round character is whether it is capable of surprising in a convincing way," Forster writes. "If it never surprises, it is flat. If it does not convince, it is a flat pretending to be round. [A round character] has the incalculability of life about it—life within the pages of a book."

Forster gives the example of Lady Bertram from Jane Austen's *Mansfield Park*. At first glance, Lady Bertram seems like the kind of character that every other writer would turn into a flat punch line. She's lazy and distractible, concerned more with her pugs than her children. But Austen rounds her out, adding in subtle flourishes to give her that extra dimension. After Lady Bertram learns that her two daughters have both brought shame to the family name—her oldest daughter was caught in an extramarital affair, while her younger daughter eloped with her lover—Austen uses the moment to reveal Lady Bertram's unexpected complexity. We assume she'll dismiss the situation, ignore the inconvenience. After all, she's never seemed to care about her family before.

But that's not what happens. Instead, Austen describes how Lady Bertram thinks "justly on all important points, and she saw therefore in all its enormity, what had happened, and neither endeavoured herself, nor required Fanny to advise her, to think little of guilt and infamy." It's a remarkable scene: the shallow Lady

Bertram has been forced to reflect on the gravity of the events, and her own role in the undoing of her family. The reader is left with a haunting image of the vain matriarch, sitting on her couch, stroking her snoring pug, sick with regret and worry about what will become of her children. We are surprised by her turn, but it's convincing in the context of her daughters. "It is a little point, and a little sentence," Forster writes, "yet it shows us how delicately a great novelist can modulate into the round."

To understand better how some writers create round characters, I met with Otto Penzler, the owner of the Mysterious Bookshop in Tribeca, specializing in crime and suspense fiction. Penzler works mostly from a windowless bunker underneath the store, the door hidden behind fake crime-scene tape. ("You're meeting Otto? Enter the crime scene, down the stairs, make a right.") That week, Penzler had just sold another lot of his acclaimed detective-fiction collection at auction. The auction had gone well—a first edition of Graham Greene's *Brighton Rock* had sold for $93,750, doubling the pre-auction estimate—but Penzler seemed forlorn, like a child who had just lost his favorite toy. "I'm depressed," Penzler told the Tribeca Citizen. "My plan was to live forever. But it occurred to me that God might not have the same plan."[19]

In 1976, Penzler coauthored the *Encyclopedia of Mystery and Detection*, a reference work that helped establish detective literature as a respected literary genre. His answers are dense and authoritative, riddled with obscure references. "If you're asking why you can reread a good detective story, but not a bad one, it all comes down to the characters," he tells me. "If you don't have good characters, you don't have a good book. That's why the best mystery writers, they really begin with the characters and work the plot from there." Roundness is everything.

Penzler tells me a story about Elmore Leonard, perhaps the greatest contemporary crime writer. "Dutch [that was Leonard's nickname] was one of my best friends," Penzler says. "When he was writing, he could not wait to talk about his books. He'd call me up and say, 'Otto, Otto, I got a problem.'" Penzler imitates Leonard's raspy smoker's voice. "So I say, 'What is it, Dutch? What's wrong?'" Penzler slips back into character: "'My hero got killed last night.' Now I'm confused, so I say, 'What do you mean, Dutch?' 'Oh, man, my character was in the bar, and all of a sudden out of nowhere this Mexican guy comes up and shoots him in the head. I don't know what I'm going to do. I'm on page one hundred and thirty, and the main character in my book is dead.' And so I said, because I'm trying to be helpful, 'Dutch, why don't you just rewrite that chapter?' And he acts like I was crazy. 'What do you mean rewrite that chapter? I told you, he was dead!'"

For Penzler, the story captures the genius of Elmore Leonard. Although he worked in a genre defined by its mechanistic plots, Leonard still found ways to inject mystery into his characters. Leonard filled his noir worlds with unpredictable people that he invented but refused to control. Sometimes this meant his hero died in the middle of the book, a victim of tragic circumstance. But these writerly headaches were worth it: Leonard's rounded cast of loan sharks, bank robbers, cynical cops, and trigger-happy marshals is what helps set his fiction apart.

And this returns us to the mental benefits of literature, which seem to depend on its rounded characters. These fictional beings don't just change the way we read—they change the way we think and feel. In a recent paper, the scientists David Kidd and Emanuele Castano apply the flat-versus-round distinction of Forster to explain why the best literature boosts our care for others by reminding us of their inherent mystery.[20] Flat characters, the scientists say, can be understood in terms of "category-based perception." The character is a type, not an individual; there is no need to enter his mind because we already know what he'll do next. These are the obvious kinds of people in a pulp fiction, or a summer action movie: we know what they'll do before they do it. This helps explain why reading genre fiction (which is often less focused on the internal states of characters) doesn't lead to improvements in theory-of-mind performance.

Round characters, however, cannot be reduced to a category—they exceed every caricature. It doesn't matter if it's Hamlet or an Elmore Leonard detective: readers must pay attention to the character's subtle emotional cues, inferring a theory of mind from the words on the page. Because these characters resist our mental shortcuts, we have to go through the long process of imagining their thoughts and feelings. It's the opacity that gets us inside their head.

The result is that stories with round characters allow us to practice the act of mind reading. Cecilia Heyes, a psychologist at the University of Oxford, compares mind reading to print reading, noting that both are part of our cultural inheritance and not hardwired into the infant cortex.[21] Print reading takes years of "scaffolding and explicit instruction"—we have to be taught the alphabet and phonics. Mind reading almost certainly requires the same sort of training. As Heyes notes, human babies are no better at mentalizing than chimp babies. The difference is that we grow up in environments rich with stories that take us inside the minds of others. The rounded fictional character, in this sense, is an essential human technology, augmenting our natural abilities.

But practice alone is not enough. According to Rorty, literature doesn't just let us simulate the act of empathy—it also helps us overcome our natural weaknesses, many of which are rooted in the failure to accept the mystery of other people. Consider a common mistake known as the fundamental attribution error. The error itself is straightforward. When we assess the behavior of others, we tend to ascribe all their actions to their inner character. If he's speeding, it's because he's a reckless driver. If she slips, it's because she's clumsy. If he's slow to reply to that text, it's because he's a rude person. Rather than accept their inherent roundness, we treat them like flat characters, reducing them to a short list of predictable qualities. They're easier to blame that way.

However, when we assess our own behavior, we're much more forgiving. It's not that we wanted to do the wrong thing—we were just in a tight spot. If we're speeding, it's because we're late for an important meeting. If we slip on a wet path, it's because the rocks were slippery. If we're slow to reply to a text, it's because we had a busy day at work. We understand that much of our own behavior is driven by context, that we are moody creatures, with a mercurial edge.

The psychologist Walter Mischel spent decades studying how circumstance shapes behavior. His breakthrough began with a failure. In the early 1960s, Mischel was hired to help the Peace Corps develop a personality assessment to screen prospective volunteers.[22] (Many of the young Americans struggled with the rigors of living in developing countries.) Mischel based his assessment on the latest science, hiring experts to score the volunteers on various personality traits. He then followed up to see how these volunteers performed as teachers in Nigeria. To his surprise, the "costly personality inferences . . . did not even reach statistical significance."[23] People were not nearly as predictable as scientists had assumed. Our personalities remained a mystery.

One of Mischel's most influential studies, conducted with Yuichi Shoda, followed children at a summer camp in New Hampshire.[24] At the time, it was widely assumed that aggression was a stable trait—if you were aggressive at home, you would also be aggressive at school, and so forth. But Mischel and Shoda found that how children behaved was highly context-dependent and very sensitive to the specifics of the situation. (To measure behavior, the scientists enlisted the help of seventy-seven camp counselors, who recorded the behavior of campers everywhere except the bathroom.) The same child might fight with other campers but obey the warnings of counselors. Another might react badly to criticism from adults but calmly handle provocations from peers. And it wasn't just aggression: the same nuanced model also applied to traits such as extroversion, agreeableness, and whining.

As Mischel notes, this theory of human personality contradicts thousands of years of scientific thinking. Ever since the ancient Greeks developed a theory of the four humors, we've described other people in terms of stable and static qualities. Human beings are supposed to be like flat characters, defined by their levels of yellow bile, extroversion, and agreeableness. (The adjectives change, but Myers-Briggs shares a conceptual foundation with the humorism of Hippocrates.) This is who they are; this is how they will act.

However, the work of Mischel and others has shown that human beings are much more mysterious than that. As the psychologist Todd Rose writes, "If you want to understand a person, descriptions of their average tendencies or 'essential nature' are sure to lead you astray. . . . If you are conscientious and neurotic while driving today, it's a pretty safe bet you will be conscientious and neurotic while driving tomorrow. At the same time, what makes you uniquely you is that you may *not* be conscientious and neurotic when you are playing Beatles cover songs with your band in the context of your local pub."[25]

Literature is one of the best antidotes to the fundamental attribution error. A good novel doesn't describe its characters in terms of general traits—it reveals them as a function of their context, showing us who they are in different situations. In many respects, the narrative is a series of if-then patterns, full of surprising scenes and encounters. After all, if the characters were predictable—if they always acted the same way—then they'd quickly become tedious. Why keep reading about someone we already understand?

And this returns us to Rorty's sentimental education. His point is that the qualities that make literature interesting are also what make it edifying. By showing us round people acting in mysterious ways, it trains us to see them everywhere. We realize that human beings are complicated and that circumstance can bend us in surprising ways.

Once we do that, Rorty says, we discover that we're not so different after all. Instead of blaming people's fixed character, we offer them the kind of forgiveness that we usually save for ourselves. "This process of coming to see other human beings as 'one of us' rather than 'them' is a matter of detailed description of what unfamiliar people are like and of redescription of what we ourselves are like," Rorty writes. "That is why the novel, the movie and the TV program have, gradually but steadily, replaced the sermon and the treatise as the principal vehicle of moral change and progress."[26] The ironic power of fiction is that it features pretend people who teach us how to deal with real ones.

## The Mystery of Talent

The Philadelphia Eagles football team was established in 1933, a replacement for the bankrupt Frankford Yellow Jackets, named for one of the city's working-class neighborhoods. The team was led by Bert Bell, a former college quarterback and part-time football coach who had pitched in $1,250 for the team rights. Bell came from old money—his father had been the state attorney general, and the family had significant real estate holdings—but Burt had no interest in the family business. "All I ever wanted to be was a football man," Bell said.[27]

The Eagles got off to a rough start. Their first game was against the Giants at the Polo Grounds—they lost 56–0. In their next game, against the Portsmouth Spartans at home, they were routed 25–0. The team was so bad that, according to John Eisenberg, Bell had to offer a free car wash to anyone who bought an Eagles ticket.[28] The stadium was still mostly empty.

The 1934 season was no better, with the team losing five of their first six games. Bell was despondent, but he didn't know how to fix the situation. He tried recruiting top prospects—he routinely outbid the other teams—but players didn't want to sign with the lowly Eagles. "The league is no stronger than its weakest link, and I've been a weak link for so long that I should know," Bell concluded. "Every year the rich get richer and the poor get poorer."

Bell's solution to this problem would transform professional sports. In May 1935, Bell proposed the creation of a football draft. It was a simple idea, at least in theory. All the top college prospects would be placed in a pool. The worst team in the league, which in this case was the Eagles, would get to choose a player first, followed by the second-worst team, and so on. The goal was to create parity, or at least to shrink the gap between the dominant New York Giants and the dismal Eagles. (Think of it as a reverse meritocracy, with the worst getting rewarded.) Even the Giants' owner, Tim Mara, grasped the need for Bell's proposal. While

Mara knew the draft would make it harder for his team to win, that "was a hazard we had to accept for the benefit of the league, of professional football, and of everyone in it," Mara said. "People come to see competition."[29]*

Bell's draft helped create the modern NFL, a sports league with annual revenues in excess of $15 billion.[30] Although the 1936 draft was an informal affair—the team owners gathered in a hotel suite, choosing players based on a scattering of newspaper stories and hearsay—the draft would soon become one of the most important events on the football calendar. For losing teams, the stakes are massive: the difference between years of success and failure often comes down to a single draft pick. Choose the right player—say, Tom Brady, Patrick Mahomes, or Lamar Jackson— and you've got a chance at the title. Choose the wrong player, and you're likely to keep losing for several more years.** You've squandered the consolation prize.

Given the impact of the draft, NFL teams have come to invest heavily in draft intelligence. They hire legions of scouts, who watch the college players in person, and employ data analysts to pore over the statistics. During the draft combine, the teams administer a battery of personality and intelligence tests, desperate to identify the factors that predict success in the pros.

But here's the shocking finding: these investments are mostly a waste of money. Although NFL teams have been drafting col-

---

* The increased parity also boosted the chanciness of the sport, which made it more entertaining.
** The hard salary cap, which went into effect in 1994, has only made draft decisions more consequential. Because NFL rookies are significantly underpaid, at least compared to their veteran colleagues, selecting a productive college player can free up salary space for other talented teammates.

lege players for more than eighty years, they still haven't found a way to choose the best ones, at least not reliably. A recent analysis of the football draft by Cade Massey and Richard Thaler found that picking athletes is basically a crapshoot, no more scientific than betting on dice in Las Vegas.[31] For instance, Massey and Thaler looked at the likelihood that a given player performs better in the NFL than the next player chosen in the draft at his position. This is the practical question that teams face in the draft, as they debate the advantages of trading up to acquire a specific athlete.

Unfortunately, there is little to no evidence that teams know what they're doing: only 52 percent of picks outperform those players chosen below them. "Across all rounds, all positions, all years, the chance that a player proves to be better than the next-best alternative is only slightly better than a coin flip," write the economists. Or consider this statistic, which should strike fear into the heart of every NFL general manager: over their first five years in the league, draft picks from the first round have more seasons with zero starts (15.3 percent) than seasons that end with a selection to the Pro Bowl (12.8 percent).

If teams admitted their ignorance, they could adjust their strategy accordingly. They could discount their scouting intelligence and remember that college performance is only weakly correlated with NFL output. Alas, teams routinely act as if they can identify the best players, which is what leads them to trade up for more valuable picks. The main culprit is what Massey and Thaler refer to as "overconfidence exacerbated by information." Teams assume their judgments about prospective players are more accurate than they are, especially when they amass large amounts of data and analytics. What they fail to realize is that much of this information isn't predictive, and that it's almost certainly framed by the same biases and blind spots that limit our assessments of other people in everyday life. As Massey and Thaler write, "The problem is not that future performance is difficult to predict, but that decision makers do not appreciate how difficult it is."

There is something sobering about the limits of draft intelligence in professional sports. (Researchers have found that other professional sports leagues, such as the NBA and Major League Baseball, also struggle to identify the most talented young players.)[32] These are athletes, after all, whose performance has been measured by a dizzying array of advanced statistics; they have been scouted for years and run through a gauntlet of scientific assessments. (As the economists write, "Football teams almost certainly are in a *better* position to predict performance than most employers choosing workers.") However, even in this rarefied domain, the mystery of human beings still dominates.

But there is hope. The secret is to remember our fundamental ignorance when it comes to other people. To borrow the literary framework of E. M. Forster, we should treat these college players like round characters in a good novel, always keeping in mind their ability to surprise and confound.

Knowing what we don't know appears to be one of the essential talents of the best football executives. Take Bill Belichick, the coach of the New England Patriots. If Belichick has a signature move in the NFL draft, it's trading down, swapping a high pick for multiple, less valuable ones. If teams could reliably assess talent, this strategy would make little sense, since it would mean giving up on superstars. However, given the impossibility of predicting player performance—Tom Brady was selected with the 199th pick in the 2000 draft—gaining more picks is an astute move. Belichick realizes that the draft is mostly a random gamble; the only way to win is to place as many bets as possible. His crucial edge doesn't come from solving the mystery of football players. It's realizing that the mystery exists.

## The Mystery of Desire

In 1912, Sigmund Freud wrote an obscure paper about sexual impotence. He wrote about impotence because it was an extremely common affliction: "apart from anxiety in all its many forms," it was the condition that he was most frequently asked to treat.[33] For these patients, the sex organs refused to perform under certain conditions, even though there was nothing wrong with their physical function. The failure was in the mind.

Freud referred to this as "psychical impotence." While entire sections of his paper now feel outdated and obsolete—Freud spends a lot of time worrying about the incestuous fixations of the unconscious—the medical issue he identified is still extremely prevalent.[34] According to the Massachusetts Male Aging Study, 52 percent of men between the ages of 40 and 70 suffer from episodes of impotence.[35] Even young men are not immune: according to a study of more than 9,000 Swiss men between the ages of 18 and 25, 30 percent have experienced at least one episode of impotence.[36]

What accounts for this epidemic of impotence? Freud's greatest insight occurred as he considered less severe cases, those patients still capable of performing the physical act but incapable of enjoying it. According to Freud, their lack of pleasure wasn't due to a lack of love; these people were often deeply attached to their partners. They just didn't want to have sex with them. "Where they love they do not desire, and where they desire they cannot love," he wrote.

For Freud, psychical impotence revealed the tragic conflict at the center of adult relationships. We crave the adventure of romance, the kind of intense desire that accompanies flirting and courtship. It's a desire rooted in mystery—we are still learning about our partner, discovering her pleasures, mapping his moods. All those secrets make for good sex.

If we are lucky, however, this initial uncertainty will eventually give way to the security of attachment. We'll come to rely on the relationship, finding safety in the predictable comforts of flannel pajamas and Netflix on the couch. Such are the unintended consequences of intimacy—it often leads to unromantic habits, fixed routines that remove the risk from a relationship. Before long, we stop closing the bathroom door.

Freud believed that the conflict between love and desire was an inescapable fact of life.* Lasting passion was impossible. Marriage meant a renouncement of romance. Our best hope was to avoid neuroses and divorce.

In recent years, however, many psychoanalysts and psychologists have come to believe that Freud was too pessimistic. They've discovered that many couples experience lasting sexual attraction, even though they've had sex thousands of times.[37] In a sense, these relationships violate the law of habituation, which holds that repetition ruins pleasure, and that our nerves get bored by the familiar.

How do these couples do it? When the psychoanalyst Stephen Mitchell revisited Freud's essay on impotence, he began with the observation that sexual experience is inherently private, the most

---

* According to Freud, the unsatisfactory nature of sex does come with a consolation prize: humans must seek out other gratifications, such as art and science. The root of culture, then, is the mediocre orgasm.

opaque pleasure of all. "Although it is one of our most common experiences, none of us knows quite what sex is like for anyone else," Mitchell writes. "The more or less standard equipment has been hijacked by the human imagination."* This hijacking means that sex is never just a physical act. It is bound up with our most mysterious desires. "In this sense, there is always an unknown, an otherness in the experience of sexuality in both one's partner and in oneself," Mitchell observes. "This unknown and unknowable dimension of sexual passion contributes to both its excitement and its risks."[38]

According to Mitchell, the sheer mysteriousness of sex is the reason some couples are able to maintain their desire over time. The key, he says, is to remember that even sex with a spouse can contain surprises. It doesn't matter how intimate we are with our partner, how many diapers we've changed, or how often we've done this before: sex should become "a journey into the otherness of the other," as Mitchell puts it. Because the act is so unknowable, it can puncture the illusion of knowing, showing us that we still have much to learn.[39] While Freud imagined love as the enemy of desire—security spoils eros—Mitchell argues that the right kind of desire can save our love, waking us up from the slumber of habit. Sex, in this sense, can serve as an effective form of relationship therapy.

But it's also not enough. As Mitchell points out, even couples with a creative sex life won't last if they can't take that same attitude outside the bedroom. The best relationships do this by

---

* The inability to comprehend someone else's sexual experience, Mitchell says, helps explain the "startling durability of pornography," which results in part from a "voyeuristic longing to find out what sex is like for others."

cultivating our need for *self-expansion*, a fundamental human motivation to grow, explore, and develop ourselves in new ways. In one longitudinal study, led by Arthur and Elaine Aron, couples that engaged in more self-expanding activities—examples include trying a new hike, attending a concert, or starting a hobby—also reported greater relationship quality. Another study randomly assigned married couples to either participate in an exciting activity (such as taking ballroom-dancing lessons) or a pleasurable activity (such as watching a movie). After ten weeks, those couples assigned to the exciting activities reported much larger increases in relationship satisfaction. Because they experienced self-expansion together, they were more likely to stay together.[40]

Self-expansion also leads to more sex. In a recent study led by Amy Muise, more than two hundred people completed relationship diaries about their levels of self-expansion, answering questions such as "How much did being with your partner expand your sense of the kind of person you are?"[41] They also listed any activities that led to feelings of self-expansion, like learning to skateboard, or shucking oysters for the first time. Finally, they reported their levels of sexual desire and sexual activity. The correlation was clear: on days that couples reported greater self-expansion, they also experienced much more sexual desire, which led to a 34 percent increase in sexual activity. (The sex was more fun, too.) Furthermore, the couples sustained this increase in desire over time, leading to lasting boosts in relationship satisfaction.

The benefits of self-expansion are rooted in the power of mystery. Freud assumed that the diminishment of desire was inevitable, but the research on self-expansion shows that desire can be rekindled, provided we engage in activities that reveal new sides of each other. Because self-expansion doesn't just expand the self—it also exposes its surprises. We remember that our partner is a rounded being, and not nearly as predictable as we assumed. Our curiosity is aroused, and the libido often follows.

When we acknowledge the mystery of other people, our behavior is transformed. We become better lovers, more attentive to the needs and nuances of our partner. We have more sex. But we also become more compassionate and forgiving, more likely to judge friends and strangers as we judge ourselves. People are complicated. The self is unknowable. If art taught us nothing else, that would be enough.

# CHAPTER 5

# THE DUCK-RABBIT

I want to beg you, as much as I can, dear sir, to be patient
toward all that is unsolved in your heart and to try to love the
questions themselves like locked rooms and like books that
are written in a very foreign tongue.

—RAINER MARIA RILKE, *Letters to a Young Poet*

## The Voynich Mystery

Wilfrid Michael Voynich was an unlikely owner of one of the
most famous medieval manuscripts in the world. Trained as a
chemist, Voynich was sent to a Siberian prison camp in 1885 for
inciting Polish nationalism. He escaped after five years with a
forged passport, before selling off his glasses and winter coat to
pay for a boat ticket to England. Once there, he became close to
Richard Garnett, the "Keeper of the Printed Books" for the British
Museum Reading Room, who persuaded Voynich to enter the
rare-book business. Before long, Voynich had turned his flam-
boyant personality, photographic memory, and fluency in seven
languages into a successful shop in London for antiquarian books.[1]

In late 1912, Voynich traveled to Italy in search of more in-
ventory. He found his way to the Villa Mondragone, a run-down
castle outside Rome. Voynich was in the cobwebbed attic, search-

ing through forgotten wooden chests, when he found a stack of illuminated medieval manuscripts. Many of the vellum pages were gorgeous, full of lush art and delicate typography; they bore the red wax seals of some of Italy's most illustrious families. Knowing the value of what he had found, Voynich bought the chests.

When Voynich got back to England, he began auctioning off his Italian haul. But there was one manuscript he refused to sell. This particular book appeared rather shabby: less than ten inches tall, it was filled with a mixture of botanical illustrations and bizarre drawings of naked women bathing in green pools. The few scholars who'd looked at the manuscript dismissed it as a strange collection of medieval herbal recipes, an atlas of obsolete medicine.

Voynich wasn't convinced. Although he referred to the codex as the "ugly duckling" of his collection—the flax spine was cracking and the paint was faded—he was fascinated by the cursive text. More specifically, he was intrigued that nobody could make sense of it. Voynich latched on to an enticing possibility: the inscrutable writing was a secret code. A masterful promoter, Voynich told the *New York Times* that his little book would "prove to the world that the black magic of the Middle Ages consisted in discoveries far in advance of twentieth-century science."[2] Of course, revealing that black magic meant cracking the code.

Alas, Voynich's initial attempts were failures; the writing remained indecipherable. Eager for help, Voynich gave the manuscript to MI-8, the cryptographic unit of the US Army. He assumed they'd break the code in no time, since they'd be able to match the text to the drawings and reverse engineer the cipher. But these professionals made no progress, either. (The botanical drawings, it turned out, were all make-believe.) "The more the cryptologists looked," write Lawrence and Nancy Goldstone in their book on the Voynich manuscript, "the more obscure the cipher became."[3]

After seven years of fruitless struggle, Voynich turned to William Romaine Newbold, an eminent scholar specializing in old philosophical texts at the University of Pennsylvania. Newbold's breakthrough came on the last page. There he spotted three faint lines of Latin. He concluded that these lines must be the cryptographic key, the secret instructions that could decrypt the rest of the text.

In April 1921, at a meeting of the American Philosophical Society, Newbold described his astonishing discoveries. He announced that the manuscript was the work of Roger Bacon, a thirteenth-century English polymath and early pioneer of the experimental method. (Bacon insisted that, whenever possible, our "theories supplied by reason should be verified by sensory data, aided by instruments, and corroborated by trustworthy witnesses."[4] It was a worthy aspiration; it also didn't stop Bacon from spending much of his career researching alchemy and astrology.) According to Newbold, Bacon's text anticipated engineering marvels such as the telescope and steam power; Bacon described the swimming style of sperm and the swirl of distant nebulae in the sky. Given these remarkable discoveries, the Bacon codex became one of the most important scientific texts in the world. It proved that Bacon was hundreds of years ahead of his time, a scientific prophet stuck in the dark ages.

So how did the cipher work? According to Newbold, it was incredibly sophisticated; Bacon must really have wanted to hide his secrets. Newbold argued that Bacon's system involved something like three different ciphers operating in conjunction. Some sections, Newbold said, could be understood by combining pairs of Latin letters into new letters that spelled out sentences; elsewhere, he believed the letters formed a purely phonetic alphabet. This meant that the cryptographer had to first study the calligraphic details under a microscope, attempting to parse those subtle marks. Then, once the letter was "decomposed," the abbreviations had to be expanded according to a long list of rules, including syllabification, commutation, and reversion.[5] This elaborate process allowed Newbold to turn each line of cipher into several paragraphs of Latin. The short book was actually an encyclopedia.

When a few of Newbold's colleagues questioned his method, Newbold pointed out that his translation had to be correct since he was describing historical events and natural phenomena of which he had no prior knowledge. In September 1926, Newbold died after an attack of "acute indigestion." In 1930, Voynich followed him to the grave. In his will, Voynich asked that his most prized manuscript—the "ugly duckling" that changed the history of science—be sold to a public institution capable of protecting its pages.

But the manuscript never sold. And it never sold because the Voynich cipher was never cracked. Although Newbold was convinced he'd solved the mystery, he was wrong. The mystery won.

———

In 1913, business tycoon George Fabyan asked John Matthews Manly, a professor of English literature at the University of Chicago, to investigate a series of codes that had supposedly been embedded in Shakespeare's work. Manly liked codes, and he liked Shakespeare, so he agreed to take a look.* It took six weeks for Manly to reject the idea. The codes were not codes. They were coincidences.

---

* Fabyan was a leading proponent of the so-called Baconian theory, which held that Sir Francis Bacon was actually the author of Shakespeare's plays.

A few years later, as World War I consumed Europe, the US government realized that it was in desperate need of code break-ers. Manly was recruited by the US Army's Military Intelligence Division, tasked with applying the same methods to secret German army telegrams that he'd previously used on Shakespeare.[6]

When the war ended, Manly returned to teaching. But he couldn't stop thinking about codes, which led him to the Voynich manuscript. This quixotic interest soon took over his life. In 1931, nearly ten years after Newbold first announced his solution for the cipher, and five years after Newbold's death, Manly published a forty-six-page paper on the medieval book. He made his thesis clear: "In my opinion, the Newbold claims are entirely baseless and should be definitely and absolutely rejected."

The rest of the paper was a wrecking ball, dismantling New-bold's claims one by one. Those microscopic signs that Newbold saw in the cursive? They were due to the cracking of the ink on the vellum. In one instance, Newbold had miscopied the actual text—but still somehow ended up with an "accurate" message. Manly criticized the malleability of Newbold's decryption rules, detailing how Newbold had generated three different translations from the same Latin lines. There were historical details that didn't add up and basic errors in spelling. And then there was Newbold's insistence that he didn't know about the science or the history in the text. Manly argued that it was self-delusion, and that New-bold's "decipherments were not discoveries of secrets hidden by Roger Bacon but the products of his own intense enthusiasm and ingenious subconsciousness."[7]

In retrospect, the problems with Newbold's decryption seem obvious and undeniable. Nevertheless, academic journals and the *Times* had praised his work; the Voynich manuscript had tempo-rarily changed the entire time line of early scientific history. It's not that Newbold set out to deceive anyone. It's that he deceived himself.

Since Newbold, hundreds of other scholars, code breakers, and hobbyists have tried to crack the manuscript. (In 1969, it was donated to Yale University.) The vellum pages have been analyzed with supercomputers by the NSA. Gordon Rugg, head of the Knowledge Modelling Group at Keele University in England, has published several recent papers showing that the basic features of the Voynich script can be replicated in a short time using a Cardan grille, a sixteenth-century method for encryption.[8] According to Rugg, the manuscript is almost certainly a hoax, generated by plugging meaningless syllables into a grille system. (This helps explain why many of the world's best cryptologists, including William Friedman, couldn't even identify the language used in the text; scholars refer to it as Voynichese.) Rugg suggests that the manuscript was probably invented to trick a rich medieval prince, possibly by selling the encrypted book as a how-to guide for alchemy.

Yet the beautiful hoax continues to fascinate. (Since the beginning of 2019, there were more than 200 academic publications about the Voynich manuscript. It's also been featured in countless novels, several movies and television shows, and even a few video games.) Which raises the obvious question, Why has this meaningless manuscript titillated kings, scholars, and code breakers for centuries? What is it about the gibberish writing that people find so endlessly interesting?

One likely explanation is the ambiguity of the text, which serves as an effective mystery hook. When Voynich discovered the codex, he was drawn to its enigmatic qualities. The book was written in an alphabet he didn't know, spelling out a language he'd never heard of, featuring drawings of plants that didn't exist.

Nevertheless, the words and pictures implied a solution, featuring consistent symbols, regular repetitions, and plenty of convincing botanical detail. The result was a work of staggering ambiguity: every word seemed pregnant with meaning. It was interesting because it demanded interpretation.

But there's a paradox here. Although people might be drawn to ambiguous medieval manuscripts, they tend to avoid ambiguous conditions in real life. In 1961, Daniel Ellsberg, an analyst working on nuclear war strategy at RAND, published a highly influential article about our reaction to ambiguity.[9] (A decade later, Ellsberg would leak the *Pentagon Papers*, a top-secret history of the Vietnam War.) Ellsberg's paper featured a gamble involving two urns, both of which contained one hundred balls. The first urn contained a mixture of red and black balls in unknown proportions. The second urn contained fifty red and fifty black balls. If a person could successfully predict the color of the ball drawn from one of the urns, he would receive a prize of $100. The question is which urn the subject wanted to bet on.

As Ellsberg predicted, and as subsequent research confirmed, the vast majority of people prefer to gamble on the urn with the known distribution of balls.* Although the mathematical odds are identical, we tend to avoid gambles with an excess of uncertainty, a tendency that came to be known as ambiguity aversion. More recently, scientists at Caltech have shown that asking people to make decisions in ambiguous conditions leads to increased brain activity in the amygdala, a brain area associated with the emotions of fear and anxiety.[10]

---

* Children, interestingly, don't show an aversion to ambiguity—they accept the uncertainty of the universe.

It's a mental tendency with serious consequences. Ambiguity aversion can lead people to make poor financial choices, as they panic sell during periods of market uncertainty. (Nobody wants to keep their savings in the ambiguous urn.)[11] It can skew our medical decisions, as we opt for treatments with more certain outcomes, even if they come with reduced potential benefits. Legal scholars, meanwhile, argue that ambiguity aversion can cause defendants to accept bad plea deals, as a bad deal is still less scary than the uncertainty of a jury trial.[12]

Or look at what happened with the Voynich manuscript. If we're not careful, ambiguity aversion can trick us into seeing conclusive answers that don't exist, just like William Newbold. Instead of enjoying the ambiguity, we insist the code has been cracked. It's disturbingly easy to deceive oneself.

In this chapter, we'll learn how good art turns ambiguity into entertainment, hooking us with content that's shifting and unsettled. We want to solve the text. We want to erase the ambivalence. We want to know *for sure*. However, by denying us definitive answers—by insisting that there are multiple interpretations—the art teaches us how to live with uncertainty.

In other words, it teaches us how to live.

## "Pretty Mouth and Green My Eyes"

In the winter of 1948, J. D. Salinger was a divorced writer living in a converted barn with his schnauzer in the suburbs of Stamford, Connecticut. He'd had a few short stories published in the *New Yorker* and *Good Housekeeping*, but he was struggling to pay his bills. When he wasn't writing, Salinger was studying Zen Buddhism. He was drawn to Buddhism mostly because of meditation, which had helped him recover from the trauma of fighting in World War II. (He'd landed at Utah Beach on D-Day, fought in the Battle of the Bulge, and cataloged the horrors of Dachau as an intelligence officer.) But the Zen aesthetic, which emphasized paradox and ambiguity as tools for reflection, entranced Salinger. He would often quote Zen koans, those short riddles that defy rational understanding. For Salinger, the best writing was itself a kind of koan, allowing the reader to meditate on the perplexing text. When he published *Nine Stories*, his first and only short story collection, Salinger chose the following koan for the epigraph: "We know the sound of two hands clapping. But what is the sound of one hand clapping?"[13] The point of the question is that nobody knows.

Salinger's most Zen story is "Pretty Mouth and Green My Eyes," which takes the form of a phone call between two friends, Arthur and Lee. It's late at night; the men are somewhere between drunk and hungover. Arthur has just returned from a party where he lost track of his wife, Joanie. He's angry and rambling. Lee, meanwhile, is lying in bed next to a woman. The conversation unfolds amid this backdrop of uncertainty. Who is the woman? Is she Joanie? How crazy is Arthur?

What makes the short story a koan is that these questions never get answered. Salinger leads us to suspect that Joanie is the unnamed "girl" in the bed. However, at the end of the story, Arthur calls back with the news that Joanie has just returned. It's a surprising twist, but the surprise doesn't bring clarity—it brings the opposite. The more we know about these characters, the less we understand. It's like thinking about the sound of one hand clapping.

Uri Hasson, a neuroscientist at Princeton, was interested in Salinger's "Pretty Mouth and Green My Eyes" precisely because of its ambiguity.[14] Hasson has spent the last several years studying the neural anatomy of narrative. He's shown people in a brain scanner

Hitchcock movies and tracked their eyes as they watch a Sergio Leone western. He's looked at the mechanics of character development in fiction—we think about pretend people the same way we think about real people—and identified the parts of the cortex that allow us to tell stories about our own life.[15] With the Salinger text, Hasson wanted to understand how we deal with a text that can't be deciphered. "The impressive thing about the story is that it encourages you to interpret it, but it also makes clear that your interpretation might be wrong," Hasson says. "Salinger has left out the lines that would make any single version the right one."[16]

How does the mind deal with such ambiguity? By searching for resolution. Ludwig Wittgenstein, in his *Philosophical Investigations*, observed that ambiguity was inevitably linked to the act of interpretation.[17] He used a classic duck-rabbit visual illusion to make his point:

Welche Thiere gleichen einander am meisten?

Kaninchen und Ente.

Some people see a duck. Some people see a rabbit. Some people can switch back and forth between the images in serial fashion. However, as Wittgenstein pointed out, these single interpretations were all incorrect. The right description, he said, was that the picture was a *duck-rabbit*. Although we can only see one image at a time, we should remember that there are other interpretations. The ambiguity isn't something to solve on the way to the answer. The ambiguity *is* the answer.*

Hasson watched this interpretive process unfold in the brain scanner. To explore the psychology of interpretation, Hasson began his experiment by making a few slight alterations to Salinger's tale. In the "cheating" condition, he rewrote the opening to make it clear that Joanie is in bed with Arthur. In the "paranoia" condition, he rewrote the first lines to suggest that Arthur is delusional. Hasson then looked to see how these minor edits shaped the way people decoded the rest of the story. The effects of the edits were profound, allowing Hasson and his colleagues to predict which version a subject had seen based solely on their brain activity. "You can really see how interpretation colors everything," Hasson says. "Once you think you know what's happening, you read the story very differently." Interestingly, these neural differences persisted throughout the entire text, even though the only changes occurred in the first four lines. It didn't matter that the rest of the story was identical: subjects in the different groups ended up processing the narrative in distinct ways. "This really shows us that the brain is an interpretive machine," Hasson says. "Once it has a frame, it tends to see everything else through that frame."

---

* As the art historian Ernst Gombrich observed, we can "remember the rabbit while we see the duck, but the more closely we watch ourselves, the more certainly we will discover that we cannot experience alternative readings at the same time."

The power of Salinger's story is that it refuses to settle on any single interpretation. It's resolutely a duck-rabbit. As a result, readers of the text must shuttle back and forth between these explanations, unsure if Joanie is cheating or Arthur is crazy. Literary scholars refer to this process as a hermeneutic circle. The circle exists when a work is so ambiguous that we can only understand the parts by anticipating their relationship to the whole. Of course, that sense of the whole itself depends on an interpretation of the parts. (Think of the duck-rabbit picture—you notice different details depending on the animal you are trying to see.) So we are stuck in a loop, forced to construct meaning by searching for fleeting patterns and subtle themes, switching between the granular and the gestalt.

This sounds frustrating, but it's an effective hook. Because the mind is so eager to find the best interpretation, the mystery of the ambiguity holds our attention. "If you're reading this story the way it was written, then you're trying to figure out the conversation for yourself," Hasson says. "The fact that it stays confusing is part of the reason you keep reading." When no answers are forthcoming, we read the words closer. Maybe Joanie is sleeping with Lee? Then we read the words again. Maybe she's not? "That ambiguity makes it more taxing for the brain, but it also makes it more interesting," Hasson says. "You can't make any one interpretation stick, no matter how badly you want it or how many times you go back to it. There is no end to it."

## Schrödinger's Cat

The critic William Empson observed, in his 1930 classic, *Seven Types of Ambiguity*, that the power of poetry depends on its ambiguity, which he defined as the ability to incite "alternative views . . .

without sheer misreading."[18] According to Empson, the obscurities of verse are what pull us in. The force of the words depends on their simultaneous truths.

Empson gives the example of Shakespeare's Sonnet LXXXIII.[19] The poem begins with flattery:

I never saw that you did painting need,
And therefore to your fair no painting set;

So far, so obvious: the subject of the sonnet is too lovely for words. This is what a sonnet is supposed to sound like. It's a poem of praise, a rhyme to our beloved. But simple compliments bore Shakespeare. As Jay-Z notes, the sonnet is a clear precursor for the braggadocio rap, which also limns a strict structure to force the writer "to find every nook and cranny in the subject and . . . invent new language for saying old things."[20] So the verse becomes a metaphor for itself: "If you can say how dope you are in a completely original, clever, powerful way," Jay-Z writes, then "the rhyme itself becomes proof of the boast's truth."

In Sonnet LXXXIII, Shakespeare shows off his skills by exploding the clichés of the standard sonnet. What begins as a love song turns into an Elizabethan braggadocio rap: Shakespeare is using the confining form to show off his creative genius. He does this by infusing the short poem with an astonishing amount of ambiguity, starting with the next lines.

I found, or thought I found, you did exceed
The barren tender of a poet's debt;

Shakespeare here is taking advantage of language's innate subtleties, deploying words with a multiplicity of possible meanings.

There is, to start, the problem of "tender," which can either be an adjective ("caring") or a noun ("offered payment for what is due"). And then there's the issue of the "debt." Shakespeare has crafted the line so that we can't tell if the debt is owed *by* the poet or *to* the poet. If it's owed *by* the poet, the line means that the beauty of the subject exceeds what the poet could express in verse. How romantic. However, if it's a debt owed *to* the poet, as a payment for his writing, it implies a sense of loss: the poet used to be a friend, but now he's just a hired hand. Either way, Empson says, the use of "barren," along with the parenthetical "or *thought* I found," hints at feelings of bitterness. Something has gone wrong with the relationship.

As the sonnet winds to an end, the gap between these interpretations turns into a chasm.

> For I impair not beauty being mute,
> When others would give life and bring a tomb.

It's a couplet ripe with questions. For one, it's not clear whose tomb this is. "This might be Shakespeare's tomb," Empson writes, in which case the line suggests that the poet brings a lifetime of devotion. But it could also be the subject's tomb. In this reading, what seems like flattery is actually a veiled threat: the poet is choosing to be mute so that he doesn't destroy the superficial appeal of his subject. Because if the poet did try to write about his subject, he would be forced to reveal their ugly secrets, those dark truths that are hidden by those "fair eyes."

The ambiguity of the sonnet captures Shakespeare's uncanny talent. What could easily be a shallow poem of praise instead becomes a demonstration of poetry's potential: even a short verse with a strict rhyme scheme can become a duck-rabbit, giving rise to two contradictory interpretations. In the romantic version, the subject is too pretty for adjectives, which is why the poet is writing about his inability to write a proper sonnet. However, in the aggrieved version, the poem captures the complexity of a broken friendship. This uncertainty of meaning cannot be escaped—even if you find one interpretation more persuasive, Shakespeare makes sure that your reading will be shadowed by its opposite. As James Baldwin noted in *The Cross of Redemption*: "That is why he [Shakespeare] is called a poet. And his responsibility, which is also his joy and his strength and his life, is to defeat all labels and complicate all battles by insisting on the human riddle."

For Empson, ambiguity is not just an intellectual game—it's also the source of the poetic emotion. A recent study by scientists at the Max Planck Institutes supports his theory.[21] By reading people dozens of different poems inside an fMRI machine—selections included Shakespeare sonnets, "Psalm" by Paul Celan, and lines from Rilke—the scientists could detect the particular aspects of poetry that led to chills, goose bumps, and spikes in blood flow to reward areas in the brain. According to the scientists, one of the most important aspects of poetic form was the "closure effect," that ability of poetry to "exploit our brain's inclination towards rhythmicity, periodicity, and the resulting prediction of upcoming events." The best poems encourage our need to make sense of things, but then subvert it with ambiguity. The words trick us into seeking the closure they refuse to yield.* In this respect, poetry echoes the subversive structures of music, which also generates feelings from the uncertainty contained within its form.[22]

---

* A meaningful poem, writes Donald Hall, is like a house with a secret room at the center. "This room is not a Hidden Meaning, to be paraphrased by the intellect," he says. Rather, "the secret room is where the unsayable gathers."

This helps explain another puzzling finding from the study, which is that the magnitude of goose bumps *increases* with repeated exposure to the poem. While familiarity usually leads to adaptation—we become less sensitive to the stimulus—good poetry escapes this trap, making us more sensitive instead. One possibility is that such sensitization reflects the intrinsic mysteriousness of the verse, which only expands with rereading. We might think Paul Celan's "Psalm" is decipherable; the words are simple, dancing on the edge of clarity. But then we are shown the poem again—"A Nothing / we were, are now, and ever / shall be, blooming"—and realize that these words are a duck-rabbit, just like Shakespeare's sonnet. There is no single answer.

The rewards of ambiguity aren't limited to literature. We live in the golden age of television, which is another way of saying we can watch countless shows full of difficult characters, complex plots, and mystery hooks. The golden age is often said to have begun with the arrival of *The Sopranos*, created by David Chase. Tony was a complicated antihero, but Chase wasn't willing to limit the mystery to his cast of mobsters. He wanted the *entire show* to be ambiguous, endlessly rewatchable because it had no settled interpretation.

The infamous series finale reflects this strategy. Tony is waiting at a diner for his family. He passes the time looking at the jukebox. He settles on "Don't Stop Believin'," by Journey. As the pop song begins, his wife walks through the door, followed by Tony's son. The camera lingers on a few suspicious strangers. There's a man in a hat drinking coffee, and a shifty-eyed customer in a Members Only jacket sitting at the counter. Then a series of quick shots: Meadow Soprano in the parking lot, the man in the jacket entering the bathroom, onion rings at the table.

The door of the diner opens again and Tony looks up. Smash cut to black.

The abrupt ending inspired countless theories, at least once people realized their cable didn't go out. Some were convinced that Tony was murdered by the man in the jacket. (According to this theory, the man retrieves a gun from the bathroom; the last shot is from Tony's point of view, and the sudden blackness is the mark of his death. As Tony's mother says, "It's all a big nothing.") Others insisted that Tony was still alive, but forced to live a life of chronic fear. (In this version, there is no assassin in the diner, but Tony suspects everyone; the suspense we feel is his eternal punishment.) In search of answers, viewers analyzed every frame, searching for allusions to earlier episodes; they mined the lyrics of the Journey song; they kept asking Chase if Tony was really dead.

Chase refused to answer. Or rather, he kept reminding people that there was no answer. "Whether Tony Soprano is alive or dead is not the point," Chase insisted in a public letter. "To continue to search for this answer is fruitless. The final scene of *The Sopranos* raises a spiritual question that has no right or wrong answer."[23] Although we want to know what happened to Tony—we've spent more than eighty hours watching him and his cronies—Chase insists that we're stuck with the mystery.

The critic Alan Sepinwall has compared the ending of *The Sopranos* to the famous thought experiment of Erwin Schrödinger.[24] In Schrödinger's example, a cat is trapped inside a cardboard box with a vial of poison. It is either dead or alive, but you can't know until you look inside: the act of observation creates the reality. While Schrödinger devised the thought experiment as a critique of quantum indeterminacy, it also captures the ambiguous state of Tony Soprano. The only difference is that his mystery box can never be opened.

## The Mystery of Meaning

It was another slow Sunday afternoon in the WKNR-FM studio in Detroit. Russ Gibb, a garrulous music promoter with a mop-top and thick circular glasses, was spinning prog and garage rock, taking calls from listeners in between sets. (When he wasn't a part-time DJ, Gibb was running the Grande Ballroom, a repurposed dance hall that helped launch such local acts as Alice Cooper, MC5, and the Stooges.) He'd just finished playing some songs off *Abbey Road*, the new Beatles album, when Tom from Ypsilanti called in to the studio.

Tom had alarming news: *Paul McCartney was dead*. Gibb gave off a skeptical laugh. He'd just listened to a beautiful new Lennon/McCartney song. How could Paul be gone? "Listen," Gibb said, "that story is always floating around about somebody, but it's just not true." But the caller wouldn't quit. "There are clues to McCartney's death in the records," Tom insisted. "What you've got to do is play 'Revolution Number Nine' backwards."

Gibb was intrigued. This silly conspiracy could be falsified on air, which would make for excellent radio. The DJ grabbed his copy of the *White Album* and slipped disc two onto the turntable.

"Now what part am I supposed to play?" Gibb asked.

"Right at the beginning. Play the part where the voice keeps saying, 'number nine . . . number nine.'"

Gibb found the groove on the record and began carefully rotating the vinyl backward. A ghostly voice emerged from the static, only it wasn't talking about numbers anymore. This is what Gibb heard: "Turn me on, dead man . . . turn me on, dead man."

Tom from Ypsilanti came back on the air, his voice mingled with feedback: "So did you hear it, Uncle Russ?"

"Yeah, man, I sure did."[25]

Gibb knew that Paul McCartney wasn't dead. But he also knew how to entertain his audience. The same kids who came to the Grande Ballroom to watch Alice Cooper in clown makeup would eat up this dead-Beatle nonsense.

He was right. Toward the end of Gibb's radio show, a teenager came running into the studio clutching a copy of *Magical Mystery Tour*. According to the writer Andru Reeve, who chronicles the "Paul Is Dead" conspiracy in *Turn Me On, Dead Man*, the freckle-faced kid promised that he could show Gibb "a clue that really proves McCartney is dead." All Gibb had to do was slow down the last few seconds of "Strawberry Fields Forever." Without hesitating, Gibb grabbed the record and turned it on.

Amid the distorted screeches and swirling strings, one could make out the hazy voice of John Lennon. At first, it sounded as if he were saying "cranberry sauce" or maybe "I'm very bored." But if you played the record again, and you listened closely, you could hear the secret message: "I buried Paul."[26]

It didn't take long before Gibb's radio act became national news. On October 14, 1969—just two days after Gibb played "Revolution Number Nine" backward on the air—a sophomore at the University of Michigan named Fred LaBour decided to turn his review of *Abbey Road* for the *Michigan Daily* into a detailed accounting of all the clues pointing to McCartney's death. (If it was satire, nobody got the joke.) LaBour cited the backward code of "Revolution," and Lennon's morbid confession on "Strawberry Fields Forever," but he also added in visual evidence. In the *Magical Mystery Tour* booklet, the other Beatles were wearing red roses on their lapels; Paul's is black. Or look at the cover of *Abbey Road*, which told the story of Paul's funeral procession. The other Beatles were wearing shoes. Only Paul was walking barefoot, as if he were about to be buried. (On the album cover, Paul was holding a cigarette in his right hand. As LaBour notes, "The original [Paul] was left-handed.") The parked Volkswagen Beetle had a license plate that includes "28IF," which alluded to the fact that McCartney would be twenty-eight years old *if* he hadn't died.* And then there was the music itself. " 'Octopus's Garden' is British Navy slang for the cemetery in England where naval heroes are buried," LaBour wrote. " 'I Want You (She's So Heavy)' is Lennon wrestling with Paul, trying to pull him out of the earth."

LaBour's article was syndicated in dozens of other student publications, including the *Harvard Crimson*. As Andru Reeve documents, students began placing classified ads in underground newspapers, asking strangers for additional information about Paul's death. "How do you know Paul is dead?" began one spot. "What raps and clues have you heard? Will exchange clues."[27] Hundreds of letters were mailed in response; the evidence was everywhere. Did you know *walrus* is Greek for "corpse"? Or that the chirps on "Blackbird" are actually a grouse, which is the bird of death in English folklore? Or that reversing the mumbles after "I'm So Tired" reveals a voice saying, "Paul is dead, man, miss him, miss him"?

The conspiracy that emerged was persuasive in its precision. The story went like this: On November 9, 1966, after a late-night recording session at Abbey Road Studios, Paul spun out in his Aston Martin and smashed into a light pole. He was "officially pronounced dead" at the scene, which is why he's wearing an O.P.D. badge on *Sgt. Pepper's*. However, given the huge value of

---

* Beatleologists would later discover additional clues in the imagery of *Sgt. Pepper's*. There's a bloody driving glove, which alludes to the car accident that killed Paul; an open palm hovers over his head, as if he's being blessed before interment; if you hold the album up to a mirror, the "Lonely Hearts" inscribed on the drum spells out "11/9 he die," which must be the date of McCartney's fatal crash.

the Beatles franchise, the three remaining band members decided to keep the death a secret, sublimating their grief into secret hints and backward recordings. To keep up public appearances, they hired the winner of a Paul look-alike contest. John Lennon went on to write "Hey Jude" and "Let It Be" in the style of Paul. Linda McCartney married someone else.

On the one hand, Paul's death was a ridiculous rumor, started by a part-time radio DJ and mischievous college student.* Nevertheless, the "Paul Is Dead" story became a cultural phenomenon. *Life* magazine devoted a cover to Paul's purported demise—they sent a reporting crew to his Scotland farm—while defense attorney F. Lee Bailey hosted a "mock-trial" television special on the "controversy." Hundreds of radio stations regularly debated the story, playing every Beatles record in reverse, while mainstream newspapers covered its viral spread, quoting credulous teenagers such as Pat Rogalski, who told Cleveland's *Plain Dealer*, "There's so much evidence that it couldn't be coincidental. I believe Paul's dead."[28] Years later, McCartney explained to *Rolling Stone* why he didn't do more to disprove the story: "They said, 'Look, what are you going to do about it? It's a big thing breaking in America. You're dead.' And so I said, 'Leave it, just let them say it. It'll probably be the best publicity we've ever had, and I won't have to do a thing except stay alive.' So I managed to stay alive through it."

The viral spread of the "Paul is dead" rumor exposes the dark side of ambiguity. It highlights the way our aversion to uncertainty can create a cascade of misreadings, just like with the Voynich

---

* In many respects, the "Paul Is Dead" story was an early warning for our current age of mass disinformation, in which tens of millions of people fell for the Obama birther hoax and 9/11 truther conspiracies.

manuscript. By the late 1960s, the Beatles had become auteurs of the abstruse. They'd always enjoyed the clever allusion—was "Norwegian Wood" about "knowing she would"?—but their discovery of THC and LSD led them to experiment with ambiguity to an unprecedented degree. So tracks about girls and sex gave way to lyrics about Polythene Pam and yellow submarines. These were chart-topping pop songs that were also silly and surreal. As the Beatles sang in "Tomorrow Never Knows": "Turn off your mind, relax and float downstream."

Yet, the Beatles were also immaculate artists. It's easy to create gibberish—what's much harder is to write lyrics that are both cryptic and evocative. We might not understand "The Fool on the Hill" or "You Never Give Me Your Money," but we're still filled with feelings, which we try to explain. The ambiguity begs for an interpretation, just as with the duck-rabbit illusion. As Lennon later reflected, "In those days I was writing obscurely, à la Dylan, never saying what you mean but giving the *impression* of something, where more or less can be read into it."[29]

Consider "I Am the Walrus," a Lennon masterpiece born out of his amusement that an English teacher at his old high school was having students analyze Lennon's songs in class. The song begins with some imagery borrowed from acid trips and an old playground nursery rhyme:

Sitting on a cornflake, waiting for the van to come
Corporation T-shirt, stupid bloody Tuesday
Man, you've been a naughty boy, you let your face grow
　　long

The song gets weirder from there, breaking down into a verse about "yellow matter custard" and "crabalocker fishwife."

The music echoes the obscurity. The opening melody was inspired by a passing police siren. Swirling strings give way to bellowing static, snippets of a *King Lear* radio play and the background shrieks of Paul and George. "I am the egg man," chants John. "I am the walrus, goo goo g'joob." After he'd finished writing down a line about semolina pilchards and the Eiffel Tower, his boyhood friend Pete Shotton recalled Lennon uttering one of his signature taunts: "Let the fuckers work that one out."[30]

Of course, the fuckers began working it out as soon as "I Am the Walrus" was released as a single. Critics noticed the allusion to the Lewis Carroll poem "The Walrus and the Carpenter," about a devious walrus who befriends a crew of oysters only to devour them. They speculated about his "elementary penguin singing Hare Krishna" line—Lennon later said he was mocking those who put all their "faith in one idol"—and tried to understand his references to Edgar Allan Poe.[31] (Lennon would also put Poe's face on the cover of *Sgt. Pepper's*.) And then there was the *Lear* fragment: What did that have to do with cornflakes?

Let's be clear: this isn't the razor-sharp ambiguity of a Shakespeare sonnet or Salinger short story. Rather, it's messy and freeform; the allusions are an atmosphere, not a map. " 'I am the egg man'? It could have the pudding basin for all I care," Lennon declared, when asked to explain the ambiguities of the song. "It's not that serious."[32] Lennon would later admit that he hadn't actually read "The Walrus and the Carpenter," or else he would have realized that the walrus was the bad guy, an evil symbol of capitalism. He should have called the song "I Am the Carpenter." ("But that wouldn't have been the same, would it?" John quipped.) He also wasn't trying to say anything with that *Lear* excerpt—it was just playing on the BBC when he was in the studio with Ringo and Lennon liked its trippy mood. Was "Semolina Pilchard" a sly reference to Sergeant Pilcher, the London cop who sent the Stones to jail on drug charges? Or was it just a gibberish reference to a fried little fish?

At times, Lennon grew cynical about this process, the way the audience insisted on finding the secret meaning in every verse. "We're a con," he told Hunter Davies. "We know we're conning them, because we know people want to be conned. They've given us the freedom to con them. Let's stick that in there, we say, that'll start them puzzling. I'm sure all the artists do, when they realize it's a con. I bet Picasso sticks things in. I bet he's been laughing his balls off for the last eighty years."*

But John exaggerated his cynicism: he loved creating ambiguous music. The Beatles used to be a boy band singing songs about holding hands. Now they were quoting Shakespeare and trolling the cops. They also discovered an astonishing talent for the suggestive line. Hunter Davies was sitting with Lennon during the writing of "I Am the Walrus." According to Davies, Lennon was improvising lyrics as he worked out the rhythm. He originally sang, 'Sitting on a cornflake, waiting for the *man* to come.' Davies, however, thought he said "*van* to come," so he wrote that down in his notebook. But Lennon preferred the mistake—it was weirder, less obvious, more ambiguous. It made Davies think about "when someone thought to be potty or mad would be told that a van would come and take them away. John liked the image."[33] And so a potential cliché about The Man gave rise to a much darker allusion to mental illness.

---

* As Ian MacDonald observes in *Revolution in the Head*, Lennon began leaving mistakes in his recorded lyrics. On "You've Got to Hide Your Love Away," for instance, Lennon sang "feeling two foot small," instead of "two foot tall." When the studio engineer suggested a fix, Lennon "laughed and said, 'Leave that in, the pseuds'll love it'" (312).

It was a typically brilliant move. During the Beatles' unprecedented run of greatness, John and Paul consistently chose the more mysterious possibility when crafting their songs. It was "van" over "man," and "hold you in his armchair" instead of "hold you in his arms," or the strange assurance that "the movement you need is on your shoulder" in "Hey Jude."* In their late masterpieces, the Beatles expressed the belief that understanding was overrated. The pleasure was in the mystery.

This creative approach worked splendidly until Tom from Ypsilanti decided to play the *White Album* backward. Although the Beatles had experimented with so-called backmasking during the making of *Rubber Soul*—while stoned, Lennon listened to "Rain" in reverse and fell for the strange sound—they'd never engaged in phonetic reversal, which is far more difficult to pull off. (Among other challenges, it requires the singer to learn how to speak backward.) Nevertheless, the human gift for linguistic interpretation ensured that the occasional Beatles track would still sound like real speech, even when played in the wrong direction. It might even include morbid references to Paul.

But here's the problem with this interpretative approach—it removes the ambiguity. The layers of potential meaning have been stripped away, replaced by a code that can be decrypted with a phonograph. Instead of accepting the mystery, the song becomes

---

* It really is "armchair," as the demos reveal. Paul tells a candid story about the first time he played "Hey Jude" for John and Yoko: "I was in the music room upstairs when John and Yoko came to visit, and they were right behind me over my right shoulder, standing up, listening to it as I played it to them, and when I got to the line 'The movement you need is on your shoulder,' I looked over my shoulder and I said, 'I'll change that, it's a bit crummy. I was just blocking it out,' and John said, 'You won't, you know. That's the best line in it!'"

a confession of a cover-up. We forget about the duck-rabbit and only see the duck.

As such, the "Paul is dead" rumor remains a cautionary tale about the combustible relationship between mass media and ambiguity aversion. Tom and his followers didn't have Facebook or Reddit—they just had radio stations and student newspapers and classified ads. But it was enough to convince strangers all across the world that these ambiguous lyrics could be solved, that they didn't have to live with not knowing.

It's a tragic misreading. The real meaning of those Beatles songs is that there is no single meaning, just meaningful interpretations. Even John couldn't explain the egg man, or why those kids on the cornflake were waiting for the van.

Certainty is certainly easier. But what keeps us coming back to the *White Album* and Salinger and Shakespeare's sonnets is not some secret Delphic message. Rather, it's the pleasure of their possibilities. Their truth is alive and ever-changing, just like us.

The art is a mirror.

# CHAPTER 6

# THE INFINITE GAME

The artist cannot and must not take anything for granted,
but must drive to the heart of every answer and expose the
question the answer hides.

**—JAMES BALDWIN, "THE CREATIVE PROCESS"**

When James Carse was growing up in Arlington Heights, a suburb
of Chicago, in the 1940s, the neighborhood boys played baseball
in an empty lot. "You'd wake up, have breakfast, hear the crack of
a hit ball, and couldn't wait to get out there," Carse remembers.
Although the game followed the basic rules of the sport—three
strikes and three outs—nobody kept track of the innings, or even
the score. "All day long we'd be out there," Carse says. "People
would come in and out and the teams would change depending
on who was around. But we didn't care about that. We didn't
care who won. We just wanted to keep playing."[1] In the evening,
the boys' parents would join them in the empty lot for a hot dog
dinner.

Forty years later, when Carse was a professor of religion at
NYU, he would remember how much he loved playing baseball
in that sandlot. These memories, along with a close reading of

Wittgenstein,* would inspire Carse to a write an academic book about the nature of games. His essential insight was that there are two kinds of games: finite games and infinite games.**

Finite games are everywhere. They are those activities, Carse says, in which the participants are bound by rules and regulations, and there are clear winners and losers at the end. These games are finite because the goal of the players is victory; they definitely keep score. It's eighteen holes of golf, Monopoly, forty-yard dashes, and *Call of Duty*. There are strict regulations in finite games—to break them is to cheat—and clear conditions for winning. The game ends once those conditions have been met.

The infinite game, in contrast, is more like sandlot baseball: it's a pursuit in which the only goal is to keep playing. While finite games have fixed rules, the players in infinite games often bend their rules to keep going. (In that sandlot game, for instance, players would switch teams to ensure competitive balance.) The play isn't a means to an end. The play is the means *and* the end.[2]

Carse believes in the beauty of infinite games, whether it's players in a democracy—elections are a game without end—or

---

* "There's a line in *The Brown Book* by Wittgenstein that really shaped my thinking," Carse remembers. "It goes something like 'the meaning of the word is what comes of it, not what is defined for that word.' I read that and realized that the consequences are quite dramatic. Because if the meaning of anything is what comes of it, then when the word is spoken, you don't know what it means until there is a reaction to it, until you see how it plays out." Language, in this analysis, is like a game.

** Carse's first draft of the book was dense and academic and ran to more than 350 pages. "As it happened, I had a sabbatical in Paris as I was finishing the manuscript," Carse remembers. "I took the pages to my favorite café and somehow lost it. All of it. I was heartbroken." Carse was ready to give up when he decided to write a summary of his lost text, just in case he wanted to return to it someday. "In about six weeks I ended up writing the book as it is," he says. "Easiest book I ever wrote. Thank god I lost that other one."

the process of evolution. (There is no perfect species.) He's convinced that games played for the sake of playing are the best kind, and that they can bring out the best in their players. As a religion scholar, known for his work on Christian mysticism, Carse is particularly drawn to the theological implications of infinite games. "The great religions have been around for a long time," Carse says. "Hinduism is six thousand years old. Judaism is four thousand years old. Within each of these religions, of course, there are powerful finite elements. You've got people who want to win an argument, create a cult, people who insist that they've finally got it all figured out." These people, Carse says, are playing finite games with God.

But Carse argued that these finite games could not explain the endurance of the great religions. "The sages, the big ones, the ones that matter over time, they know that when you think you're finished with the religious text, all you've really done is open another chapter," Carse says. "The argument goes on, which is a good thing. Look at Judaism. The Jewish people never had a powerful army or empire. They were scattered for thousands of years. But they had this text, the Talmud, that kept the rabbis busy, and that was enough." We turn to religion for answers, but what sustains religion are the infinitude of questions.

And it's not just religion—Carse believes that infinite games also explain the endurance of the best culture, whether it's Shakespeare or *Sgt. Pepper's*. "The best literature is never solved," Carse says. "You might see *Hamlet* once and think you get it, but then you see it again and you realize you didn't get it, or that you got it wrong. So you keep returning, you keep playing." The canon isn't composed of texts with clear takeaways. It's composed of texts whose meaning is mercurial and unstable. Such infinite games probably sound frustrating. Why bother with a mystery box that can't be opened? Why read a whodunit that never tells you who did it? Why believe in a religion that keeps changing the rules?

Yet, as Carse points out, there is joy in such eternal pursuits. "You try to describe an infinite game to a grown-up and they get this skeptical look on their face," Carse says. "They can't imagine playing a game you can't win. But then you look at a child, at when they're happiest, and it's usually when they're playing in their own world, making up their own rules, engaged in an activity that has no stopping point. They're happiest playing in an infinite game."

This chapter explores the techniques of the best infinite games. How do they hold our attention? How do they keep us playing pursuits we never win? The key, it turns out, is to use multiple mystery hooks, creating a work of culture that keeps confounding in different ways.

## The Game Is Afoot

In the summer of 1998, Jason Hallock was working as a reader for a movie production company. He devoured multiple books and scripts every day, looking for content that could become the next big Hollywood hit. He rejected the vast majority of his reading. "You see enough and you learn the tells of the derivative stuff," Jason says. "Most stories are a copy of a copy, and the original was better."[3]

One day, a bound galley of a British children's novel landed on Jason's desk. He was told there was a little "heat on it"—the book was getting buzz—so he added it to his pile. The cover looked cute, but not particularly promising, at least for a movie studio. "I mean, it had *philosopher* in the title," Jason remembers. "That doesn't scream blockbuster."

But then he began reading. By page five, he was entranced. By the end of the third chapter, he was in love. Jason finished the book a few hours later and immediately wrote a rare review. Here are the key lines from his coverage:

"A wonderful, creative children's fantasy that is bursting with imagination and big screen potential. It has the appeal of a classic fairytale combined with an eye-popping visual environment. . . . Ultimately, all of these elements work together to create an incredibly engaging narrative."

Jason's praise grabbed the attention of his boss, who called him on the phone. "She asked me if I was serious about this," Jason remembers. "I told her I was dead serious, that it was really great. So she went in to her boss, who was a senior vice president, and her boss thought it sounded strange. But she also knew that I didn't give very many positive endorsements, so she canceled her lunch and read the book." The senior vice president also fell in love and rushed into the office of the head of production. She slammed the book down on his desk and told him that they had to buy the rights immediately. "He glances at the book and reads the jacket copy," Jason remembers. "Then he shakes his head and says, 'I don't know . . . wizard school?'"

The book was *Harry Potter and the Sorcerer's Stone*. (The title had been tweaked from the original British version, *Harry Potter and the Philosopher's Stone*.) When Jason and the other executives tried to convince the head of production to change his mind, he responded that even if the book was good, the reported asking price of $500,000 was way too high for a first-time fantasy author.

He was wrong. The movie adaptation of *Harry Potter and the Philosopher's Stone* has grossed more than $1 billion, with the total series bringing in more than $7 billion at the box office. "The head of production is a smart guy, but he said no to buying one of the most popular story franchises in history," Jason says. "And all because he didn't think wizard school sounded interesting."

Jason Hallock is now the top story analyst at Paramount Pictures, tasked with identifying blockbuster plots and fixing those broken ones that have already been paid for. I met him on a late-spring day at the sprawling studio on Melrose Avenue; he gave me the full tour, showing me the New York City back lot and the massive Blue Sky Tank, which allows filmmakers to shoot elaborate water scenes in the middle of Los Angeles. To see the sets up close is to learn how much the camera can hide, and how easily we overlook its tricks. The streets of Manhattan, for instance, are all stucco facade—even the bricks are hollow—while most of the cinematic backdrops are just garishly painted walls. "It's a bit much in person, but it works on film," Jason says. Prop artists hustle fake furniture around; we peek into a soundstage and watch as an imaginary paradise is disassembled. Plastic palm trees are loaded on trucks. Golden sand is shoveled into wheelbarrows. A lonely tiki hut waits in the corner.

When it comes to movies, Jason is one of the last romantics. Although he's been a studio insider for years, his voice still vibrates with delight when he discusses Fredric March's performance in *The Best Years of Our Lives*—"Maybe the best drunk acting *ever*," Jason says—or the perfect comic notes in *Raiders of the Lost Ark*. "Movies have always been a hard sell. You're asking people to spend fifteen dollars a ticket to sit for a few hours in a dark room with strangers," Jason says, a few months before a pandemic would shut theaters down. "They're an even harder sell now, when everyone has all this content available on their phones. The only way that ticket is worth it is if you give them something enthralling."

Jason cites the beginning of *Harry Potter* as an example. "What is it about those first pages that sucked me in? J. K. Rowling doesn't begin at wizard school, which would be the obvious place. She begins instead on a very ordinary suburban street, but it's an ordinariness that highlights these little details we don't understand." There's a cat reading a map, and tawny owls flying around, and these odd professors in long robes talking about someone who can't be named. None of it makes sense, at least not yet, but these puzzling specifics activate our curiosity. Who are these people? And what are they doing on Privet Drive?

These questions are mystery boxes. Like *Star Wars*, which also throws us into a strange world full of unknowns, Rowling triggers our curiosity by depriving us of explanation.* "My job is to read fiction, but there are a lot of books and scripts where by page three, I'm like, 'I already know what's going to happen,'" Jason says. "'I have no more questions.' But with *Harry Potter* it was the opposite. I just kept turning the page."

---

* A similar technique is used by Marvel, the most successful movie franchise in history. The superhero genre is defined by its utter lack of narrative mystery: the good guys always win. (*Avengers: Endgame* was never going to end with the triumph of Thanos.) The triumph of Marvel is to create mystery boxes within its closed universe, thus ensuring our attention even when the plot is predictable.

The tradition began with a post-credits scene in *Iron Man*, as Tony Stark walks into his mansion and is greeted by Nick Fury. "You think you're the only superhero in the world?" Nick asks. "You've become part of a bigger universe. You just don't know it yet." Subsequent credit scenes continued the tradition, implying even bigger universes. The after-credit sequence for *Captain America: Civil War* references *Black Panther*—a movie that wouldn't be released for another two years—while the after-credits for *Avengers: Infinity War* anticipate *Captain Marvel*. Meanwhile, the Infinity Gauntlet, a weapon that plays a crucial role in a 2018 Marvel film, is first glimpsed in *Thor*, released in 2011. As the researchers Spencer Harrison, Arne Carlsen, and Miha Skerlavaj observe, in their analysis of Marvel's success, these subtle references "provoke an intense interest in characters, plotlines and entirely new worlds. Its whole universe has the feel of a puzzle that anyone can engage with."

Rowling's use of mystery boxes is not an accident. In interviews, she's described the *Harry Potter* novels as obeying the basic detective-story structure: "I think the *Harry Potter* books are in many ways whodunits in disguise," Rowling said. (Since completing the *Potter* series, Rowling has written a series of adult detective stories under a pseudonym.) Like a good crime mystery, a central unknown propels each Potter novel, whether it's the bad guy searching for the philosopher's stone, or the location of the last Horcrux. The reader is led to a certain suspect—it must be Snape!—before Rowling delivers a reversal worthy of Agatha Christie. (It's Quirrell! And Harry himself is the last Horcrux!) In retrospect, the necessary clues have been there all along. We just didn't know how to read them.

These surprising reversals are made possible by a narrative style that Rowling also borrows from detective fiction: the "third person limited omniscient view." She describes her characters in the third person—Harry Potter is not the voice of *Harry Potter*—but her narrative voice shares their limited, blinkered perspective. The style allows the writer to draw out the mystery, tricking readers with errant suspects and other prediction errors. We never know more than Harry, and he never knows very much.

The power of these mystery boxes is temporary. We eventually learn that the cat is Professor McGonagall, and that Voldemort is hiding inside Quirrell. To create a more meaningful mystery—to invent an infinite game—it's essential to include mysteries that aren't unboxed at the end. These questions persist, no matter how many times we reread the novels.

*Harry Potter and the Philosopher's Stone* starts creating those kinds of mysteries in chapter 2, which jumps ten years into the future. Harry is now a small and skinny boy, living in a dark cupboard under some stairs. His glasses are held together with tape. "On the one hand, Harry is a character you've seen a million times before," Jason says. "He's the frog who turns out to be a prince. In the hands of a lesser writer, he would be a boring cliché. But what makes him so compelling are those little particulars. The glasses. The strange scar. The snake in the zoo." These are iconic details because they perfectly describe a character while also filling in his world; we get a glimpse of Harry, but also his precarious existence. He's a wizard messiah who doesn't even know wizards exist.

As the story unfolds, Rowling complicates Harry's character. He might be the hero, but he's got some uncanny connections to Voldemort, the villain. Harry, too, can speak with snakes, and the wands of the two are brothers. They can eavesdrop on each other's thoughts. The result is a blurring of the boundaries between good and evil. While Rowling could have given us the flat characters typical of the fantasy genre, she instead gifts us a rounded cast, each with surprises and opacities.

Just look at Severus Snape, the potions teacher at Hogwarts. On a first read, Snape is an obvious nemesis, a bad guy from the bad house. He is cruel toward the kids from Gryffindor. He murders Dumbledore. He gives away Harry's escape plan. (Are you worried I just spoiled the book for you? Keep reading.) However, once we know how Snape's story ends—in one of the most stunning reversals, he turns out to be a brave double agent—we're able to see the sly logic behind his sins. His mean streak might be sincere, but it might also be an act for Voldemort. It's a question that never gets fully resolved. The result is that Snape becomes more interesting with each rereading. His opaqueness increases.

As Jason notes, complicated characters are a defining feature of all replayable stories. He cites *The Godfather* trilogy as an example of another epic that highlights the mystery of its imaginary people. "People can see *The Godfather* twenty times because it's an incredible world, populated by these really interesting people," Jason says. "And when you rewatch it, that means you keep noticing new things. The characters keep changing." Take a scene from the first *Godfather*. Michael is meeting Sollozzo and McCluskey at a popular Italian restaurant in the Bronx. A gun has been hidden in the bathroom. (Michael is planning on killing Sollozzo and McCluskey since they tried to kill his father.) Michael excuses himself, retrieves the weapon, and—just as an elevated train comes to a loud halt—fires three bullets at point-blank range. His face is panicked as he drops the gun and runs out of the restaurant.

It's an iconic few minutes of cinema, and not just because it's the pivotal moment when Michael crosses over to the dark side. (David Chase was heavily influenced by this scene when creating the last moments of *The Sopranos*.) What makes this suspenseful scene so rewatchable are the revealing details—McCluskey, the corrupt cop, distracted by his veal chop, Sollozzo's obvious contempt, Michael struggling to contain his nerves. As the film and sound editor Walter Murch observes, one of the reasons we pay such close attention to these character details is because Francis Ford Coppola, the director of the *Godfather* movies, had Michael and Sollozzo speak in Italian but refused to provide subtitles. "It's very bold, even today, to have an extended scene between two main characters in an English-language film speaking another language with no translation," Murch said in an interview with the writer Michael Ondaatje. "As a result you're paying much more attention to *how* things are said and the body language being used, and you're perceiving things in a very different way."[4]

Coppola also focuses our attention by not using music during the scene. "Most movies use music the way athletes use steroids," Murch says. "It gives you an edge, it gives you a speed, but it's unhealthy for the organism in the long run."[5] The reason it's unhealthy, according to Murch, is that music in movies is often used to strip away the mystery. Instead of having to decode the subtext for ourselves, the music dictates our feelings, telling us to be scared or happy, nervous or sad. By denying us this emotional shortcut, Coppola forces the audience to grapple with the complexity of his protagonist. The silent soundtrack heightens the suspense; we have no idea what Michael will actually do. "I feel differently about these characters every time I rewatch the movie," Jason says. "That's the genius of it. I've got the shots memorized, but it's always a different experience watching it."

The infinite games of *Harry Potter* start with mystery boxes and opaque characters. But Rowling doesn't stop there: she also makes extensive use of the ambiguity hook. Consider the famous prophecy that sets the story in motion, leading Voldemort to murder Harry's parents. Rowling was inspired by *Macbeth*. In that play, Macbeth receives a prophecy from the witches that "no man that's born of a woman / shall ever have power upon thee." This prediction gives Macbeth a reckless confidence, but only because he ignores the ambiguity of the words. In the end, Macbeth is vanquished by Macduff, who was born by cesarean section. (He was "from his mother's womb / untimely ripped.") For Rowling, the moral of *Macbeth* is that prophecies are full of ambiguities. They require interpretation, just like a literary text.

In *Harry Potter*, the prophecy is revealed by Professor Sybill Trelawney, a rather unreliable professor of divination. A few months before Harry was born, Trelawney announces that "the one with the power to vanquish the Dark Lord [Voldemort] approaches . . . Born to those who have thrice defied him, born as the seventh month dies . . . and the Dark Lord will mark him as his equal, but he will have power the Dark Lord knows not . . .

and either must die at the hand of the other for neither can live while the other survives."

Like Macbeth, Voldemort misinterprets the prophecy by ignoring the ambiguity. He assumes that the prophecy is about the newly born Harry Potter, which is why he tries to kill the baby boy. (He ends up killing Harry's parents instead.) It's not until the sixth book that we fully learn the prophecy wasn't prophetic at all. Dumbledore explains:

"Harry, never forget that what the prophecy says is only significant because Voldemort made it so. . . . Voldemort singled you out as the person who would be most dangerous to him—and in doing so, he *made* you the person who would be most dangerous to him!"

In an interview, Rowling refers to the ambiguous prophecy as "the Macbeth idea: the witches tell Macbeth what will happen and he then continues to make it happen."[6] And so Trelawney's prediction becomes a lesson in interpretation. Rowling (via Dumbledore) is reminding us that the most interesting texts must be unpacked, that they contain ambiguities that can't easily be solved. As Shira Wolosky, a professor of English literature at Hebrew University, writes in *The Riddles of Harry Potter*, "In many ways the Potter books are classically patterned as quests, but in the broadest sense, what Harry and those around him pursue are secrets and riddles. In this sense the 'quest' is the act of interpretation itself."[7]

"Why did you have to make it so difficult?" Harry asks Dumbledore, near the end of the series. This question could also be asked of Rowling, who fills her young adult novels with mystery boxes, prediction errors, opaque characters, and ambiguity. She makes it difficult, of course, because the pleasure resides in the search. It is not the solution that entertains and edifies—it's the mystery. This, perhaps, is Dumbledore's greatest teaching. After he dies, the headmaster leaves behind a final will dense with riddles, gifting his favorite students with items that, at first glance, seem rather useless. (Ron, for instance, is left with a deluminator, an object that can suck all the light from a room.) Not until Voldemort is defeated do the students understand the point of Dumbledore's bequest. It was never about the things themselves. The real gift was the interpretative journeys they inspired.

The same could be said of the *Harry Potter* novels. They are densely plotted whodunits—our first read is inevitably rushed, as we race to open all the mystery boxes. However, the true genius of the novels is that they exceed their intricate plots. Even after we know how the stories end, we are still compelled to reread them, parsing the text the way Dumbledore taught us to.* We realize that everyone is more complicated than we thought, and that the prophecies are not actually prophecies at all. As Wolosky writes, what the *Harry Potter* books show "is that such interpretation is never-ending, since the world we live in is one of inexhaustible meanings."[8] And so the text remains an infinite game, full of mysteries that never get old. Not bad for a book about wizard school.

## Spoiler Alert

There is a simple test to determine if a text is an infinite game: *spoil it*. Tell an eager nine-year-old that Harry defeats Voldemort. Does she put down the book? Whisper to a seatmate that *Hamlet* is a tragedy—everyone dies. Does he leave the theater? Put on

---

* Harry Potter has also inspired near-infinite amounts of fan fiction, as readers seek new ways of continuing the game.

*The Godfather* and announce that Michael can't escape the family business. Is the movie ruined?

The answer is that these spoilers don't matter. The best art is unspoilable, an infinite game that doesn't require an ignorant audience. It's a basic fact of entertainment that we seem to have forgotten. We live in a time of constant spoiler alerts: it's nearly impossible to read a review about a piece of entertainment without encountering the requisite warning.* The logic behind such warnings is straightforward: If we know what will happen, then we'll lose interest in the story. The power of *Harry Potter* depends on the secrets of its end.

The good news is that there's solid scientific evidence that spoilers are not nearly as ruinous as we think. In a study published in *Psychological Science*, Jonathan Leavitt and Nicholas Christenfeld gave hundreds of undergraduates twelve different short stories.[9] The stories came in three different flavors: ironic-twist stories (such as Chekhov's "The Bet"), whodunits ("A Chess Problem" by Agatha Christie), and "literary stories" by writers such as John Updike. Some subjects read the story as is, without a spoiler. Some read the story with a spoiler carefully embedded in the actual text, as if Chekhov himself had given away the end. And some read the story with a spoiler disclaimer in the preface.

Here's the shocking twist: the scientists found that almost every single story, regardless of genre, was *more* pleasurable when

---

* The philosophy professor Richard Greene, in his history of spoilers, writes that "spoiler alerts" are intertwined with technology. The first "spoiler alert"—a warning about the ending of a forgotten *Star Trek* film—happened in 1982 on a Usenet news group. However, Greene writes, "It wasn't until 2000 that the term 'spoiler alert' became commonplace across the Internet," a ubiquity that parallels the sprawling reach and speed of the internet.

prefaced with a spoiler. Although we've long assumed that our pleasure depends on not knowing the ending, this new research suggests that the tension actually detracts from our enjoyment. An easy way to make a good story even better is to spoil it at the start.

When I first read this study, I was skeptical. Wasn't it the suspense that kept us engaged? How could our intuitions about spoilers be so incorrect? Christenfeld assured me that such skepticism was quite common: "I'd say ninety percent of people, when I tell them our results, just don't believe it. They all tell me about the time someone spoiled this or that for them."

However, as Christenfeld points out, his spoiler study wouldn't be nearly as counterintuitive for premodern audiences. For thousands of years, mass culture consisted entirely of stories whose endings were foretold, from the Greek tragedy to the Shakespearean comedy. Homer's audience knew who won the Trojan War (and what happened to Achilles), while Jane Austen's readers never doubted that her books would end with a wedding. Even George Lucas wasn't afraid of spoilers: in 1976, a year before *A New Hope* was released, he told the *New York Times* that the Death Star would be destroyed at the movie's end.[10] "Genre fiction is, by definition, very predictable," Christenfeld says. "But nobody complained that Shakespeare spoiled *All's Well That Ends Well* with his title."*

Why don't spoilers ruin the story? According to Christenfeld, it's because the splendor of the imaginary world matters more than the uncertainty of the ending: "When you read or watch a

---

* The scholar Allen Redmon, at Texas A&M University–Central Texas, argues that the concept of the spoiler is rooted in the myth of "a pure or virginal text." We bring the same moralistic assumptions to the movies that we bring to sex, supposing that something is lost after the first time.

fiction, you willfully enter into it. You're suspending your disbelief, choosing to get emotionally invested in this place that doesn't exist and might not even be possible. My argument is that if you can trick yourself into believing in aliens or dragons or whatever, then you can also suspend knowledge of what happens next." Put another way, we're so good at slipping into fictional universes that spoilers are mostly irrelevant. The imagination is more powerful than we think.

This still doesn't explain why spoilers can make certain stories *more* enjoyable. One hypothesis is that spoilers draw our attention to the lasting mysteries of the art, much like Coppola withholding subtitles so we notice the subtleties of Pacino's performance. Or look at *Harry Potter*: once we know what happens to Snape, we're free to appreciate his complex motivations. The flat nemesis becomes a rounded character. "Spoilers make it better because they free you to notice more of everything else, since you're not just focused on what's going to happen next," Christenfeld says. "And that everything else"—those insoluble elements that draw us into the fictional world—"are a big source of what we enjoy."* We think spoilers reduce the mystery. But when it comes to great art, they actually *increase* it.

Plot is a finite game—every story has a beginning, middle, and end. Yet, even within this limited structure, some writers find a

---

* *Citizen Kane* begins with a classic mystery box, as the tycoon Charles Foster Kane utters "Rosebud" with his last, dying breath. When we watch the movie for the first time, we are pulled along by our curiosity: What could *Rosebud* possibly mean? The answer, given away in the final shot, is that Rosebud was the name of the sled Kane played with as an eight-year-old. It's an underwhelming reveal, a seemingly random scrap of memory. But that's also the point. When we rewatch the movie, the insignificance of Rosebud forces us to ponder the larger mystery of Kane. We might know the secret of his final word, but we understand even less about the man.

way to encompass the infinite. They do this by inventing questions that never get answered, no matter how many times we reread the text or rewatch the movie. "I don't go back to my favorite films because I forgot the story," Jason Hallock says. "I go back to them because there's something there that I still don't get. There's a sense with them that I'm always missing something, that there's more going on than I can ever see."

## "The Figure in the Carpet"

In 1896, Henry James published a short story called "The Figure in the Carpet."[11] At first read, the story is a simple questing tale: the unnamed narrator is determined to divine the true meaning of the novelist Hugh Vereker's work, a hidden theme the writer compares to "a complex figure in a Persian carpet." Despite spending a "maddening month" searching for this secret, the narrator discovers nothing. Then tragedy strikes: Vereker dies, taking the secret with him to the grave. The narrator's quest ends in failure. The figure in the carpet is never found.

James almost certainly intended the story as a criticism of those searching for concealed themes in his own art. The ambitious narrator wants to solve Vereker's fiction, but the secret is there is no secret. He didn't fail because he couldn't find the key. He failed because there was nothing to find. Literature is an infinite game.

The failure to appreciate mystery is a common error, and not just for literary critics. Gregory Treverton, the former chairman of the National Intelligence Council, makes an important distinction between puzzles and mysteries.[12] The Cold War, he said, was defined by its puzzles: American intelligence agencies were seeking answers to solvable questions: How many nuclear warheads did the Soviets have? Where were the missiles located? How far could they travel? Such puzzles, he says, are about missing information. The answer is out there—it just needs to be located.

But not every intelligence question has a settled answer. Take the threat of terrorism. As Treverton writes, "Terrorists shape themselves to our vulnerabilities: the threat they pose depends on us."[13] The attackers on September 11 were not trained pilots or aviation experts—they simply noticed a weakness in our airport screening procedures. Treverton's point is that trying to identify a terrorist attack is very different from counting Soviet missiles, since the answer depends on "the future interaction of many factors, known and unknown." The lack of a clear answer means that it's not a puzzle—it's a *mystery*. It's not about finding the missing piece of information, but about dealing with uncertainty and ambiguity.* When it comes to mysteries, Treverton notes, "the analysis begins where the evidence ends."[14]

Unfortunately, intelligence agencies often attempt to turn mysteries into puzzles. Like Henry James's narrator, they're playing an infinite game, but they keep trying to find definitive solutions. Treverton cites the hunt for Iraq's weapons of mass destruction as an example. The intelligence agencies were searching for hidden caches—that's the puzzle approach—when they should have been trying to grapple with Saddam's complicated psychology. (Because he was so scared of insurrection and other "local threats," Saddam bragged about weapons he didn't have.) As a result, they imposed an overconfident conclusion onto some fuzzy satellite evidence.

---

* The psychological literature distinguishes between *epistemic* uncertainty (puzzles) and *aleatory* uncertainty (mysteries).

Convinced they'd glimpsed Saddam's chemical weapons tankers, they were actually looking at fire trucks.[15]

How do we avoid these mistakes? Philip Tetlock and Barbara Mellers, psychologists at the University of Pennsylvania, have shown that it's possible to dramatically improve our predictions of the future. The scientists began by identifying a promising set of amateur forecasters, tasked with predicting the outcome of various events. These people came from all walks of life. There was a computer science teacher and a bureaucrat with the Department of Agriculture, a mathematics professor and a struggling filmmaker. What made these people so promising was their "active open-mindedness." As Tetlock puts it, they treated their "beliefs as hypotheses to be tested, not treasures to be protected."[16]

After picking those promising amateurs, Tetlock and Mellers asked them to make forecasts about various world events, from the conflict in Syria to the likelihood of a trade war with China. The scientists gave the volunteers extensive feedback about their predictions, along with a quick introduction to the most common cognitive errors. After three years, this simple training system generated some incredible results. In particular, it has led to the emergence of what Tetlock calls "super-forecasters," amateurs who are able to consistently beat experts and algorithms. In many instances, the victories were resounding, with the super-forecasters proving to be 35 to 65 percent more accurate than their competitors. They even beat intelligence analysts at the CIA with access to classified information.[17]

What accounts for the success of these super-forecasters? Tetlock and Mellers emphasize their humility. They know what they don't know. They are constantly revising their beliefs, updating their opinions. When discussing their predictions with others, they disagree gently, aware that the future is open to endless interpretation. Because they treat prediction like an infinite game, and not like a finite puzzle, they end up making far more accurate forecasts.

James Carse appreciates the practical benefits of infinite games. In conversation, he seems tickled that his little treatise has gained a second life, cited by cognitive psychologists, business consultants, and the progressive Silicon Valley set. "I do think there's an increasing recognition that treating the world like a finite game can come with negatives," he says. "Finite games tend to induce a style of thinking that sees the world in very black-and-white terms. They create the kind of status competitions that make a lot of us miserable."* If our sense of worth comes from finite games, Carse says, then we're setting ourselves up for a lifetime of disappointment: "You're never going to be rich enough, never going to win enough."

This is why we need infinite games and their infinite mysteries. Because there are no winners and losers, just players, infinite games show us how to live within the moment, embracing experience as an end unto itself. It's not about defeating anyone or solving anything—it's about admiring the layers and enjoying the unknown. It's about playing the game with other people. "Think of that sandlot baseball," Carse says. "We weren't concerned with the score. Even at our age we realized that playing was the fun part. Not winning. Just the playing."**

---

* Consider social media. Instead of bringing us closer together, the sharing platforms become a competition for likes and followers and retweets.

** A good story is like that never-ending baseball game, bringing us together around a shared experience. In a series of studies, the Uri Hasson has looked at what happens to the brain when people are engrossed in complex narratives. He's shown them Hitchcock scenes, Larry David sketches, and Sergio Leone westerns. His results are remarkable. Within seconds of the story beginning, the brains of the subjects start to converge on the same patterns of activity. Hasson refers to this process as "neural entrainment." In his talks, he uses the example of five metronomes to show how

That's also the lesson of unspoilable texts, whether it's the Talmud or *Hamlet* or the bounteous world of *Harry Potter*. We will not decipher these writings—there is no figure to be found—but that doesn't mean they aren't full of wisdom, or that we can't learn from their impenetrable mysteries. "The real value in teaching these old books is to show students how to confront the unknown," Carse says. "I never cared if my students remembered what I taught. I cared about how they approached the subject. Did they accept the mystery? Did they have a sense of modesty? The best teaching is really teaching students how to live with ignorance."

## Awe Is the Ubermystery

Why do infinite games exist? One answer is that they're useful. They keep us humble. They help us cope with uncertainty. They teach us how to think more effectively. But then the same could be said of statistics, and our cultural canon isn't full of statistical manuals.

The real reason infinite games have been celebrated for thousands of years is because of how they make us *feel*. Their cognitive benefits are a side effect. It's our emotions that keep us playing these games, even if we never find a way to win.

---

the entrainment happens. At first, the metronomes are all ticking at different times, just like those individual brains before the story. But then he places the metronomes on a pair of vibrating cylinders. Within seconds, the external vibrations start to synchronize the metronomes, bending them all to the same beat. Stories work the same way. "There are so many things in life that exaggerate our differences," Hasson says. "But the best stories give us an experience that we can share with strangers at a pretty fundamental level."

So what feelings do infinite games inspire? The most important one is awe. Much of the scientific research on awe has been led by psychologist Dacher Keltner at the University of California, Berkeley. As Keltner notes, awe can be triggered in countless conditions. "If I think about my own experience of awe, I think about Chichen Itza, down in the Mayan culture, or Sainte-Chapelle in Paris," he says. "I think about the leek soup I had at Chez Panisse that one time."[18]

These different sources might seem as if they have nothing in common. But Keltner says they actually share two fundamental properties: "The first property of awe is that it feels vast. It has vastness built into it." Think of a layered text, or the view of Yosemite Valley, or a soup with an uncommon depth of flavor: there is a sense of infinity, a feeling that we will never know it all.

The second property, Keltner says, is that the source "transcends our understanding of the world." It's confusing and confounding, requiring a process that psychologists refer to as "accommodation," as we adjust our old ideas and expectations to the awesome experience. We don't know how to read this poem. We can't begin to explain this magic trick. We have no idea how this painting was made or this church was built, or why we're crying as we reread *Harry Potter* for the third time. *The mystery is manifest.*

In ordinary life, such conditions can make us uncomfortable, even scared. What is that unknowable thing? And why is it so vast? Every other animal is wired to run away in these situations, to flee from the surfeit of ambiguity and prediction errors. But humans are capable of experiencing a different feeling: given the right context, and the right content, we can turn our fear into wonder. The trembling becomes goose bumps. The dread is transformed into awe.[19]

In recent years, Keltner and colleagues have documented the

psychological benefits of awe experiences. "The first thing you find is that awe really transforms your mind, and how you look at your social world," Keltner said in a recent lecture. "We have big parts of the frontal lobes that help us think about the interests of other people . . . What we're finding is that brief doses of awe move us from a model of self-interest to being more engaged with the interests of others."

You can track this shift in the brain. One fascinating piece of evidence involves the default mode network, a circuit of brain areas that's associated with self-representation and personal goals. As Keltner wrote in an email, the default mode network "is engaged by processing information from an egocentric point of view. It is the neural substrate of your default self."

According to research by Michio Nomura and colleagues, awe hushes this egocentric network.[20]* When the scientists showed people videos of awe-inspiring natural sights, they found a significant reduction in activity in areas associated with the default mode. But the brain wasn't going silent. Although the default mode was less active, the scientists observed a surge of activity in the cingulate cortex, an area associated with the processing of rewards. "What this means," Kelter says, "is that our pure experiences of awe . . . feel rewarding, good, and delightful." The ego fades away, replaced by a sprawling sense of wonder.

The dissolution of the ego also changes our behavior. In one experiment, Keltner and colleagues divided students into two groups. Some students were asked to look up at a grove of towering eucalyptus trees for one minute. "When you gaze up at these

---

* Other experiences that silence the default mode network include meditation, prayer, and various psychedelic drugs such as psilocybin.

trees, with their peeling bark and surrounding nimbus of grayish green light, goosebumps may ripple down your neck, a sure sign of awe," Keltner writes. Other students were asked to look in the opposite direction, at the facade of a science building. Then, all of the students encountered a stranger who fell to the ground, dropping his pens in the dirt. The people who were awed by the trees were more likely to help.

Along with Craig Anderson, Keltner has begun studying the chemical sources of the awe experience.[21] The scientists have found that people with a genetic mutation affecting the D4 type of dopamine receptor are significantly more likely to report awe after watching a short film about the universe. (The mutation is believed to make dopamine more potent.) They're also more likely to feel awe while white-water rafting, and during the course of a normal week. This builds on previous research linking the D4 mutation to exploratory behavior, with the mutation appearing more frequently in human populations that migrated farther in the distant past.[22] One possibility is that humans evolved the capacity for awe so that we could venture into the vast unknown. Instead of being scared by new places, we are moved by their mystery. The horizon beckons.

Most of us aren't explorers. We live in cities and suburbs, far removed from astonishing natural scenes. This means that the most likely place we experience awe is our own creations. By engaging with material we can't understand—content that feels infinite and requires accommodation—art hijacks these ancient exploratory instincts. Keltner has shown, for instance, that inducing awe in the laboratory makes people far more interested in abstract paintings. They also spend longer on difficult puzzles. They are more curious about the novel and strange.

This research helps reveal the virtuous feedback loop between mysterious art and the emotion of awe. When we pay attention to content defined by its vast unknowns, we are filled with a powerful and uplifting feeling. That feeling, in turn, makes us want to keep exploring the work, which leads to even more awe.

The game goes on and on.

# CHAPTER 7

# THE HARKNESS METHOD

The secret of Education lies in respecting the pupil.
It is not for you to choose what he shall know,
what he shall do. It is chosen and foreordained,
and he only holds the key to his own secret.

—RALPH WALDO EMERSON, "EDUCATION"

## Emerson in Cabrini-Green

To get to the Noble Academy from downtown Chicago, you take one of the broad boulevards that begin at the lake, amid the fancy stores of the Gold Coast. Eventually you'll hit Clybourn Avenue, a diagonal street that cuts across the grid like a scar. For decades, Clybourn was the northern boundary line of Cabrini-Green, a notorious public housing development that became a symbol of urban dysfunction. The red-and-white towers were patrolled by members of the Gangster Disciples, wielding automatic weapons and selling crack in the courtyards.

Those buildings are gone; the last Cabrini-Green project was demolished in 2011. The neighborhood has been replaced by the so-called "new city," a splotchy sprawl of low-rise condos, hold-out bodegas, and strip malls anchored by a Starbucks. There's a new Target, but also plenty of shuttered factories covered in faded

NO TRESPASSING signs. Empty grass fields surround a supermarket selling poke bowls and kombucha.

The Noble Academy is across the street from that supermarket, in a squat brick building that used to be the elementary school for the Cabrini-Green projects. The school has since been renovated, but original details remain, such as the bulletproof glass, heavy security doors, and black metal bars.

The academy began as an unlikely experiment. In 2007, an anonymous donor paid for a freshman from the Noble Network of Charter Schools in Chicago to spend the summer at Phillips Exeter Academy, the elite boarding school in rural New Hampshire. Exeter's campus is one of genteel beauty. For a student visiting from inner-city Chicago, the manicured lawns and painted white window frames probably felt like a faraway foreign country.

The first summer exchange with Exeter was a disaster—the Noble student insisted on returning to Chicago after two days. Nevertheless, Ethan Shapiro, the director of the Exeter summer school, stayed in contact with leaders at the Noble Network. At the time, the Noble Network had just three campuses—it's now seventeen high schools and one middle school, serving over twelve thousand students—but it was already recognized as a model charter program, with graduation rates and test scores that far exceeded the average at Chicago public schools. Despite the initial mishap, Exeter and Noble decided to try again. In the summer of 2008, twelve students from Noble schools visited Exeter. This time, they stayed.

Their experience had lasting consequences. When school resumed in the fall in Chicago, the Noble teachers noticed that the students who had attended Exeter had a certain swagger in the classroom. They were more likely to raise their hands; they weren't easily intimidated by hard texts; they showed poise during group discussions.

What accounted for this newfound confidence? One possibility was the Exeter pedagogy, which is known as the Harkness method. In 1930, the philanthropist Edward Harkness gave $5.8 million to Exeter (roughly $99 million in current dollars) to transform the school's approach to education. Although Harkness had gone to the best schools in the country, he felt his education had been a disappointment, full of tedious lessons and forgotten facts. He wanted to pioneer a better way.[1]

The Harkness gift led Exeter to pioneer the Harkness method. In the typical school, the teachers perform for the students. They are responsible for breaking down the material and constructing the knowledge. In a Harkness class, the cognitive load is designed to be on the students, who are tasked not just with memorization but with figuring out what they need to remember. "Harkness teaching can take many different forms, but it's really student-centered, student-led discussions," says Meg Foley, an instructor of history at Exeter affiliated with the Exeter Humanities Institute, which trains teachers in the Harkness method. "The philosophy is really that the students are doing the heavy lifting and the teacher is there to nudge, facilitate, make sure the dynamic is a good one."

The shift from the passive lecture required a new curriculum. While the traditional classroom focused on the delivery of answers, the Harkness method emphasized open-ended questions, which could generate lively conversations. Students were given problems, not facts. They were expected to disagree and discuss, to delve into the mystery on their own.

It's a radical approach with deep roots. In Ralph Waldo Emerson's nineteenth-century writings on education, he frequently lamented the soul-crushing strictures of American schooling. "I call our system a system of despair," Emerson wrote. The typical class "sacrifice[s] the genius of the pupil, the unknown possibilities of his nature, to a neat and safe uniformity."[2] In place of these rules, Emerson emphasized the need for student independence; children learn best when they teach themselves. "Everybody delights in the energy with which boys deal and talk with each other, the mixture of fun and earnest, reproach and coaxing, love and wrath." His point was that teachers should harness this youthful energy, not suppress it by delivering sermons and insisting on silence.

The Noble administrators were determined to bring Emerson's philosophy to their Chicago schools. They were persuaded by the anecdotal experience of those summer students, but also a larger belief in social justice. As Pablo Sierra, one of the Noble administrators who led the initial Exeter collaboration, told the *American Scholar*, "I wanted to give my kids what Exeter kids get."[3] Classroom discussion shouldn't be a luxury reserved for students at fancy private schools.

But the leaders of the Noble Network wanted to experiment with the Harkness method for another reason also: their test scores had hit a ceiling, a problem the administrators had come to call "the Noble Plateau." In 2003, when Noble began tracking achievement tests, their students had an average score of 17.3 on the ACT, a test of college readiness. By 2011, that score had risen to 20.3, which was 3.1 points higher than the students' peers in the Chicago public schools. But then the progress stalled: by 2014, three years later, the Noble ACT scores had failed to increase significantly.

This test score plateau was a symptom of a larger disappointment. Although nearly 90 percent of Noble graduates started at a four-year college, only 40 percent ended up graduating. What's more, Noble's own surveys showed that less than 10 percent of graduates ended up in "high-powered careers," such as law or medicine. The Harkness method helped Exeter students prepare for these professions. Could it also help students at Noble?

Implementing the Harkness method on a Noble campus, and not at an elite prep school, had challenges. Because all Noble campuses are nonselective—they take every student who applies, as long as there's space—the incoming students often reflect the broader struggles of the Chicago public school system. Many freshmen are years behind grade level. They lack effective study habits. Eight-five percent come from low-income families. Fifteen percent are special-needs students. While Emerson imagined students conversing about the mysteries of Shakespeare and astronomy, most students starting at Noble are not proficient in reading and math. How could they possibly teach each other?

And there's the problem of class size. The typical Exeter class has twelve students, all of whom fit around the Harkness table; the intimacy of the setup was deemed essential for an effective conversation. At Noble, most classes are closer to thirty students. It's one thing to celebrate the "energy of youth" in a small group. It's something else when the teacher is vastly outnumbered.

Despite these obstacles, the Noble Network began a Harkness experiment in 2009 featuring two groups of fifteen honor students. The administrators chose students with the highest reading scores because these students would be advanced enough to stay on grade level even if the Harkness experiment failed. Most people expected it to fail.

The results were stunning. After a semester of Harkness, thirteen of the thirty students aced the reading portion of the ACT; as a group, their reading scores increased by 30 percent more than their peers at the same Noble campus. The experiment was so successful that one of the teachers, Ms. Clark, decided to try out Harkness in two of her regular classes the next semester. Because these classes had more than thirty students, she had to create three separate Harkness tables; the room was a din of talking teenagers. But the trend remained the same: these students displayed a dramatic increase in reading scores.

Based on these exciting preliminary results, the Noble Network leaders decided to start the Noble Academy, which aimed to build on the promising early results of the Harkness experiments. The school opened in 2014, in a temporary location in downtown Chicago. Two hundred students signed up, most of them poached from the wait lists at other Noble campuses. Lauren Boros was the founding leader. "The first year was incredibly rocky," Lauren says. "We put the kids right away at Harkness tables and it didn't work. The conversations weren't effective. And they weren't effective because we hadn't created the culture yet. The kids didn't know how to work together. They didn't know how to ask questions. They didn't know how to listen." Lauren pauses, as if she's remembering that difficult first year. "Listening is really hard."

## The Noble Academy

Lauren Boros grew up a few blocks from the Cabrini-Green projects, on the nice side of North Avenue. "That street was our dividing line," she says. "You stayed north of North Avenue and you were fine. You were in nice Lincoln Park. You went south and you were in Cabrini-Green. Growing up north of North Ave., you knew you never go south." Lauren attended elite Chicago private schools before going to Columbia University. She was on the premed track when her New York City taxi smashed into a car making a left; Lauren was ejected from the vehicle. She needed eighteen stitches and twelve staples to close the wound in her head. Lauren was riding in the taxi with her best friend, who was African American. Two ambulances showed up. Lauren was taken to New York-Presbyterian, a hospital on the Upper East Side affiliated with Columbia and Cornell. Her friend was taken to a run-down hospital in the Bronx. "It was one of those moments where you realize that these injustices are not accidents," Lauren says. "And even though I was premed, I decided that I wanted to work on these injustices, because I knew that they were keeping kids from reaching their potential."

After graduation, Lauren signed up for Teach for America. She was assigned to a middle school in Gary, Indiana, and commuted from Chicago, leaving her apartment at six in the morning and returning fifteen hours later. "I grew some thick skin very quickly," she remembers. "The very first day I walk in and the students called me 'Barbie.' I said, 'You can't call me that.' So they said, 'Fine. *Miss* Barbie.'"

It was an exhausting job, but Lauren had found her calling. After Teach for America, she worked at her first Noble campus, teaching algebra to ninth graders. Before long, she became the assistant principal. Two years later, she founded the Noble Academy.

I first met Lauren on a gorgeous late-September day, a month into the school year. It was Monday morning, and the hallways were bustling with students in the Noble uniform: black dress shoes, khaki pants, tucked-in navy polo shirts. After countless high fives in the hallway, and an emergency conversation with an assistant principal about a new student who was missing credits, Lauren led me to her office. We sat at an oval table—it's the only official Harkness table at the school, since each one can cost more than $10,000—and Lauren got out her breakfast of a green smoothie.

The best educators have a natural charisma; for whatever reason, you want to listen to them tell you things. Lauren has that charisma. She has long wavy hair, an encouraging smile, and a jaunty, caffeinated energy. There are 450 kids at the academy; Lauren doesn't just know their names, she knows which ones are struggling in which classes, where they want to go to college, and who has recently had a "LaSalle," the Noble slang for after-school detention. When she spots a student with detention—he didn't do his homework—she doesn't admonish him. She tells him that she's looking forward to spending the afternoon together. He smiles in relief.

The Noble Network of schools is high-performing because of its No Excuses culture, which instills a sense of self-discipline and accountability in its students. Although elements of this approach are controversial—if a student receives more than thirteen demerits during the school year, the student has to attend a "character development" class that costs $140—the success of the Noble Network is not. (In 2015, the Noble Network was named the best charter school system in America by the Broad Foundation.) "It all starts with culture," Lauren says. "Before you can do anything else, you have to give students a sense of responsibility. It's learning how to do your homework every night. How to respect your classmates. How to pay attention. These are foundational skills, and they're the foundation of the success of the Noble culture."

But what the ACT ceiling and low college graduation rate revealed is that the focus on discipline is necessary but not sufficient, at least if you want students to reach their full potential. "We were really good at giving students the skills to deal with familiar material," Lauren says. "But I think what the [ACT] ceiling showed us is that that's not enough. If you don't give them the skills to also deal with the unfamiliar, if you don't teach them how to be curious, then you're doing them a real disservice."

The Noble Academy was an attempt to combine that No Excuses culture with the Harkness method, which engages students by confronting them with questions. "In real life, you don't get the answers served up to you," Lauren says. "You get problems, which you have to solve with your peers." Lauren then puts her hand on the Harkness table. "This table is what a staff meeting looks like. It's what a board meeting looks like. It's what a lot of college classes look like. We're preparing you for those places."

Lauren leans forward in her chair; her voice gets quieter, as if she's about to tell me a secret. "Everyone in education likes to use the word *rigorous*. But what does it mean? What people usually mean is that something is 'hard,' so you're a rigorous school if you give out lots of bad grades." She shakes her head in dismay. Lauren then begins sketching two invisible lines with her fingers. "Imagine a graph with two axes. One axis is risk and the other is ambiguity. So you've got this corner here"—she points to the bottom left quadrant—"which is low risk and low ambiguity. That's a math class where you just give the kids the algorithm and they plug and chug. There's no ambiguity and no risk because the teacher knows exactly what she wants. She's got the Platonic ideal of an answer in her head and is pushing the kids to that end."

Lauren then touches the top right corner of her imaginary graph. "What we aim for here is this: high risk and high ambiguity. For us, that's what it means to be rigorous. It means giving the students material that is hard and complex and trusting them to find their own way, to take risks and make mistakes and learn from them." It seems logical that the academy's curriculum might help students build a set of soft skills, such as self-esteem and public speaking. Lauren, though, knew the academy would be judged by the same metric as every other public school: standardized test scores. "That's the game our kids have to play," she says. "You can complain about it, you can scream about the unfairness of it all, how they don't get tutors or any help, but they need that score, otherwise no college is going to give them a chance. That score is what sets them up for a life rich with options."

Most public schools respond to the pressures of standardized testing by teaching to the test, drilling students on the most likely answers. The students practice multiple-choice exams and follow a strict curriculum. Why bother with ambiguity when the tests are so literal? Curiosity is a luxury they can't afford.

The Noble Academy is proof that there's a better way. Although their curriculum does *not* teach to the test—it pretty much does the exact opposite—the academy has seen the largest growth in student scores in the entire Chicago public school system. Among ninth and eleventh graders, Noble Academy students are in the 98th and 97th percentile for "student growth" based on their PSAT and SAT scores.[4] The academy consistently has one of the highest ACT scores of any nonselective school in Chicago, with a college enrollment rate above 91 percent.[5]

Lauren's explanation for this remarkable improvement is rooted in the benefits of mystery: "When you teach kids to be excited about hard questions, when you teach them that not knowing the answer is something to embrace, then you are also giving them a crucial skill for testing. What normally happens when a student sees something on a test they're unfamiliar with is that they freeze and panic. They don't know how to deal. But I think because our kids are used to ambiguity, they find it a little exciting, so they're more willing to tackle those problems first."

It's a training we need. As Lauren notes, ambiguity and uncertainty are inescapable facts of life, and not just on the SAT. "If you have a high-powered job, then you're going to be faced with situations you've never seen before," she says. "There's no rule book you can follow. You're going to have to know how to handle problems that are new and maybe a little scary."

The Noble Academy teaches students how to think about the unknown. By making ambiguous material a central feature of the curriculum, the school shows them that ambiguity isn't just frightening—it's also what makes the classroom such an interesting place, giving rise to all sorts of unpredictable conversations. It's the mystery that keeps us engaged. "We want students to always be at the edge of what they know," Lauren says. "If we can teach them to push themselves, to go to the place where it's going to feel challenging and mysterious, then we're teaching them more than just something to remember for a test. We're teaching them how to keep getting better, no matter where they are or what they do."

Lauren then tells me a story about a senior named Danny. "Danny took a practice [math] SAT and bombed it. And he's a really high performer, so I was like, 'Danny, what happened?' And it turned out that he'd found a hard math problem, one he'd never seen before, and was just really determined to figure it out. He eventually did, but then he had no time left for all the easy questions." Lauren smiles. "That's the monster I created, you know? But as monsters go, I'll take it. We can teach them a few testing hacks. What's much harder to teach is the confidence that comes from dealing with difficult and ambiguous material all day long."

After talking with Lauren, I get a chance to wander around the academy, dropping in on classes to observe the Harkness method in action. I watch students in an AP Environmental Science class working together to assign trophic levels to various animals; when they run into problems, they don't bother Ms. Hanson—they turn to each other and Google. In AP Government, taught by Ms. Traubert, the students were engaging in a line-by-line "translation" of the US Constitution in their Harkness groups. One table was trying to make sense of article I, section 9, which prevents the government from outlawing the slave trade but never uses the word *slave*. ("You can tell they're embarrassed about slavery because they won't say it," says one of the students.) Another table was struggling with why the founding fathers kept suspending the civil rights of anyone "engaged in insurrection or rebellion." "These guys were just rebels, and now they're like, 'If you do what we did, you'll have no rights,'" says a senior named Minerva. "But I guess that's what happens when you get the power."

In AP Calculus, the students worked on a word problem featuring Pascal's triangle. When some of the students got stuck and asked Mr. Rothgeb for help, he didn't give them the answer, or even a useful hint. Instead, he pretended that he didn't know either. Lauren refers to this as "modeling vulnerability" and says it's an important way for teachers to show students the fun of mystery and experimentation. "When I teach my math class, I like to put up a hard problem and tell the kids that I can't solve it, so let's do it together," Lauren says. "That gives you a chance to praise the process, and not just the end result. When we snap"—group snapping is how Noble students applaud one another—"it's never because someone got it correct. We snap because someone is willing to share how they got it wrong, or because they're willing to stand up in front of their friends and give it a shot."

There's empirical proof for the effectiveness of this technique.[6] In the psychology literature, it's called the self-explanation effect, and it results from giving students the freedom to generate answers and explanations for themselves, even if it takes longer and leads to mistakes along the way. (The alternative is "instructor scripted" education, in which teachers don't just give their students the questions—they also tell them how to solve them.) For instance, in a study of the self-explanation effect among third, fourth, and fifth graders, students who got the wrong answer to a math problem were encouraged to "think of a new way to solve the problem."[7] If they still couldn't figure it out, they were shown a wrong answer by another child and asked to explain why it also was incorrect. They were never given the solution by the adult—their struggle was part of the lesson. According to a recent meta-analysis of sixty-nine experiments, self-explanation is a "powerful intervention," capable of enhancing learning across a wide range of subjects, from algebra to reading comprehension.[8]

One of the reasons self-explanation works is because it forces people to acknowledge the mystery. A recent study by physicists at Harvard looked at the impact of the method among college students in an introductory physics class.[9] In the control condition, students were given a standard chalkboard lecture—"the sage on a stage" method—and were explicitly told how to solve the sample problems. In the self-explanation condition, the students were given the exact same information and handouts but had to solve the problems by themselves in small groups. As expected, students in the self-explanation condition scored significantly higher on a subsequent test of learning. They understood the physics material better.

But these educational benefits come with a twist: *the students thought they learned less.* What accounts for this discrepancy? Because the students had to solve the problems on their own, they became "painfully aware of their lack of understanding, in contrast with fluent lectures that may serve to confirm students' inaccurately inflated perceptions of their own abilities." Self-explanation forced them to acknowledge the mystery, all those slippery concepts they still didn't understand. And that's why they learned so much more.

Unfortunately, the typical American classroom is often designed to make learning as easy as possible, which minimizes self-explanation. That, at least, is the conclusion of the TIMSS study, which has been gathering data on the teaching of math and science across the world since 1995. After filming hundreds of classrooms in seven countries in the late '90s, it became clear that American students were usually given simple rules to solve their math problems, or what the researchers described as lessons built around the "use of procedures." (This is what Lauren dismisses as the "plug and chug" method.) According to the data, 55 percent of American eighth-grade math lessons featured the use of procedures; in another 36 percent the teacher gave away the answer without any additional explanation. Less than 10 percent of all lessons tasked students with any sort of self-explanation.

Imagine getting the following problem in math class: you have to draw and define an isosceles right triangle, or a triangle with one ninety-degree angle and two legs that are equal in length. In the American classrooms, the teachers would usually just draw the triangle—this is what it looks like. They might also give the students a straightforward rule for getting the answer. ("Draw two congruent legs and connect them with a right angle.") Such an approach makes the lesson easy. There is no ambiguity, just the efficient delivery of answers.

The downside is that the ease minimizes long-term learning. According to more recent TIMSS results, Japanese students are consistently some of the highest performers on math and science tests in the world. (Only Singapore, Taiwan, and South Korea can compete.)[10] One explanation for the success of Japanese students is the strategies employed by their teachers. When the TIMSS researchers cataloged their classroom time, they found that less than 3 percent of Japanese lessons involved plug and chug or teachers delivering the answers. Instead, their lessons were built around "making connections." While American teachers drew the isosceles right triangle for their students, the Japanese teachers would focus on more fundamental concepts, such as the properties shared by all these triangles, or the meaning of Pythagoras's constant.[11] The eighth graders weren't shown the solution, or even a set of procedures for finding the solution. They were given a problem that they had to solve for themselves. "Part of the reason US students don't do as well on international measures of high school knowledge is that they're doing too well in class," said the cognitive psychologist Nate Kornell, in an interview with David Epstein. "What you want is to make it easy to make it hard."[12*]

Later in the day, I sit down with Danny, that student who bombed the SAT because he couldn't let go of a hard problem. Danny has a mop of unruly curls, a delicate face, and large doe eyes; he speaks quietly, but with the assurance of a teenager used to sharing his thoughts. After college, he wants to be a band teacher. I ask Danny why he thinks the Harkness method leads to such a dramatic boost in test scores. "When you go to a school that teaches

---

* There's a parallel here with social media, and the way it makes it easy for us to overestimate our knowledge, just like those students in typical American classrooms. Facebook is a primary news source for more than 40 percent of Americans. Why is Facebook so popular? Much of the credit belongs to the algorithm that personalizes the News Feed, delivering a unique stream of content to every user. Here's the dismal twist: the software has learned that an efficient way to keep our attention is to serve up content that confirms what we already believe. If you make people feel secure in their opinions, if you filter out the complexity and dissent, they end up spending more time on the social network. The problem is that this leads people to have faith in false beliefs.

to the test, it gets pretty boring because it's just about remembering this or that," he says. "But here you can really dive deep into stuff, and then you get to hear what everyone else thinks, too. It's more work, I guess, but you don't really mind because it's not boring."

The lack of boredom became a consistent theme in my conversations with the students. For them, there was nothing counterintuitive about the success of Harkness at the Noble Academy. Simply put, the high-risk, high-ambiguity method worked because it made their education more *interesting*. "If you are immune to boredom, there is literally nothing you cannot accomplish," writes David Foster Wallace. "It is the key to modern life."[13]

Erin Westgate, a psychologist at the University of Florida, has devoted her career to studying the causes of boredom. She defines boredom as an emotion that "alerts us that we are unable or unwilling to successfully engage attention in meaningful activities."[14] The key word in that definition is *meaningful*. Too often, schools take the meaning of their activities for granted. They assume that students are motivated by grades or test scores or the thrill of understanding quadratic equations. The Harkness approach, however, encourages students to find their own meaning in the curriculum. They control the conversation. They choose the topics. And what they usually end up talking about is the mystery, the material that incites the most debate and disagreement. It might be surprising, but it's not the settled answers that give us meaning. It's the questions. Not knowing is the antidote to boredom.

A senior named Gloria—she wants to major in premed or public policy—described her own transition at the academy: "At first, I didn't really like it here. I was like, 'I'm not even learning anything because all we do is talk about what we don't understand.' But then, as you do it, you realize that's the best way to learn. . . . If you're just told what a book is about, then you're going to forget it.

But if you read the book and you have to decide for yourself what it's saying, and you get to hear what all your friends think, then you're going to pay attention." Gloria laughs, flashing her braces. "Because sometimes what your friends say is totally insane. I'm like, 'Did we even read the same book? How could you possibly think that?' And then they explain and it makes you rethink what you thought."

Not until the end of the school day, as the students are getting ready to leave, do I notice the inscription on the back of their sweatshirts. It's the slogan of the Noble Academy, a mantra repeated every day in every classroom: Take Risks. No Fear. No Shame.

## Knowing What You Don't

When Aida Conroy was in eighth grade, she was awarded a full scholarship to Exeter. She'd attended public schools in Rogers Park, on the far north side of Chicago, and wasn't prepared for the transition. "I grew up just like the kids here [at the Noble Academy]," Aida says. "I thought Exeter would basically be *Harry Potter*. You learn some spells, become a wizard, stuff like that." The reality was far less romantic. Aida was too scared to talk in class. She cried herself to sleep for weeks. "It took me a while to even understand what was expected of me in the Harkness conversations," she remembers. "But over time it became this life-changing experience."

Aida is a Harkness mentor at the Noble Academy. She has a youthful face and an incandescent smile; if she were wearing the academy uniform, and not a bright orange blouse, she could easily pass for a student. Although Aida still teaches, her main focus is on supporting her fellow instructors, sitting in on their classes and offering them advice and feedback. "When you're used to standing up at the front of class and performing for fifty minutes, it can be a pretty big change to Harknessing," she says. "It can feel like you're giving up all control." Aida laughs. "Actually, you *are* giving up all control."

That lack of control often means that teachers have to spend additional time on class preparation, since they never know how the conversation will unfold. "There's no script," Aida says. "Because you're giving the students open-ended prompts, you really have to be prepared for a wide range of possible discussions. It almost never goes how you think it will go."

To deal with this uncertainty, Aida gives Harkness teachers a new set of techniques for interacting with their students. Aida offers the example of the awkward silence. "Sometimes the students are in conversation and there's a long pause. And when you're new to Harkness, it's easy to react and interrupt because you think nothing's happening. But kids have to get comfortable with silence. Sometimes you need that silence to think. That's why I always say it's not an awkward silence—it's a pregnant pause. Something good is going to come out of it."

There were plenty of those pregnant pauses in Becky Wessels's World History class. Becky is another Harkness mentor, and her classroom walls are decorated with suggested conversation prompts for the students, such as "I'd like to complicate that . . ." or "I would suggest a different way of looking at it . . ." or "I'm not entirely convinced that . . ." The students are talking about the trade-offs of empire—the prompts covered the conquests of Rome—and many of their sentences begin with gentle forms of dissent. They disagree with a smile.

Toward the end of class, Ms. Wessels encourages the students to get introspective. They stop talking about ancient Rome and start dissecting their own conversation. Lauren had told me earlier that such self-reflection was one of the key transitions for Noble students. "It's this very meta-moment," she said. "But it's also very important because it means they're taking responsibility for their learning. They realize that a good discussion isn't about the teacher or the content. It's up to them." In Ms. Wessels's history class, one student said they should have used more evidence from the text; another noted that it was hard talking about religion; a boy who stayed quiet during class said he should have asked some follow-up questions.

What struck me about these meta-conversations was the way they captured the essential culture of the Noble Academy. These students have learned that learning is a process, not something handed down by a grown-up. They critique their own conversations because their entire education is a conversation, a shared struggle to find new and better questions to ask each other. Noble Academy students don't walk into the classroom and expect to leave seventy-four minutes later with a notebook full of answers. They walk into the classroom and expect to learn that there are other ways of solving math problems and reading the Constitution and thinking about the world.

When I asked Aida Conroy whether the high test scores of academy students surprised her, she responded by highlighting the limits of the typical No Excuses public school approach: "I have seventy-four instructional minutes a day to teach students that entered high school reading at a sixth-grade level. I could do blatant reading instruction for the whole year and probably make up about two years of growth. Most educators would say that's a success. But I don't think I'd be instilling in them any love and joy of learning if I did that. And the thing about the love and joy of learning, as cheesy as it sounds, is that it transfers. With Harkness, by the end of the year my kids are sending me articles that they want to read in class. They're bringing up issues and problems that I never thought of.

They're learning from each other. And so that seventy-four minutes is expanded, because now they have a better sense of what they don't know. And that becomes what they're most interested in."

What Aida is describing is intellectual humility, a character strength that shapes how we learn and respond to new information. According to the research, those with high levels of intellectual humility are more likely to admit they're wrong or don't understand something. They're also better at seeking out new information that contradicts their beliefs.[15] Instead of embracing certainty, they enjoy the difficult delights of mystery.[16] "A lot of what schools call 'critical thinking' comes down to intellectual humility: knowing what you don't know," notes Angela Duckworth, a psychologist at the University of Pennsylvania.[17] It's an ironic fact of education, but perhaps the most important lesson we learn is the limits of our education.

Intellectual humility isn't on the Illinois state curriculum, and it's not on any standardized test, but it's an essential part of the Noble Academy education. Here on the edge of Cabrini-Green, amid the empty lots and stucco strip malls, these students are learning how to get excited by mystery. They're being trained to seek out hard problems and ambiguous content. Their teachers are celebrating curiosity, even if it leads to the incorrect answer. "The best part for me is when the students are leaving the classroom, walking out the door, and they're still talking about what was discussed at the Harkness table," Aida says. "Because that's when you know it's working. They're applying this way of thinking, of learning, and using it everywhere. It's not just something they do at school. It's become part of their life."

# THE MECHANIC AS DETECTIVE

Doubt is one of the names of intelligence.

—JORGE LUIS BORGES

The Porsche 911 came into the repair shop with a strange problem—the engine wouldn't turn off. Jeff Haugland, co-owner of EuroSpec Motoring, one of the best Porsche specialists in Los Angeles, had dealt with thousands of mechanical issues on these expensive sports cars but he'd never seen a failure like this one. "You would turn the key, take it out, but the engine would keep running," Jeff says. "Do it again, and again, but the engine just would not shut off."[1] Jeff could only stop the engine by starving it of air. "I had to cover the air intake with my bare hands. Like I was strangling it."

This Porsche had a devastating malfunction—a car that won't turn off is inoperable. (The owner had been letting it run until it ran out of gas.) Yet the car itself gave no sign anything was wrong—there were no warning lights, no error codes, no beeps or alerts. "A modern car has dozens of computers that control everything from the fuel injection to the exhaust," Jeff says. "And if anything is outside the parameters"—if, say, the engine is running a few degrees too hot—"then you get that service light telling you to take it in."

The problem with the Porsche that wouldn't turn off, however, was that its computers thought the car was running perfectly. "The computers have to be programmed to detect the problems," Jeff says. "And nobody ever thought to program an error code for an engine that wouldn't stop. I mean, that's *insane*."

Jeff looks like a mechanic out of central casting: gray Dickies, neck tattoos, backward baseball hat, grease marks on his hands and cheeks. When I arrive at EuroSpec, he's still underneath an old Porsche, banging away at a rusted joint. I pass the time by admiring the contradictions of twenty-first-century car repair. One side of the shop features the traditional tools of the mechanic—greasy lube tubes, wrenches and sockets in every shape and size, stacks of motor oil. But there's also a wall of digital tablets—black mirrors with dirty fingerprints—that give Jeff and his team access to the hidden guts of these incredibly sophisticated machines.

"In the old days, everything was analog," Jeff says. "You pressed on the gas, your foot causes a hole to open, more fuel is squirted into the engine. Now you press on the gas, you move your foot this much"—Jeff holds his fingers an inch apart—"and the electronic sensor tells the computer you want sixty-two percent throttle. So instead of the fuel injectors pulsing at 1.3 milliseconds, they're going to pulse at 1.8 milliseconds. The point is that your little movement is being translated by a bunch of computers into extremely precise instructions to the engine." Jeff sighs, as if he misses the analog days. "That precision leads to much better performance, but the trade-off is that there's a lot of shit that can break. And none of it is cheap."

In many respects, the rise of computers has diminished the mystery of car repair. Mechanics used to be detectives in the mold of Sherlock Holmes, or Tom and Ray Magliozzi from *Car Talk*. A customer would enter the shop with a vague complaint: perhaps the car was making a strange noise at cold idle, or the steering column would vibrate during left turns at slow speed. The job of the mechanic was to translate these mysterious symptoms into a diagnosis, identifying the bits of broken metal and rubber responsible for the problem.

But the modern car can now diagnose itself, sharing its error codes and malfunctions. It reports broken circuits, out-of-sync pistons, and takes its own temperature every few seconds. "You always begin with the computer," Jeff says. "A car comes in the shop, first thing you do is plug it in, let it tell you what it thinks is wrong." But as Jeff points out, these computer diagnoses are the *start* of the deductive process, not the end. Consider a common problem for Porsches, which is an error involving the ignition coils. "A crappy mechanic will see that error code and just put in a new coil," Jeff observes. They treat the computer as an oracle; there is no mystery, since the computer has already told them what's wrong.

A good mechanic, however, will understand the limits of such assessments. After all, there are countless faults that could cause the ignition-coil error code. It could be a broken computer spitting out errant warnings. Or it could be a snapped wire connecting the coil and the sensor. "That's why you got to open her up," Jeff says. "I start at the coil, but then I literally grab the wiring and start tracing it back. It's going to go under the car, and into a little crevice you can't get into, and under the seat, and all the way to the other side to the computer. And I've got to trace the entire thing because the problem could be anywhere." Jeff then shows me the wiring diagram on a recent Porsche model. It looks like a labyrinth, a network of overlapping lines running off in every direction. "There are miles of these copper wires inside the car," he says. "Not feet. *Miles.*"

So Jeff assesses the signal on the wire to the ignition coil. Then he looks at the surrounding circuit. If there's an electrical problem, he wants to understand the underlying cause. Did a rat get inside and start chewing? Did the car have bodywork done? What broke the wire? "You've got to be curious in this job," he says. "You really have to want to figure it out, otherwise you'll just do what the computer says because it's faster and you're lazy and another customer walked through the door."

Car repair is a metaphor for the modern age. Just as the mechanic is quickly told by the onboard computer that there's an issue with the engine coil, so do our gadgets offer us instantaneous answers to every conceivable question. In the age of information, there's no excuse for not knowing. Mystery is optional.

Yet, what distinguishes the best minds—whether it's in car repair or politics, art or science—is the ability to get beyond these initial answers. The Nobel laureate and psychologist Daniel Kahneman talks about a thinking mistake he refers to as WYSIATI, or What You See Is All There Is. "People are designed to tell the best story possible," Kahneman said in a 2012 interview. "So WYSIATI means that we use the information we have as if it is the only information. We don't spend much time saying, 'Well, there is much we don't know.' We make do with what we do know. And that concept is very central to the functioning of our mind."[2]

The digital world exacerbates the WYSIATI error. Those luminous screens offer up the promise of omniscience, but the world is more complicated than it appears on the first page of search engine results, or on our filtered Facebook News Feed. Likewise, those car computers are just the start of the investigation—what they tell the mechanic is rarely a complete diagnostic picture. That's why a proper understanding of the world requires that we keep asking questions, even when our devices offer us immediate results.

The psychologist Barry Schwartz captured this process at work in a clever experiment. He presented 115 undergraduates with a logic puzzle featuring a series of keys and light bulbs. To get a reward, the students had to press two keys four times each. Given the number of keys, this meant there were seventy possible solutions, each of which led to a small monetary payout. Initial groups of students were given no instructions, which meant they had to proceed randomly, learning by trial and error.

Here's where WYSIATI comes into play. When Schwartz rewarded students for finding a single solution, they almost never sought out alternative ones. They also gave up trying to find the more general rule determining the rewards. Instead, they repeated what worked in the past, pressing the same keys over and over. They acted like the mechanic who always obeys the onboard computer, blind to all the other possible answers.

Schwartz then reran the experiment with a twist. In this version, he asked the students to find the general rule, thus encouraging them to look beyond their initial success. This minor difference changed everything. Now, every single student found the larger pattern. Because the students were less vulnerable to the WYSIATI fallacy—they had been told that the first payout was *not* all there was—they kept asking questions, which led them to the real answer. Being aware of the mystery made them much better problem solvers.[3]

This is Jeff's competitive advantage: he knows what he doesn't, which makes him less vulnerable to the curse of WYSIATI. "I'm real stubborn," he says. "My partner is always telling me to give up, cut my losses, but I gotta get to the bottom of it." Jeff then smiles, chuckles to himself. "This is gonna sound bad, but it's like when the Lakers are down with two minutes left and Kobe just opens up, just starts hitting shots. That's pure determination, you know? He's not going to lose, and I'm not going to lose."

And that's why the Porsche 911 that wouldn't turn off was so upsetting. Jeff had been working on the car for *three months*. He'd spent dozens of unbillable hours on the vehicle, investigating every relevant mechanical element in the engine. He'd looked at the ignition electronics and the transmission and the starter. But none of them were broken; Jeff was totally confused. "I was losing my fucking mind," he says. "I'd see that car every day and it would be taunting me, reminding me that I couldn't figure it out."

Jeff's first break came when he began looking at a series of seemingly unrelated electrical issues. The brake lights would flicker and stay on, and sometimes the convertible top would freeze. "There's no reason these should have anything to do with the engine," Jeff says. "The computer would never tell you to check them. No repair book would tell you to check them. But I didn't know what else to do, so I figured I might as well try."

## Mindfulness

Ellen Langer is a scientist of the mind who became famous for studying our mindlessness. People do so many seemingly stupid things, Langer says, but most of these errors share a common cause: we don't like to think. Thinking is hard work. It's easier to be thoughtless. "Social psychology is replete with theories that take for granted the 'fact' that people think," Langer wrote in one of her first papers. With her usual audacity, she then went on to insist that most of those theories were false.[4]

Langer backed up these bold claims with a series of highly influential studies.[5] In one classic paper, she showed that allowing subjects to choose their lottery tickets led them to assign the tickets a much higher value, even though the randomness of the game meant their choice was meaningless. They knew this—they just didn't think about it. In another experiment, Langer and a colleague approached a student at a copy machine in the university library. As the subject was about to insert his coins into the copier, Langer asked if she could use the machine first. If people were thoughtful creatures, then we'd be far more likely to let a person with a valid reason ("I'm in a rush") cut in line. But that's not what Langer found. Instead, she discovered that offering people *any reason at all*, even an utterly meaningless one ("I have to make copies"), led to near-universal submission. It's not that people aren't listening, Langer says—it's that they're not thinking. Most of life is lived on autopilot.[6] "We're not just *not there*," she says. "We're often not even there enough to know we're not there."[7]

One of the primary symptoms of mindlessness—and a leading reason it leads to thinking mistakes—is that it causes us to neglect mystery, even when it's blindingly obvious. In the 1960s, the psychologist John Yellott began conducting a new kind of intelligence test on students at Stanford University.[8] He ushered each subject into a small, soundproofed room containing a chair, a table with two keys, and a Sylvania electroluminescent display, the same sort of monitor used on the Apollo command module.

Yellott would then explain the study. For every trial, there were two possibilities: the display would either show an *X* or a *Y*. The subject was to predict which letter would appear next, signaling his guess by pressing one of the keys.

Two distinct strategies can be used during this task. The first is called the maximizing strategy. It goes this way: after watching the letters turn on for a few rounds, maximizers decide always to pick the one that appears most frequently. In the Stanford study, for instance, the letter Y was programmed to appear 80 percent of the time. This means that a maximizer would press Y again and again; she'd never touch the X key.

When you give an animal this sort of test, they tend to act like maximizers. Monkeys, goldfish, pigeons, rats—they all use this rudimentary yet effective strategy. Instead of trying to solve the pattern, they accept the mystery and settle for being right most of the time.[9] One species, however, doesn't engage in maximizing behavior: human beings. We rely on what's called a matching approach. In Yellott's experiment, the students tried to "match" their guesses to the average probability of the letters, so they guessed Y about 80 percent of the time and X the remainder.

After the experiment was over, Yellott interviewed the students about their strategies. Most said the matching was an attempt to decipher the pattern; they wanted to solve the system, not just keep pressing a single letter. Unfortunately, their clever solutions were illusions. While Ys appeared 80 percent of the time, the exact distribution of letters followed an utterly random sequence. The overconfidence of the human subjects impacted their performance, so that they only guessed the correct bulb around 68 percent of the time. What's worse, they never changed course; they failed to learn from their failures, even after watching hundreds of letters on the screen. As the Nobel laureate Kenneth Arrow wrote in a review of the literature, "The remarkable thing about this is that the asymptotic behavior of the individual, even after an indefinitely large amount of learning, is not the optimal behavior."[10] When it comes to this guessing game, goldfish routinely outsmart us.

Why are humans so bad at predicting the letters? *Because we mindlessly deny the mystery.* We treat it like a puzzle instead. We've got these big brains, Langer says, but we often use them in ways that minimize their powers. "If we admit there's mystery, then we also have to admit that we don't have as much control as we'd like," Langer says. "And that's scary. So instead we just repeat our mistakes. That's the sort of behavior that mindlessness leads to."

But Langer wasn't content to document our mental sins. After becoming the first tenured female psychologist at Harvard, she became increasingly interested in studying the solution to mindlessness, which she refers to as *mindfulness*. When we're mindful, we are "actively drawing distinctions, making meaning, or creating categories," Langer wrote.[11] In other words, *we're paying attention*. But this isn't the sterile attention of the traditional classroom, in which being attentive means "holding something still," or memorizing the facts recited by the teacher. Instead, Langer sees mindfulness as a way to realize that reality is never still, and that what we know is only a small sliver of what there is. Mystery abounds. "Mindfulness is really about noticing new things," she told me. "When you notice things, that puts you in the present, but it also reminds you that you don't know nearly as much as you think you know. . . . We tend to confuse the stability of our attitudes and mindsets with the stability of the world. But the world outside isn't stable—it's always changing." Mindfulness helps us see the change. Even better, it turns ordinary life into an infinite game, helping us enjoy the uncertainty that is everywhere.

How can we become more mindful? For Langer, the answer isn't yoga or Transcendental Meditation or some expensive ritual that involves a top-secret mantra. ("The people I know won't sit still for five minutes, let alone forty," she told *Harvard Magazine* in 2010.)[12] It doesn't require unplugging from the internet or going to a mindfulness-certified therapist. Instead, Langer's advice for those seeking mindfulness begins with an acknowledgment of their ignorance. If mystery neglect is a problem caused by mind-lessness, its treatment involves mystery *appreciation*. "I always ask people, 'How much is one and one?'" Langer says. "And they say 'Two,' of course. And then I remind them that one and one isn't *always* two. You put one pile of snow on top of another pile of snow, you still have one pile of snow. Add two pieces of gum together and you've still got one piece of gum. And so on." Langer isn't arguing with arithmetic—she just wants people to recognize that the truth is conditional and the universe is full of surprises. "When we're mindless, we rely on absolutes," she says. "It was like this before, it will always be this way in the future. But that's not the way the world works. It's much more mysterious than that."

In one study, conducted with Alison Piper, Langer introduced a new object in two different ways. Sometimes, the object was de-scribed in absolute terms ("This is a dog's chew toy"), and some-times it was described conditionally ("This *could* be a dog's chew toy"). The subjects were then asked to use the object to solve a prob-lem, such as erasing a mark on a piece of paper. The question was whether the subjects would think to use the dog toy to accomplish the task. The results were clear: only those introduced to the object in a conditional manner were able to use it creatively, finding ways to use the chew toy as an eraser.[13] Because the conditional script introduced a hint of the unknown (it might *not* be a dog's chew toy), subjects were far more effective at dealing with the challenge.

Mindfulness is often described as a practical thinking tool, a trendy productivity hack. But for Langer, mindfulness is about the experience of delight. "Do you remember how much fun tic-tac-toe used to be, until you mastered the game?" Langer asks. "Or look at the little kid in the elevator. They're so excited to press the buttons because they can't reach the buttons. How many adults are excited to be in an elevator?" Langer's point is that mastery is tedious—it's the *mastering* that compels our attention. "I always tell people the easiest way to be mindful is to throw yourself into a new activity that fully engages you. It's going to engage you because you don't know how to do it. It's still a mystery. And when you're fully engaged, you should remind yourself that that's the way you should feel *all the time*. Not knowing is what makes you feel alive. Not knowing is what gives you energy. Not knowing is the fun part."

Langer has followed her own advice. When she was fifty years old, she decided to start painting. It had been a rainy summer, too rainy for tennis, and Langer found herself telling a friend that she'd always wanted to try painting, so why not now? The subjects of her art are varied—she paints her dogs, the Cape Cod sunset, friends in funny poses, old furniture. Sometimes she paints on old wood shingles; other works are done on vast stretched canvases, bought on sale at the local art-supply store. Langer is now an accomplished artist, represented by fancy galleries, but she still mostly paints because of how it makes her feel. ("When I don't want to paint, I don't paint," she says.) For Langer, the creative act allows her to confront the world in a more mindful manner; the art reinforces her science. "It's not until you try to make a painting that you're forced to really figure out what you're looking at," she says. "I see a tree and I say that tree is green. Fine. It is green. But then when I go to paint it, I have to figure out exactly what shade of green. And then I realize that these greens are always changing, and that as the sun moves across the sky, the colors change, too. So here I am, trying to make a picture of a tree, and all of a sudden I'm thinking about how nothing is certain and everything changes. I don't even know what a tree looks like."

For Langer, a good painting is a model for the good life. Not the work itself, but the making of it. When Langer settles down with her brushes and oil paints and that intimidating blank canvas, she doesn't expect perfection. Perfection would be boring. She knows that she will make mistakes, that she will put down paint in the wrong places, that her portrait will never match her vision. Her simple goal is to stay interested in the artwork for as long as possible, to somehow see what she's never before seen. In one study, Langer instructed artists to persist with their art regardless of what happened. It didn't matter if they made an errant line or got the color wrong—they had to "keep going forward." And you know what happened? These pictures, full of accidents and flaws, ended up being preferred by everyone else. "If you're doing it right, then the mistakes can be a window into something new and genuinely beautiful," Langer says. "Instead of just following some plan, they force you to exist in the present. They force you to really look at what you're doing. And when you look closely, when you *really look*, you realize that you don't know as much as you think you do. When it comes down to it, you don't know much at all. That, right there, is the start of mindfulness."

## Corrosion

Jeff's first car was a 1963 Ford Ranchero that he bought for $1,500. Two weeks after he bought it, the car broke down. "The problem was, I spent all my money buying it," Jeff says. "But I had girls to see, things to do. I was fifteen. I needed a car!" So Jeff begged the owner of an auto-parts store to let him work in exchange for inventory. (The Ranchero needed a new fuel pump and radiator.) After scrubbing the bathroom and mopping the floors for a few months, Jeff graduated to the service center, where he changed oil and repaired brakes. It was satisfying work—"I learned that I liked fixing stuff," Jeff says—and the paychecks led him to drop out of high school.

After a decade toiling in various repair shops, Jeff decided to open his own garage, specializing in Porsches. He found a small space on Craigslist and waited for customers. "Sat on my hands for a month, and I was like, 'What did I do? Was this a huge mistake?'" But then a few Porsches came in; word spread that Jeff could fix anything. Before long, he was working on those repairs that even the dealers couldn't figure out. People started shipping him their Porsches from all over the country.

Which brings us back to that 911 that wouldn't turn off. Jeff spent the first few weeks checking all the obvious suspects: "A problem like that, you assume it's an ignition issue. Maybe a faulty fuel pump, starter, stuff like that." But all those parts were working perfectly. "I opened up that engine and put it back together, but it still didn't work." Or rather: the engine still wouldn't *stop* working.

At this point any other mechanic would have given up. The car was hopelessly broken. But not Jeff. If he couldn't find the fault in the engine, then he'd have to look at everything else in the car. He began by investigating the wonky convertible top. He accessed the convertible control unit—a green electrical circuit the size of a VHS tape in the back of the car—and began tracing out the wires. Jeff remembered that the convertible control unit had a communication link to the engine. This was for safety reasons: "You don't want some jerk raising the roof on his car when he's going eighty on the highway. So the top is disabled at certain speeds."

When Jeff opened up the convertible control unit, he noticed a small amount of white corrosion on the circuit board. "Corrosion is pretty common, but this corrosion was bridging the gap between two different terminals. Now, one of the problems with corrosion is that it's semiconductive, which means power can travel across it." Jeff saw that rusty bridge and suddenly had a crazy theory—power from the convertible control unit might be back-feeding voltage to the engine. "It probably wasn't a lot of power, but maybe, just *maybe*, it was enough to keep the engine control unit from turning off. And if the engine control unit won't turn off, neither will the engine."

To test his hypothesis, Jeff began pulling the wires that connect to the convertible control unit. "It's got like five plugs going into it. I pull the first plug and the brake lights turn off." That was intriguing, since the brake lights had also been acting strangely. So Jeff pulled another wire. And another. And then, when he pulled that last wire heading into the convertible control unit, the engine suddenly went silent. "I was never so happy to hear an engine die." After he replaced the corroded circuits, the engine worked perfectly. The car was fixed. "Only took me three months of hell," he says with a smile.

For Jeff, the saga of the 911 that wouldn't turn off is a testament to the limits of computer diagnostics. "The computer was never programmed to worry about voltage leaking through that circuit. It didn't even know there was a problem, so it was never going to help me find the solution."

This broken Porsche might be an extreme example, but it's a reminder to Jeff to always look beyond the initial fixes suggested by the car's microchips. (What they report is not all there is.) "The computers know what they know, but they don't know what they don't," Jeff tells me. It's a line that sounds very Zen, but it also contains an essential insight into how to think effectively in the information age. If we are going to rely on these powerful gadgets, then we need to be vigilant about their frailties and blind spots. The machines aren't aware of their own shortcomings. Google never admits its ignorance—almost every search generates some search results—and those microchips inside your car can't conceive of problems beyond their narrow parameters. Our job is to remember all the unknowns they ignore.

Look at a recent study of how GPS technology changes the

way we interact with the world. The experiment was conducted in Kashiwa, Japan, a dense suburb outside Tokyo. A third of the subjects were taken on a winding route by a human guide. Another third used a paper map. The final third were given a programmed GPS unit—they just had to follow the electronic instructions. While the subjects given the paper maps and human guides could generally navigate the path, the GPS subjects struggled to reach the destination. They walked slower and made more mistakes. They stopped more frequently. What's more, when asked to draw a map of the route after the experiment, those who used GPS drew maps that were much less accurate.[14]

What explains this failure? The problem with technology that promises answers is that it often leads people to stop asking questions. We disengage from the world. Instead of paying attention to the route, we just obey the machine. The technology encourages our mindlessness, allowing us to pretend we know where we're going even when we don't.

The solution isn't to avoid GPS. Jeff, after all, still relies on those computers in his shop. It's just that he also insists on staying mindful amid the machines, looking beyond their fast fixes. What are they not noticing? What else could be going wrong? What questions are not being asked?

Albert Hirschman, a developmental economist and essayist, devoted much of his writing to the virtues of doubt. Along with his best friend and brother-in-law, Eugenio Colorni, Hirschman came up with a professional goal: *he wanted to prove Hamlet wrong*. He believed that Hamlet had given doubt a bad reputation. The melancholic prince had led people to associate doubt with inaction, paralysis, soliloquies that led nowhere.[15]

Hirschman, in contrast, saw doubt as liberating. When we doubt, we give ourselves the freedom to see the world differently.

We can consider new perspectives and solutions. We learn to act without the need for certainty.

When explaining the virtues of doubt, Hirschman often used the example of creativity. If we actually knew what the creative act would require—the endless drafts, iterations, and failures—we'd never pursue creative problems. The cost would seem too high. Why make ourselves miserable?

Take Jeff. If he'd known that the Porsche 911 would take him a few months to fix, he probably would have declined the repair. But he said yes because he didn't know. Because nobody knew. And it was that *not knowing* that unleashed Jeff's potential. As Hirschman put it, in a letter to his daughters, "The secret of creativity is then to place yourself in situations where you've got to be creative, but this is done only when one doesn't know in advance that one will have to be creative."[16]

Jeff had no idea how to turn off that Porsche engine. But he didn't let his doubt stop him. To paraphrase Hirschman, he found a way to prove Hamlet wrong.

Mindfulness has always been a struggle, but it's never been more necessary. To deal with the hard problems of life, we have to accept the mystery. We have to embrace our doubts. "There are two secrets to being good at this job," Jeff says. "You gotta think for yourself and you gotta give a shit."

## The Fifteenth Rock

The Ryoan-ji rock garden in Kyoto looks, at first glance, like a pile of rocks. There are fifteen large stones, stained by time and moss, scattered around a groomed gravel lawn. The scattering is not an accident: each of these boulders has been positioned so that the viewer can only see fourteen of the fifteen rocks at a time, regardless of where he or she stands. You can circle the garden. You can stand on your tiptoes and crane your neck. But you will not see every boulder. The temple garden is a subtle lesson in mystery, the rocks reminding us that even the simplest spaces can contain the unknown.

This is one of the essential functions of art: it teaches us how to live with mystery. By giving us suspenseful twists and layered worlds, opaque characters and obscure lines, it trains us to enjoy our prediction errors. Instead of seeking out confirming evidence, art reminds us that doubt is more useful and mindfulness is more fun. We realize that the joy is in the verb—not the understanding, but the trying.

It's a necessary mindset because there is no escaping mystery: the unknown will always be an essential part of our knowledge. We want perfect truths, but the reality is there's no such thing. Our best theories get disproven; facts get falsified; in the long run, we are wrong about nearly everything. It's the secrets that survive.

This idea was summarized by the American philosopher Willard Van Orman Quine in his seminal paper "Two Dogmas of Empiricism." As Quine noted, many of our most fundamental scientific principles—the ideas upon which so much else depends— are actually the most mysterious. Take gravity, a force of physics so basic it's celebrated on *Sesame Street*. Yet, the sheer simplicity of gravity—it makes objects fall down—obscures its profound unknowns. It has been nearly 350 years since Newton described the force, and more than a century since Einstein redefined gravity in terms of space-time, but we still have no idea what gravity is made of or where it comes from or how it fits with quantum mechanics.* We can measure its pull on the universe, but the force itself is utterly mysterious. Everything we know depends on things we never can.

The art of being human is learning to deal with these limits. In *To the Lighthouse*, Virginia Woolf describes how Lily Briscoe, the abstract painter, has for years been working on a particular landscape painting. She keeps redoing the water, moving the tree, changing the color of the shadows. It's a maddening process: the more Lily rages against the "difficult white space" of the canvas, the less she seems to understand. But then, while staring at the lighthouse off in the distance, Lily has a breakthrough. Life is "like a work of art," she suddenly realizes. It's also full of unknowns and imperfections. The point of life and of art is not to solve these problems—it's to wrestle a little beauty and awe from the questions. So her flawed portrait of the coast returns her to the world, only now with a more mindful perspective. "The great revelation had never come," Lily thinks. "The great revelation perhaps never did come. Instead, there were little daily miracles, illuminations, matches struck unexpectedly in the dark; here was one."[18]

Lily's struggle is the struggle of creation. When we begin the creative process, all we have is the blank page. Nothing is known; the ending is unwritten. It's tempting to erase these uncertainties, to fill in the emptiness with knowledge and wisdom, to pretend we knew all along.

But the best art never forgets how it began. It remembers the mysteries that inspired the work. Because those mysteries don't

---

* Here's Richard Feynman: "What is gravity? Newton made no hypotheses about this; he was satisfied to find *what* it did without getting into the machinery of it. *No one has since given any machinery.* It is characteristic of the physical laws that they have this abstract character."[17]

just keep the artist interested in the creative process—they are also what hold the scarce attention of the audience. We are drawn to the unknown. Our awe depends upon it.

It's an astonishing fact of human culture: what lasts is what mystifies. Time is an acid that destroys answers. It ruins our certainties. What remains instead are those stories and paintings and characters that find ways to contain what they cannot fathom, hooking us with their unspilled secrets. They are alive with the mystery of the universe. Which is why they live on.

# ACKNOWLEDGMENTS

First, Ben Loehnen. My extraordinary editor. You found the structure in my ruminations, and helped me discover the book I wanted to write. I will forever be in your debt for giving me a chance.

Andrew Wylie and Rebecca Nagel have guided this book from the start, back when it was a few rambling pages on wonder and awe. They've read every draft and offered invaluable notes.

Kyle Paoletta worked tirelessly fact-checking this book. I'm so grateful he took this project on—he was meticulous and diligent. Whatever mistakes remain are all mine.

Thank you to all the brilliant people, teachers, and scientists who shared their insights with me. And if that wasn't enough, they also took the time to read and correct the text. A special thank-you to the late James Carse, who was so patient and thoughtful; our first conversation ended up inspiring an entire chapter.

Steve Boldt did an excellent job copyediting the manuscript. A huge thank-you to him and Carolyn Kelly for getting this book to the finish line.

Shlomo and Steve were the best colleagues anyone could ask for.

Two dear friends deserve special mention. Robert Krulwich has encouraged my interest in this subject for years. (He's always been a model of human wonder.) I was worried about writing a book on the beauty of questions—didn't people want answers? But on one of our long walks around New York he convinced me that mystery and its synonyms were worthy of investigation.

Bruce Nelson has patiently listened to me talk for years about mystery between bites of deli sandwiches. He's responsible for so many of the best threads of this book. And when inspiration flagged, he kept me inspired with his own beautiful art.

And then there's my family. Without whom not. My parents, my siblings, my cousins—you all kept me going.

This book, like everything in my life, has been profoundly shaped by my children. The hermeneutics of *Harry Potter*, the tricks of Ryan's ToyReview, the appeal of Sherlock, and the abiding joys of curiosity—these are all things Rose, Isaac, and Louisa have taught me. I'm very excited to learn more from you tomorrow.

And Sarah . . . There will never be words. You make me better every day. Never gonna let you go.

# NOTES

## Introduction: The Mystery of Mystery

1  Jared Cade, *Agatha Christie and the Eleven Missing Days* (London: Peter Owen, 2011), 79.

2  Tina Jordan, "When the World's Most Famous Mystery Writer Vanished," *New York Times*, June 11, 2019, https://www.nytimes.com/2019/06/11/books/agatha-christie-vanished-11-days-1926.html.

3  Laura Thompson, *Agatha Christie: A Mysterious Life* (New York: Pegasus, 2013), 166.

4  Cade, *Agatha Christie and the Eleven*, 97.

5  Ibid., 81.

6  Ibid., 81–83.

7  Ibid., 99.

8  Ibid., 98.

9  Ibid., 103.

10  Thompson, *Agatha Christie*, 222.

11  "Mrs. Christie Found in a Yorkshire Spa," *New York Times*, December 15, 1926, https://timesmachine.nytimes.com/timesmachine/1926/12/15/98410135.html?pageNumber=1.

12  Cade, *Agatha Christie and the Eleven*, 130

13  Thompson, *Agatha Christie*, 209.

14  Agatha Christie, *An Autobiography* (New York: William Morrow, 2012), 437.

15  Cade, *Agatha Christie and the Eleven*, 106.

16  Thompson, *Agatha Christie*, 202.

17  Christie, *Autobiography*, 358.

18  Edgar Allan Poe, "A Few Words on Secret Writing," *Graham's Magazine*, July 1841; and Jeffrey Meyers, *Edgar Allan Poe: His Life and Legacy* (Lanham, MD: Rowman & Littlefield, 1992), 122.

19  Kenneth Silverman, *Edgar A. Poe: Mournful and Never-Ending Remembrance* (New York: Harper Perennial, 1992), 172.

20  Ibid., 173.

21  Interview, September 26, 2019.

22  Wystan Hugh Auden, "The Guilty Vicarage," *Harper's Magazine*, May 1948.

23  Wolfram Schultz, "Dopamine Reward Prediction-Error Signalling: A Two-Component Response," *Nature Reviews Neuroscience* 17, no. 3 (2016): 183.

24  Scott Waddell, "Dopamine Reveals Neural Circuit Mechanisms of Fly Memory," *Trends in Neurosciences* 33, no. 10 (2010): 457–64; Wolfram Schultz and Anthony

Dickinson, "Neuronal Coding of Prediction Errors," *Annual Review of Neuroscience* 23, no. 1 (2000): 473–500; and Wolfram Schultz, Leon Tremblay, and Jeffrey R. Hollerman, "Reward Prediction in Primate Basal Ganglia and Frontal Cortex," *Neuropharmacology* 37, no. 4–5 (1998): 421–29.

25  Clifford Geertz, *The Interpretation of Cultures* (New York: Basic Books, 1973), 5.

26  John Berman, Deborah Apton, and Victoria Thompson, "Stephen Sondheim: My 'West Side Story' Lyrics Are 'Embarrassing,'" ABCNews, December 8, 2010, https://abcnews.go.com/Entertainment/stephen-sondheim-west-side-story-lyrics -embarrassing/story?id=12345243.

27  John Keats, *The Complete Poetical Works and Letters of John Keats* (New York: Houghton Mifflin, 1899), 277.

## Chapter 1: The Mystery Box

1  Stefan Zweig, *Burning Secret* (London: Pushkin Collection, 2008), 52.

2  Madeline Berg, "How This 7-Year-Old Made $22 Million Playing with Toys," *Forbes*, December 3, 2018, https://www.forbes.com/sites/maddieberg/2018/12/03/how-this -seven-year-old-made-22-million-playing-with-toys-2/#3f11a21f4459.

3  J. J. Abrams, "The Mystery Box," filmed March 2007 at TED200, Monterey, CA, video, 17:50, https://www.ted.com/talks/j_j_abrams_mystery_box?utm_campaign= tedspread&utm_medium=referral&utm_source=tedcomshare, accessed January 10, 2019.

4  Steve Jobs, keynote address, Macworld San Francisco, January 9, 2009, Moscone Center, San Francisco, CA, https://www.youtube.com/watch?v=vN4U5FqrOdQ.

5  Leonard Mlodinow, *The Upright Thinkers* (New York: Vintage, 2016), 21–23; Ian Leslie, *Curious: The Desire to Know and Why Your Future Depends on It* (New York: Basic Books, 2014), 28; and Paul L. Harris, *Trusting What You're Told: How Children Learn from Others* (Cambridge, MA: Harvard University Press, 2012).

6  Michelle M. Chouinard, Paul L. Harris, and Michael P. Maratsos, "Children's Questions: A Mechanism for Cognitive Development," *Monographs of the Society for Research in Child Development* 72, no. 1 (2007): 1–129.

7  P. E. Shah et al., "Early Childhood Curiosity and Kindergarten Reading and Math Academic Achievement," *Pediatric Research*, 2018, https://doi.org/10.1038/s41390 -018-0039-3.

8  Matthias J. Gruber, Bernard D. Gelman, and Charan Ranganath, "States of Curiosity Modulate Hippocampus-Dependent Learning via the Dopaminergic Circuit," *Neuron* 84, no. 2 (2014): 486–96.

9  Lynn Nadel and Morris Moscovitch, "Memory Consolidation, Retrograde Amnesia and the Hippocampal Complex," *Current Opinion in Neurobiology* 7, no. 2 (1997): 217–27.

10  George Loewenstein, "The Psychology of Curiosity: A Review and Reinterpreta- tion," *Psychological Bulletin* 116, no. 1 (1994): 75.

11  "Electronic Gaming Device Utilizing a Random Number Generator for Selecting the Reel Stop Positions," United States Patent, US4448419A, May 15, 1984,

https://patentimages.storage.googleapis.com/10/ac/5f/f72c55579aaabe/US4448419
.pdf.

12   Ibid.

13   John Robison, "Casino Random Number Generators," *Casino City Times*, July 28,
     2000.

14   Natasha Dow SchuÄàll, *Addiction by Design: Machine Gambling in Las Vegas*
     (Princeton, NJ: Princeton University Press, 2012), 91.

15   Schüll, *Addiction by Design*.

16   Luke Clark et al., "Gambling Near-Misses Enhance Motivation to Gamble and
     Recruit Win-Related Brain Circuitry," *Neuron* 61, no. 3 (2009): 481–90.

17   Dave Hickey, *Air Guitar* (New York: Art Issues Press, 1997), 23.

18   D. E. Berlyne, *Aesthetics and Psychobiology* (New York: Appleton-Century-Crofts,
     1971).

19   D. E. Berlyne, "Novelty, Complexity, and Hedonic Value," *Perception & Psychophys-
     ics* 8, no. 5 (1970): 279–86.

20   Raymond Loewy, *Never Leave Well Enough Alone* (Baltimore, MD: Johns Hopkins
     University Press, 2002), 280.

21   "The Year in Sports Media Report: 2015," Nielsen, February 3, 2016, http://www
     .nielsen.com/us/en/insights/reports/2016/the-year-in-sports-media-report-2015
     .html.

22   Pedro Dionisio, Carmo Leal, and Luiz Moutinho, "Fandom Affiliation and Tribal
     Behaviour: A Sports Marketing Application," *Qualitative Market Research* 11, no.
     1 (2008): 17–39; Marieke de Groot and Tom Robinson, "Sport Fan Attachment
     and the Psychological Continuum Model: A Case Study of an Australian Football
     League Fan," *Leisure/Loisir* 32, no. 1 (2008): 117–38; and Marco Iacoboni, *Mirroring
     People: The New Science of How We Connect with Others* (New York: Farrar, Straus
     and Giroux, 2009).

23   Nicholas Christenfeld, "What Makes a Good Sport?," *Nature* 383 (1996): 662.

24   Stanley Schachter et al., "Speech Disfluency and the Structure of Knowledge,"
     *Journal of Personality and Social Psychology* 60, no. 3 (1991): 362–63.

25   Nicholas Christenfeld, "Choices from Identical Options," *Psychological Science* 6, no.
     1 (1995): 50–55.

26   Michael M. Roy and Nicholas J. S. Christenfeld, "Do Dogs Resemble Their
     Owners?," *Psychological Science* 15, no. 5 (2004): 361–63.

27   Christine R. Harris and Nicholas Christenfeld, "Can a Machine Tickle?," *Psycho-
     nomic Bulletin & Review* 6, no. 3 (1999): 504–10.

28   Nicholas Christenfeld, David P. Phillips, and Laura M. Glynn, "What's in a Name:
     Mortality and the Power of Symbols," *Journal of Psychosomatic Research* 47, no. 3
     (1999): 241–54.

29   A. Clauset, M. Kogan, and S. Redner, "Safe Leads and Lead Changes in Competi-
     tive Team Sports," *Physical Review E* 91, no. 6 (2015): 062815.

30   "1892 NL Team Statistics," Baseball Reference, http://www.baseball-reference.com
     /leagues/NL/1892.shtml.

31  John Thorn, "Who Were the Fastest Pitchers?" *Our Game*, February 18, 2014, https://ourgame.mlblogs.com/who-were-the-fastest-pitchers-c453890d0516.

32  Leonard Koppett, *Koppett's Concise History of Major League Baseball* (New York: Carroll and Graf, 2004), 72–74.

33  Bill Deane, *Baseball Myths* (Lanham, MD: Scarecrow Press, 2012), 10.

34  Rodney J. Paul, Yoav Wachsman, and Andrew P. Weinbach, "The Role of Uncertainty of Outcome and Scoring in the Determination of Fan Satisfaction in the NFL," *Journal of Sports Economics* 12, no. 2 (2011): 213–21.

35  Interview, Studio City, December 28, 2017.

36  Coltan Scrivner et al., "Pandemic Practice: Horror Fans and Morbidly Curious Individuals Are More Psychologically Resilient during the COVID-19 Pandemic," *Personality and Individual Differences* 168, no.110397 (2020).

## Chapter 2: The Magic Gasp

1  "Do Lotteries Do More Harm than Good?" *Chicago Booth Review*, January 30, 2020, https://review.chicagobooth.edu/economics/2020/article/do-lotteries-do-more -harm-good.

2  Thank you to Mohan Srivastava for supplying the image of the lottery tickets.

3  Jonah Lehrer, "Cracking the Scratch Lottery Code," *Wired*, January 31, 2011, https://www.wired.com/2011/01/ff-lottery/.

4  A. H. Danek et al., "An fMRI Investigation of Expectation Violation in Magic Tricks," *Frontiers in Psychology* 6 (2015): 84–85.

5  Sian Beilock, "Why a Broken Heart Really Hurts," *Guardian*, September 13, 2015.

6  Anne-Marike Schiffer and Ricarda I. Schubotz, "Caudate Nucleus Signals for Breaches of Expectation in a Movement Observation Paradigm," *Frontiers in Human Neuroscience* 5 (2011): 38.

7  Jessica A. Grahn, John A. Parkinson, and Adrian M. Owen, "The Cognitive Functions of the Caudate Nucleus," *Progress in Neurobiology* 86, no. 3 (2008): 141–55.

8  Gustav Kuhn, *Experiencing the Impossible: The Science of Magic* (Cambridge, MA: MIT Press, 2019), 19–20.

9  Karl Duncker, "On Problem-Solving," *Psychological Monographs* 58, no. 5 (1945): 1–113.

10  Tim P. German and Margaret Anne Defeyter, "Immunity to Functional Fixedness in Young Children," *Psychonomic Bulletin & Review* 7, no. 4 (2000): 707–12.

11  Jim Steinmeyer, *Hiding the Elephant: How Magicians Invented the Impossible*, (New York: Random House, 2005).

12  Theodor Adorno, *Minima Moralia: Reflections on a Damaged Life* (New York: Verso, 2005), 222.

13  Stephen Kaplan, "Perception and Landscape: Conceptions and Misconceptions," USDA Forest Sevice, General Technical Report PSW-GTR-35 (Berkeley, CA: Pacific Southwest Forest Range Experiment Station, 1979), 241–8, https://www.fs .usda.gov/treesearch/pubs/27585.

14 Ross King, *Brunelleschi's Dome: How a Renaissance Genius Reinvented Architecture* (New York: Bloomsbury, 2000), 35–37.

15 John Berger, *Ways of Seeing* (London: Penguin UK, 1972), 16.

16 David Hockney, "Through the Looking Glass: David Hockney Explains How a Question about Some Ingres Drawings Led to a Whole New Theory of Western Art," *History Today*, November 2011.

17 Lawrence Weschler, *True to Life: Twenty-Five Years of Conversations with David Hockney* (Berkeley, CA: University of California Press, 2008), 117.

18 "Robert Hughes Quotes: On Caravaggio, Warhol, and Hirst," *Telegraph*, August 7, 2012, https://www.telegraph.co.uk/culture/art/art-news/9458192/Robert-Hughes -quotes-on-Caravaggio-Warhol-and-Hirst.html.

19 David Hockney, *Secret Knowledge: Rediscovering the Lost Techniques of the Old Masters* (New York: Viking Studio, 2006), 262.

20 Weschler, *True to Life*, 180.

21 Hockney, *Secret Knowledge*, 14.

22 D. H. Younger, "William Thomas Tutte: 14 May 1917–2 May 2002," *Biographical Memoirs of Fellows of the Royal Society* 58 (2012): 283–97.

23 Michael Smith, *The Secrets of Station X: How the Bletchley Park Codebreakers Helped Win the War* (London: Biteback, 2011), location 2067.

24 Roy Jenkins, *A Life at the Center: Memoirs of a Radical Reformer* (New York: Random House, 1991), 53.

25 Smith, *Secrets of Station X*, Chapter 10.

26 W. T. Tutte, "FISH and I," University of Waterloo, https://uwaterloo.ca/combinatorics -and-optimization/sites/ca.combinatorics-and-optimization/files/uploads/files/corr98 -39.pdf.

27 Captain Jerry Roberts, *Lorenz: Breaking Hitler's Top Secret Code* (Cheltenham, UK: History Press, 2017), 78–79.

28 J. J. O'Connor and E. F. Robertson, "William Thomas Tutte," MacTutor, http:// www-history.mcs.st-and.ac.uk/Biographies/Tutte.html.

29 Tutte, "FISH and I."

30 Roberts, *Lorenz*, 89.

31 Ibid., 134.

32 Ibid., 74.

33 Central Intelligence Agency, "The Enigma of Alan Turing," April 10, 2015, https:// www.cia.gov/news-information/featured-story-archive/2015-featured-story-archive /the-enigma-of-alan-turing.html.

34 Richard Fletcher, "How Bill Tutte Won the War (Or at Least Helped to Shorten It by Two Years)," Bill Tutte Memorial Fund, Issue 1, May 2014, http://billtuttememorial .org.uk/wp-content/uploads/2014/05/How-Bill-Tutte-Won-the-War.pdf.

35 Lisa Grimm and Nicholas Spanola, "Influence of Need for Cognition and Cognitive Closure on Magic Perceptions," *Cognitive Science*, 2016; and Joshua Jay, "What Do Audiences Really Think?," *Magic*, September 2016.

36 Mike Weatherford, "Las Vegas has become 'Caveman' Central," *Las Vegas Review*

*Journal*, May 16, 2003, https://www.reviewjournal.com/entertainment/entertain-ment-columns/mike-weatherford/las-vegas-has-become-caveman-central/.

37  Kuhn, *Experiencing the Impossible*, 9.

38  Jonah Lehrer, "Magic and the Brain: Teller Reveals the Neuroscience of Illusion," *Wired*, April 20, 2009, https://www.wired.com/2009/04/ff-neuroscienceofmagic/.

## Chapter 3: The Power of Comic Sans

1  Interview with Dan Myrick, January 10, 2018.

2  Emalie Marthe, "'They Wished I Was Dead': How 'The Blair Witch Project' Still Haunts Its Cast," *Vice*, September 14, 2016, https://broadly.vice.com/en_us/article/gyxxg3/they-wished-i-was-dead-how-the-blair-witch-project-still-haunts-its-cast.

3  Connor Diemand-Yauman, Daniel M. Oppenheimer, and Erikka B. Vaughan, "Fortune Favors the Bold (and the Italicized): Effects of Disfluency on Educational Outcomes," *Cognition* 118, no. 1 (2011): 111–15.

4  Shane Frederick, "Cognitive Reflection and Decision Making," *Journal of Economic Perspectives* 19, no. 4 (2005): 25–42.

5  Ferris Jabr, "Does Thinking Really Hard Burn More Calories?" *Scientific American*, July 18, 2012, https://www.scientificamerican.com/article/thinking-hard-calories/.

6  Adam Alter, *Drunk Tank Pink: And Other Unexpected Forces That Shape How We Think, Feel, and Behave* (New York: Penguin, 2014), 195.

7  Stanislas Dehaene, *Reading in the Brain: The New Science of How We Read* (New York: Penguin, 2009).

8  Stanislas Dehaene and Laurent Cohen, "The Unique Role of the Visual Word Form Area in Reading," *Trends in Cognitive Sciences* 15, no. 6 (2011): 254–62.

9  Laurent Cohen et al., "Reading Normal and Degraded Words: Contribution of the Dorsal and Ventral Visual Pathways," *Neuroimage* 40, no. 1 (2008): 353–66.

10  Viktor Shklovsky, "Art as Technique," 1917, in *Literary Theory: An Anthology*, ed. Julie Rivkin and Michael Ryan (New York: John Wiley & Sons, 2017), 8–15.

11  Jane Hirshfield, *Ten Windows* (New York: Knopf, 2015), 207.

12  Homer, *The Odyssey*, trans. Emily Wilson, (New York: W. W. Norton, 2018), 1–2.

13  Helen Vendler, *Dickinson: Selected Poems and Commentaries* (New York: Harvard University Press, 2010), 399.

14  Emily Dickinson, *Envelope Poems* (New York: New Directions Publishing, 2016).

15  Thank you to Harvard University Press for granting permission to reproduce the poem. Thomas H. Johnson, ed., *The Poems of Emily Dickinson* (Cambridge, MA: Harvard University Press, 1955).

16  R. Morris Jr., *Gertrude Stein Has Arrived: The Homecoming of a Literary Legend* (Baltimore, MD: Johns Hopkins University Press, 2019), 5; Joseph Bradshaw, "This Week in BAM History: Gertrude Stein's American Lectures," *BAM Blog*, November 8, 2011, https://blog.bam.org/2011/11/this-week-in-bam-history-gertrude.html.

17  "Miss Stein Speaks to Bewildered 500," *New York Times*, November 2, 1934, https://nyti.ms/2CbMQeK.

18  Leonard S. Marcus, *Margaret Wise Brown: Awakened by the Moon* (New York: HarperCollins, 1992), 41.

19  Anne Fernald, "In the Great Green Room: Margaret Wise Brown and Modernism," *Public Books*, November 17, 2015, https://www.publicbooks.org/in-the-great-green-room-margaret-wise-brown-and-modernism/.

20  Aimee Bender, "What Writers Can Learn from 'Goodnight Moon,'" *New York Times*, July 19, 2014, https://opinionator.blogs.nytimes.com/2014/07/19/what-writers-can-learn-from-good-night-moon.

21  Dan Kois, "How One Librarian Tried to Squash *Goodnight Moon*," *Slate*, January 13, 2020, https://slate.com/culture/2020/01/goodnight-moon-nypl-10-most-checked-out-books.html.

22  Bob Levenson, *Bill Bernbach's Book* (New York: Villard, 1987), xvi.

23  "William Bernbach," *AdAge*, March 29, 1999, http://adage.com/article/special-report-the-advertising-century/william-bernbach/140180/; and Mark Hamilton, "The Ad That Changed Advertising: The Story Behind Volkswagen's Think Small Campaign," Medium, March 20, 2015, https://medium.com/theagency/the-ad-that-changed-advertising-18291a67488c.

24  Chip Bayers, "Bill Bernbach: Creative Revolutionary," *Adweek*, August 8, 2011, http://www.adweek.com/news/advertising-branding/bill-bernbach-creative-revolutionary-133901.

25  Levenson, *Bill Bernbach's Book*, 17.

26  Alfredo Marcantonio, David Abbott, and John O'Driscoll, *Remember Those Great Volkswagen Ads?* (London: Merrell, 2014), 11.

27  The Volkswagen Beetle image by Steven Verbruggen (@minorissues on Flickr) is licensed under Creative Commons.

28  Levenson, *Bill Bernbach's Book*, 25.

29  Ivan Hernandez and Jesse Lee Preston, "Disfluency Disrupts the Confirmation Bias," *Journal of Experimental Social Psychology* 49, no. 1 (2013): 178–82.

30  Levenson, *Bill Bernbach's Book*, 27.

31  Noah Callahan-Bever, "Kanye West: Project Runaway," *Complex*, January 2010, https://www.complex.com/music/kanye-west-interview-2010-cover-story.

32  Daniel Isenberg, "Emile Tells All: The Stories Behind His Classic Records," *Complex*, October 28, 2011, https://www.complex.com/music/2011/10/emile-tells-all-the-stories-behind-his-classic-records/kanye-west-pusha-t-runaway.

33  Cole Cuchna, "Runaway by Kanye West (Part 1 & 2)," *Dissect*, October 2017, https://podcasts.apple.com/us/podcast/runaway-by-kanye-west-part-2/id1143845868?i=1000393935936.

34  Taylor Beck, "When the Beat Goes Off: Errors in Rhythm Flow Pattern, Physicists Find," *The Harvard Gazette*, July 19, 2012, https://news.harvard.edu/gazette/story/2012/07/when-the-beat-goes-off/.

35  Jon Caramanica, "Into the Wild with Kanye West," *New York Times*, June 25, 2018, https://www.nytimes.com/2018/06/25/arts/music/kanye-west-ye-interview.html.

36 Leonard B. Meyer, "Some Remarks on Value and Greatness in Music," *Journal of Aesthetics and Art Criticism* 17, no. 4 (1959): 486–500.

37 Leonard B. Meyer, *Emotion and Meaning in Music* (Chicago, IL: University of Chicago Press, 2008), 28.

38 Norbert Wiener, *The Human Use of Human Beings: Cybernetics and Society* (New York: Da Capo Press, 1988), 21.

39 Valorie N. Salimpoor et al., "Anatomically Distinct Dopamine Release during Anticipation and Experience of Peak Emotion to Music," *Nature Neuroscience* 14, no. 2 (2011): 257.

40 Yi-Fang Hsu et al., "Distinctive Representation of Mispredicted and Unpredicted Prediction Errors in Human Electroencephalography," *Journal of Neuroscience* 35, no. 43 (2015): 14653–60.

## Chapter 4: Strategic Opacity

1 Stephen Greenblatt, *Will in the World: How Shakespeare Became Shakespeare* (New York: W. W. Norton, 2004), 293.

2 Harold Bloom and Brett Foster, eds., *Hamlet* (Langhorne, PA: Chelsea House, 2008), 41; and Harold Bloom, *Hamlet: Poem Unlimited* (New York: Riverhead, 2003).

3 Greenblatt, *Will in the World*, 294.

4 James Shapiro, *A Year in the Life of Shakespeare* (New York: HarperCollins, 2005), 285–86.

5 Greenblatt, *Will in the World*, 324.

6 Jack Miles, *God: A Biography* (New York: Knopf, 1995), 6.

7 Erich Auerbach, *Mimesis: The Representation of Reality in Western Thought*, trans. Willard R. Trask (Princeton, NJ: Princeton University Press, 1953), 11.

8 Thomas McDermott, *Filled with All the Fullness of God: An Introduction to Catholic Spirituality* (London: Bloomsbury, 2013), 15.

9 Donald Preziosi, ed., *The Art of Art History: A Critical Anthology*, Oxford History of Art (Oxford, UK: Oxford University Press, 2009), 22.

10 Giorgio Vasari, *The Lives of the Most Excellent Painters, Sculptors, and Architects* (New York: Random House, 2006), 227.

11 Ibid., 238

12 Margaret Livingstone, *Vision and Art* (New York: Harry Abrams, 2014), 73.

13 Scott McCloud, *Understanding Comics* (New York: HarperCollins, 1993), 66.

14 Richard Rorty, *Objectivity, Relativism, and Truth: Philosophical Papers*, 1 (Cambridge, UK: Cambridge University Press, 1991), 203.

15 Obrad Savić, ed., *The Politics of Human Rights* (New York: Verso, 1999), 67–83.

16 David Kidd and Emanuele Castano, "Different Stories: How Levels of Familiarity with Literary and Genre Fiction Relate to Mentalizing," *Psychology of Aesthetics, Creativity, and the Arts* 11, no. 4 (2017): 474.

17 David Comer Kidd and Emanuele Castano, "Reading Literary Fiction Improves Theory of Mind," *Science* 342, no. 6156 (2013): 377–80.

18  Edward Morgan Forster, *Aspects of the Novel* (New York: Penguin Classics, 2005).

19  "Penzler's Mystery Books on the Block," Tribeca Citizen, March 4, 2019, https://tribecacitizen.com/2019/03/04/penzlers-mystery-books-on-the-block/.

20  Kidd and Castano, "Different Stories," 474.

21  Cecilia Heyes, *Cognitive Gadgets* (Cambridge, MA: Belknap Press, 2018), 168.

22  Walter Mischel et al., *Introduction to Personality: Toward an Integrative Science of the Person* (New York: Wiley, 2007), 37; and Jonah Lehrer, "Don't!: The Secret of Self-Control," *New Yorker*, May 18, 2009, https://www.newyorker.com/magazine/2009/05/18/dont-2.

23  Walter Mischel, *Personality and Assessment* (Abingdon, UK: Psychology Press, 2013).

24  Walter Mischel and Yuichi Shoda, "A Cognitive-Affective System Theory of Personality: Reconceptualizing Situations, Dispositions, Dynamics, and Invariance in Personality Structure," *Psychological Review* 102, no. 2 (1995): 246.

25  Todd Rose, *The End of Average* (New York: HarperCollins, 2015), 106.

26  Richard Rorty, *Contingency, Irony, and Solidarity* (Cambridge, UK: Cambridge University Press, 1989), xvi.

27  Ray Didinger, *The New Eagles Encyclopedia* (Philadelphia: Temple University Press, 2014), 7.

28  John Eisenberg, *The League* (New York: Basic Books, 2018), 118.

29  Ibid. 122.

30  Ira Boudway and Eben Novy-Williams, "The NFL's Very Profitable Existential Crisis," *Bloomberg Businessweek*, September 13, 2018, https://www.bloomberg.com/news/features/2018-09-13/nfl-makes-more-money-than-ever-and-things-have-never-been-worse.

31  Cade Massey and Richard H. Thaler, "The Loser's Curse: Decision Making and Market Efficiency in the National Football League Draft," *Management Science* 59, no. 7 (2013): 1479–95.

32  D. Koz et al., "Accuracy of Professional Sports Drafts in Predicting Career Potential," *Scandinavian Journal of Medicine & Science in Sports* 22, no. 4 (2012): e64–e69; Bobby Hubley, "Signing Bonuses & Subsequent Productivity: Predicting Success in the MLB Draft," Diss. 2012; Barry Staw and Ha Hoang, "Sunk Costs in the NBA: Why Draft Order Affects Playing Time and Survival in Professional Basketball," *Administrative Science Quarterly* (1995): 474–94; and Alexander Greene, "The Success of NBA Draft Picks: Can College Careers Predict NBA Winners?," *Culminating Projects in Applied Statistics* 4 (2015).

33  Sigmund Freud, *Sexuality and the Psychology of Love* (New York: Simon & Schuster, 1997), 48.

34  Uwe Hartmann, "Sigmund Freud and His Impact on Our Understanding of Male Sexual Dysfunction," *Journal of Sexual Medicine* 6, no. 8 (2009): 2332–39.

35  Henry Feldman et al., "Impotence and its Medical and Psychosocial Correlates: Results of the Massachusetts Male Aging Study," *Journal of Urology* 151, no. 1 (1994): 54–61.

36  Anais Mialon et al., "Sexual Dysfunctions Among Young Men: Prevalence and Associated Factors," *Journal of Adolescent Health* 51, no. 1 (2012): 25–31.

37  Emily A. Impett et al., "Maintaining Sexual Desire in Intimate Relationships: The Importance of Approach Goals," *Journal of Personality and Social Psychology* 94, no. 5 (2008): 808; and Eli J. Finkel, Jeffry A. Simpson, and Paul W. Eastwick, "The Psychology of Close Relationships: Fourteen Core Principles," *Annual Review of Psychology* 68 (2017): 383–411.

38  Stephen Mitchell, *Can Love Last?* (New York: W. W. Norton, 2002), 78–79.

39  Ibid., 192.

40  Arthur Aron et. al., "The Self-Expansion Model of Motivation and Cognition in Close Relationships," *Oxford Handbook of Close Relationships* (Oxford, UK: Oxford University Press, 2013), 95–96; Charlotte Reissman, Arthur Aron, and Merlynn R. Bergen, "Shared Activities and Marital Satisfaction: Causal Direction and Self-Expansion Versus Boredom," *Journal of Social and Personal Relationships* 10, no. 2 (1993): 243–54.

41  Amy Muise et al., "Broadening Your Horizons: Self-Expanding Activities Promote Desire and Satisfaction in Established Romantic Relationships," *Journal of Personality and Social Psychology* 116, no. 2 (2019): 237.

## Chapter 5: The Duck-Rabbit

1  Raymond Ed Clemens, *The Voynich Manuscript* (New Haven, CT: Yale University Press, 2016).

2  Josephine Livingstone, "The Unsolvable Mysteries of the Voynich Manuscript," *New Yorker*, November 30, 2016, https://www.newyorker.com/books/page-turner/the-unsolvable-mysteries-of-the-voynich-manuscript.

3  Lawrence Goldstone and Nancy Goldstone, *The Friar and the Cipher: Roger Bacon and the Unsolved Mystery of the Most Unusual Manuscript in the World* (New York: Doubleday, 2005), 8.

4  As cited in A. C. Grayling, *The History of Philosophy* (New York: Penguin Press, 2019), 158.

5  M. D'Imperio, *The Voynich Manuscript: An Elegant Enigma* (National Security Agency, 1978).

6  Knox College Office of Communications, "Knox Professor Reveals Unlikely Hero in War of Secret Coders," May 4, 2016, https://www.knox.edu/news/knox-college-professor-john-dooley-book-on-codebreakers.

7  Goldstone and Goldstone, *Friar and the Cipher*, 259.

8  Gordon Rugg and Gavin Taylor, "Hoaxing Statistical Features of the Voynich Manuscript," *Cryptologia* 41, no. 3 (2016): 1–22; and Andreas Schinner, "The Voynich Manuscript: Evidence of the Hoax Hypothesis," *Cryptologia* 31, no. 2 (2007): 95–107.

9  Daniel Ellsberg, "Risk, Ambiguity, and the Savage Axioms," *Quarterly Journal of Economics* 75, no. 4 (1961): 643–69.

10  Ming Hsu et al., "Neural Systems Responding to Degrees of Uncertainty in Human Decision-Making," *Science* 310, no. 5754 (2005): 1680–83; and Benedetto De Martino, Colin F. Camerer, and Ralph Adolphs, "Amygdala Damage Eliminates

Monetary Loss Aversion," *Proceedings of the National Academy of Sciences* 107, no. 8 (2010): 3788–92.

11  Stephen G. Dimmock et al., "Ambiguity Aversion and Household Portfolio Choice Puzzles: Empirical Evidence," *Journal of Financial Economics* 119, no. 3 (2016): 559–77.

12  Uzi Segal and Alex Stein, "Ambiguity Aversion and the Criminal Process," *Notre Dame Law Review* 81 (2005): 1495.

13  Dominic Smith, "Salinger's *Nine Stories*: Fifty Years Later," *Antioch Review* 61, no. 4 (2003): 639–49, www.jstor.org/stable/4614550.

14  Yaara Yeshurun et al., "Same Story, Different Story: The Neural Representation of Interpretive Frameworks," *Psychological Science* 28, no. 3 (2017): 307–19.

15  Uri Hasson et al., "Intersubject Synchronization of Cortical Activity during Natural Vision," *Science* 303, no. 5664 (2004): 1634–40; Uri Hasson et al., "Brain-to-Brain Coupling: A Mechanism for Creating and Sharing a Social World," *Trends in Cognitive Sciences* 16, no. 2 (2012): 114–21; and Uri Hasson et al., "Neurocinematics: The Neuroscience of Film," *Projections* 2, no. 1 (2008): 1–26.

16  Interview with Uri Hasson, December 6, 2018.

17  John J. Ross, *Reading Wittgenstein's* Philosophical Investigations: *A Beginner's Guide* (Washington, DC: Lexington Books, 2009), 146; and L. Wittgenstein, *Philosophical Investigations*, ed. J. Schulte, trans. P. M. S. Hacker (Hoboken, NJ: Wiley-Blackwell, 2009), 206.

18  William Empson, *Seven Types of Ambiguity* (New York: New Directions, 1966).

19  Ibid., 133.

20  Jay-Z, *Decoded* (New York: Random House, 2010), 26.

21  Eugen Wassiliwizky et al., "The Emotional Power of Poetry: Neural Circuitry, Psychophysiology, Compositional Principles," *Social Cognitive and Affective Neuroscience* 12, no. 8 (2017), 1229–40.

22  Benjamin P. Gold et al., "Musical Reward Prediction Errors Engage the Nucleus Accumbens and Motivate Learning," *Proceedings of the National Academy of Sciences* 116, no. 8 (2019): 3310–15.

23  Emily VanDerWerff, "David Chase Responds to Our Sopranos Piece," *Vox*, August 27, 2014, https://www.vox.com/2014/8/27/6076621/david-chase-responds-to-our-sopranos-piece.

24  Matt Zoller Seitz and Alan Sepinwall, "Does Tony Live or Die at the End of *The Sopranos*?" *Vulture*, January 9, 2019, https://www.vulture.com/2019/01/the-sopranos-ending-does-tony-die.html.

25  Andru J. Reeve, *Turn Me On, Dead Man* (AuthorHouse Press, 2004), 12–13.

26  Donald A. Bird, Stephen C. Holder, and Diane Sears, "Walrus Is Greek for Corpse: Rumor and the Death of Paul McCartney," *Journal of Popular Culture* 10, no. 1 (1976): 110.

27  Reeve, *Turn Me On, Dead Man*, 35.

28  Ibid., 59.

29  Philippe Margotin and Jean-Michel Guesdon, *All the Songs: The Story behind Every Beatles Release* (New York: Black Dog & Leventhal, 2014), 428.

30  Ben Zimmer, "The Delights of Parsing the Beatles' Most Nonsensical Song," *Atlantic*, November 24, 2017, https://www.theatlantic.com/entertainment/archive /2017/11/i-am-the-walrus-50-years-later/546698/o.

31  David Sheff, *All We Are Saying: The Last Major Interview with John Lennon and Yoko Ono* (New York: St. Martin's Griffin, 2000), 184.

32  Zimmer, "Delights of Parsing."

33  Hunter Davies, ed., *The Beatles Lyrics* (New York: Little, Brown, 2014), 239.

## Chapter 6: The Infinite Game

1  Interview with James Carse, September 26, 2018.

2  James Carse, *Finite and Infinite Games* (New York: Free Press, 2013), 9.

3  Interview with Jason Hallock, March 6, 2018.

4  Michael Ondaatje and Walter Murch, *The Conversations: Walter Murch and the Art of Editing Film* (New York: Knopf, 2002), 121.

5  Ibid., 122.

6  "New Interview with J.K. Rowling for Release of Dutch Edition of 'Deathly Hallows,'" TheLeakyCauldron.org, November 19, 2007, http://www.the-leaky -cauldron.org/2007/11/19/new-interview-with-j-k-rowling-for-release-of-dutch -edition-of-deathly-hallows/; and Wilma De Rek, *De Volkskrant*, November 19, 2007.

7  Shira Wolosky, *The Riddles of Harry Potter* (New York: Palgrave Macmillan, 2011), 2.

8  Wolosky, *Riddles of Harry Potter*, 2.

9  Jonathan D. Leavitt and Nicholas J. S. Christenfeld, "Story Spoilers Don't Spoil Stories," *Psychological Science* 22, no. 9 (2011): 1152–54.

10  Donald Goddard, "From 'American Graffiti' to Outer Space," *New York Times*, September 12, 1976, https://www.nytimes.com/1976/09/12/archives/from-american -graffiti-to-outer-space.html?searchResultPosition=2.

11  Henry James, *The Figure in the Carpet and Other Stories* (London: Penguin UK, 1986).

12  Gregory Treverton, *Intelligence for an Age of Terror* (New York: Cambridge University Press, 2009), 4–5; and Gregory Treverton, "Risks and Riddles," *Smithsonian*, June 2007.

13  Treverton, "Risks and Riddles."

14  Treverton, *Intelligence for an Age of Terror*, 3.

15  Rebecca Leung, "The Man Who Knew: Ex-Powell Aide Says Saddam-Weapons Threat Was Overstated," CBSNews, October 14, 2003, http://www.cbsnews.com/news/the -man-who-knew-14-10-2003/.

16  Philip Tetlock and Dan Gardner, *Superforecasting: The Art and Science of Prediction* (New York: Crown, 2015).

17  Philip Tetlock and Dan Gardner, "Who's Good at Forecasts?," *Economist*, November 18, 2013.

18  Dacher Keltner, "Why Awe Is Such an Important Emotion," filmed June 2016 at Greater Good Science Center, UC Berkeley, video, 29:41.

19    Joerg Fingerhut and Jesse J. Prinz, "Wonder, Appreciation, and the Value of Art,"
      *Progress in Brain Research* 237 (2018): 107–28; and Dacher Keltner and Jonathan
      Haidt, "Approaching Awe, a Moral, Spiritual, and Aesthetic Emotion," *Cognition
      and Emotion* 17, no. 2 (2003): 297–314.

20    Ryota Takano and Michio Nomura, "Neural Representations of Awe: Distin-
      guishing Common and Distinct Neural Mechanisms," *Emotion* (2020), PMID:
      32496077.

21    Craig Laurence Anderson, "The Relationship between the D4 Dopamine Receptor
      Gene (DRD4) and the Emotion of Awe" (PhD diss., University of California,
      Berkeley, 2016).

22    Chuansheng Chen et al., "Population Migration and the Variation of Dopamine
      D4 Receptor (DRD4) Allele Frequencies around the Globe," *Evolution and Human
      Behavior* 20, no. 5 (1999): 309–24; and Luke J. Matthews and Paul M. Butler,
      "Novelty-Seeking DRD4 Polymorphisms Are Associated with Human Migration
      Distance Out-of-Africa after Controlling for Neutral Population Gene Structure,"
      *American Journal of Physical Anthropology* 145, no. 3 (2011): 382–89.

## Chapter 7: The Harkness Method

1    Guy Williams, "Harkness Learning: Principles of a Radical American Pedagogy,"
     *Journal of Pedagogic Development* 4, no. 1 (2014).

2    Ralph Waldo Emerson, *The Portable Emerson* (New York: Penguin, 1977), 256.

3    Lincoln Caplan, "Chicago Hope," *American Scholar*, September 6, 2016, https://
     theamericanscholar.org/chicago-hope/.

4    Chicago Public Schools, "Nobel – Academy HS," https://www.cps.edu/schools
     /schoolprofiles/400170.

5    Nobel Academy, "School History," https://nobleschools.org/nobleacademy/school
     -history/.

6    K. Bisra et al., "Inducing Self-Explanation: A Meta-Analysis," *Educational Psychology
     Review* 30, no. 3 (September 2018): 703–25.

7    Bethany Rittle-Johnson, "Promoting Transfer: Effects of Self-Explanation and
     Direct Instruction," *Child Development* 77, no. 1 (2006): 1–15.

8    K. Bisra, "Inducing Self-Explanation," 703–25.

9    Louis Deslauriers et al., "Measuring Actual Learning versus Feeling of Learning in
     Response to Being Actively Engaged in the Classroom," *Proceedings of the National
     Academy of Sciences* 116, no. 39 (2019): 19251–57.

10   I. V. S. Mullis et al., "TIMSS 2015 International Results in Mathematics," 2016,
     retrieved from Boston College, TIMSS & PIRLS International Study Center;
     and M. O. Martin et al., "TIMSS 2015 International Results in Science," 2016,
     retrieved from Boston College, TIMSS & PIRLS International Study Center.

11   James Hiebert, *Teaching Mathematics in Seven Countries: Results from the TIMSS 1999
     Video Study* (Collingdale, PA: Diane Publishing, 2003), 100–105.

12   David Epstein, *Range* (New York: Riverhead Books, 2019), 103.

13   D. F. Wallace, *The Pale King* (New York: Little, Brown, 2011), 390.

14 Erin Westgate, "Why Boredom Is Interesting," *Current Directions in Psychological Science* 29, no. 1 (2019): 33–40, https://www.erinwestgate.com/uploads/7/6/4/1/7641726/westgate.2019.currentdirections.pdf.

15 Elizabeth J. Krumrei-Mancuso et al., "Links between Intellectual Humility and Acquiring Knowledge," *Journal of Positive Psychology*, 2019: 1–16; D. Whitcomb, H. Battaly, J. Baehr, and D. Howard-Snyder, "Intellectual Humility: Owning Our Limitations," *Philosophy and Phenomenological Research* 94, no. 3 (2017): 509–39; and T. Porter and K. Schumann, "Intellectual Humility and Openness to the Opposing View," *Self and Identity* 17 (2018): 139–62.

16 Mark R. Leary et al., "Cognitive and Interpersonal Features of Intellectual Humility," *Personality and Social Psychology Bulletin* 43, no. 6 (2017): 793–813.

17 Email from Angela Duckworth, March 10, 2019.

## Coda: The Mechanic as Detective

1 Interview with Jeff Haugland, December 4, 2018.

2 Lea Winerman, "'A Machine for Jumping to Conclusions,'" *Monitor on Psychology*, February 2012, https://www.apa.org/monitor/2012/02/conclusions.

3 B. Schwartz, "Reinforcement-Induced Behavioral Stereotypy: How Not to Teach People to Discover Rules," *Journal of Experimental Psychology: General* 111, no. 1 (1982): 23–59.

4 Ellen J. Langer, Arthur Blank, and Benzion Chanowitz, "The Mindlessness of Ostensibly Thoughtful Action: The Role of 'Placebic' Information in Interpersonal Interaction," *Journal of Personality and Social Psychology* 36, no. 6 (1978): 635; and Ellen Langer, *On Becoming an Artist* (New York: Ballantine Books, 2005), xvii.

5 Ellen Langer, "The Illusion of Control," *Journal of Personality and Social Psychology* 32, no. 2 (1975): 311–28.

6 Ibid.

7 Interview with Ellen Langer, January 24, 2019.

8 John I. Yellott, "Probability Learning with Noncontingent Success," *Journal of Mathematical Psychology* 6, no. 3 (1969): 541–75.

9 Richard J. Herrnstein and Donald H. Loveland, "Maximizing and Matching on Concurrent Ratio Schedules," *Journal of the Experimental Analysis of Behavior* 24, no. 1 (1975): 107–16; and George Wolford, Michael B. Miller, and Michael Gazzaniga, "The Left Hemisphere's Role in Hypothesis Formation," *Journal of Neuroscience* 20, no. 6 (2000): 1–4.

10 Kenneth J. Arrow, "Utilities, Attitudes, Choices: A Review Note," *Econometrica: Journal of the Econometric Society* 26, no. 1 (1958): 1–23.

11 Ellen J. Langer, Benzion Chanowitz, and Arthur Blank, "Mindlessness-Mindfulness in Perspective: A Reply to Valerie Folkes," *Journal of Personality and Social Psychology* 48, no. 3 (1965): 605–607.

12 Cara Feinberg, "The Mindfulness Chronicles: On 'The Psychology of Possibility,'" *Harvard*, September–October 2010, http://harvardmagazine.com/2010/09/the-mindfulness-chronicles?page=all.

13 Ellen J. Langer and Alison I. Piper, "The Prevention of Mindlessness," *Journal of Personality and Social Psychology* 53, no. 2 (1987): 280.

14 Toru Ishikawa et al., "Wayfinding with a GPS-Based Mobile Navigation System: A Comparison with Maps and Direct Experience," *Journal of Environmental Psychology* 28, no. 1 (2008): 74–82.

15 Jeremy Adelman, *Worldly Philosopher: The Odyssey of Albert O. Hirschman* (Princeton, NJ: Princeton University Press, 2013), 117.

16 Michele Alacevich, "Visualizing Uncertainties, or How Albert Hirschman and the World Bank Disagreed on Project Appraisal and What This Says about the End of 'High Development Theory,'" *Journal of the History of Economic Thought* 36, no. 2 (2014): 137–68.

17 Richard Feynman, *Six Easy Pieces*, (New York: Basic Books, 2004), 107.

18 Virginia Woolf, *To the Lighthouse* (San Diego, CA: Harcourt Brace Jovanovich, 1989), 161.

# ABOUT THE AUTHOR

Jonah Lehrer is a writer, journalist, and the author of *A Book About Love*, *How We Decide*, and *Proust Was a Neuroscientist*. He graduated from Columbia University and studied at Oxford University as a Rhodes Scholar. He's written for *The New Yorker*, *Nature*, *Wired*, *The New York Times Magazine*, *The Washington Post*, and *The Wall Street Journal*. He lives in Los Angeles.